MAHATMA GANDHI MURDER CASE
HIGH COURT JUDGMENT

BY THE HIGH COURT OF JUDICATURE FOR THE PROVINCE OF EAST PUNJAB AT SIMLA

VOLUME ONE

Nathu Ram V Godse (Convict-Appellant) versus Rex (Respondent)

Digitised version (in Two Parts) of complete Judgment of 560 Legal-size Typed Pages delivered on 21st June 1949 by Full Bench comprising Mr. Justice Bhandari, Mr. Justice Achhru Ram and Mr. Justice G.D. Khosla, sitting at Peter Hoff, Simla.

S. PADMAVATHI & D.G. HARIPRASATH

ISBN 979-8-89544-846-5

MAHATMA GANDHI MURDER CASE

High Court Judgment [21/06/1949]

Volume One

IN THE HIGH COURT OF JUDICATURE FOR THE PROVINCE OF EAST PUNJAB AT SIMLA

CRIMINAL APPELLATE SIDE

CRIMINAL APPEAL NO.66 OF 1949

APPEAL FROM THE

ORDER OF ATMA CHARAN, ESQUIRE, JUDGE, SPECIAL COURT,

RED-FORT, DELHI, DATED THE 10TH FEBRUARY, 1949.

NATHURAM VINAYAK GODSE: CONVICT-APPELLANT

VERSUS

REX: RESPONDENT

APPEALLATE JUDGMENT OF THE DIVISION BENCH COMPRISING

**MR. JUSTICE BHANDARI, MR. JUSTICE ACHHRU RAM, and
MR. JUSTICE KHOSLA**

JUDGMENT DELIVERED ON 21ST JUNE 1949

Table of Contents

Foreword by Editors

Mahatma Gandhi was assassinated on Friday the 30th January 1948. Nathuram Vinayak Godse and 11 others were arraigned as accused. One of the accused Digambar Ramachandra Badge turned as Approver. Three of the accused were declared "absconders". Finally Nathuram V Godse and 7 others were put into the Accused Dock in the Special Court, Red Fort Delhi. The Trial Commenced on 22nd June, 1948 and the Judgment was given on 10th February 1949.

Nathuram V Godse pleaded "**guilty**" to the charges while the remaining 7 accused pleaded "**not guilty**" to the charges of murder and conspiracy. The remaining three absconders (Gangadhar Dandwati, Gangadhar Jadhav and Suryadeo Sharma all were from Gwalior) were heard in absentia.

1st Accused Nathuram V Godse and 2nd Accused Narayan D Apte were given Death Sentence plus 19 years Rigorous Imprisonment each on various counts of Arms Act, Explosives Act, and Indian Penal Code. Out of the remaining 6 Accused 7 were given varying terms of sentence - 3rd Accused Vishnu R. Karkare (Transportation for Life + 17 years RI), 4th Accused Madanlal K Pahwa (Transportation for Life + 25 years RI),5th Accused Shankar Kistayya (Transportation for Life + 25 years RI), 6th Accused Gopal V Godse (Transportation for Life + 15 years RI), and 8th Accused Dattatraya S Parchure (Transportation for Life). The 7th accused V.D. Savarkar, who was a Barrister-at-Law was acquitted on the ground of "**insufficient evidence produced by the Prosecution**".

While N.V. Godse never appealed over his "Death" sentence but appealed claiming that there was **no conspiracy**; no other was involved; the dastardly crime was his individual and independent act only, the other accused appealed against their sentences.

The appeal was entertained by the Punjab High Court located at Simla. Peterhoff the summer residence of the Viceroy was converted into the Punjab High Court. Hearing by the Three-Judge Division Bench of Punjab High Court began on 2nd May 1949. The Punjab High Court had to gone through 1131 printed pages with a supplementary volume of 115 pages of cyclostyled paper. The Appeal ended in the confirmation of Death Sentences imposed on N.V. Godse and N.D. Apte; Dattatarya S Parchure and Shankar Kistayya were acquitted. The remaining three i.e. V.R. Karkare, Gopal Godse, and Madanlal K Pawha had to face their sentence of Transportation for Life.

Privy Council, London declined to entertain the appeal from Godse and Apte on the ground that a Supreme Court of India was to be established soon in India. The Clemency petitions filed on behalf of Nathuram V Godse and by Narayan D Apte were rejected by Shri C. Rajagopalachariar, the then Governor-General of India. Thus the fates of Godse and Apte were sealed. In a swift action **Nathuram V Godse** and **Narayan D Apte** were hanged in Ambala Prison on 15th November 1949. On the otherside the incarcerated Karkare, Gopal, and Madanlal were let off in October 1964. As time rolled on all the convicts including the approver died one by one on health cause. Now remains only the history and bitter reminiscences of the Assassination of Mahatma Gandhi, the assassins and conspirators. Ironically Gandhi and Godse merged with the Nature and dissolved into the Past.

The lurking point in this case is all the accused except Shankar Kistayya and the approver Digambar Ramachandra Badge belonged to the different elite walks of life. Nathuram V Godse was an Editor cum Journalist; his brother Gopal V Godse was a Sotrekeeper in the Army Depot, Pune; Narayan D Apte was a College Mathematics Professor as well as Managing Director of Hindu Rashtra, Prakasham Limited, Pune; Vishnu R Karkare was a Restaurant Proprietor, Ahmed Nagar; Madanlal Pahwa (an erstwhile Sub-Inspector of Police) was a Refugee in the Ahmednagar Refugee Camp, Dattatraya S Parchure was an Ayurvedic Medical Practitioner in Gwalior, Vinayak D Savarkar was a Barrister-at-Law. Thus a **Lawyer,** a **Doctor,** a **Professor,** a **Sub-Inspector,** a **Journalist,** a **Hotelier,** and a **Government Servant including a Domestic Servant and an arms-dealer conspired together "to Kill Gandhi".**

Paradoxically Mahatma Gandhi breathed his last "murmuring" **"Hei Ram"** while Nathuram Vinayak Godse went to the gallows "shouting" **"Akhant Bharat Amar Rahe". One soul becomes the victim and the other soul becomes the accused. All roads lead to Rome. There ends the matter.**

This Appellate Judgment takes you to the inroads of the Mahatma Gandhi Murder and Murder Appeal with the intricacies of related facts and laws.

Thanking you

Yours historically,
S. PADMAVATHI & D.G. HARIPRASATH,
Advocates-editors
Cell: 94 860 74 220; 99 44 99 8759;, and
9487768108.
Chidambaram 608 001

15th August 2024.

Acknowledgements

The Editors of this Book are acknowledging the files and documents, photos and pictures, information and help placed at their disposal by various authorities, individuals, Companies, Institutions, Smritis, Government Institutions, Railway authorities, etc. Without their help and assistance this book would not be accomplished.

We express our gratitude to the National Archives, New Delhi (which is a repository of Mahatma Gandhi Murder Case details running to 11,000 pages); kiranbedi.com (for supply of FIR 68 of 1948); Kapur Commission Report; Birla House (Gandhi Smriti), Delhi for having accorded permission to take photographs of various places and documents available there; newspapers Daily Herald, The Hindustan Times, Indian Express, The Times of India, Pakistan Times, the Dawn, the Miami Herald, Railway Authorities (Frontier Mail Steam Loco Photo); Madurai Mahatma Gandhi Memorial Museum; Indian Post and Telegraphs Department, Indian Culture, Government Archives, Photo courtesy and credit under the CC Share alike license user: PlaneMad/email:arun.planemad@gmail.com.

The editors are extremely shocked and surprised for the warm reception accorded to them by the Godse family and friends located in Pune and neighbours in Shaniwar Peth, Budhwar Peth, Narayan Peth, Pune and residents of Shivaji Nagar apartments, Shanivarpet for having permitted us to have photograph of some important documents and exhibits connected to this work.

The editors are gratefully acknowledging Shri Arun Ganesh (arun.planemad@gmail.com) for his photograph (Rajiv Gandhi Assassination Place) available in this book.

The editors are happy to express their gratitude to the NOTIONPRESS, Chennai and their staff for the stupendous task of bringing out the work into a nice book.

We, the editors duly acknowledge the helping hand lent by Mr. D. Vedamurthi of Chidambaram and Mr. K. Kanagarajan erstwhile Station Master of Indian Railways from Salem in materialising this daunting work as a compact volume in yours (readers') hands.

Last but not the least the editors' full-fledged thanks go to Mr. D. Ganesh, M.A., LL.B., Advocate for his valuable suggestion and guidance from the conception to the publication in documentation of a landmark Judgment of Independent India.

S. PADMAVATHI & D.G. HARIPRASATH,

advocates-editors
15th August 2024.

Red-Fort Trial Court Judgment Repercussion on the Accused and Appellants

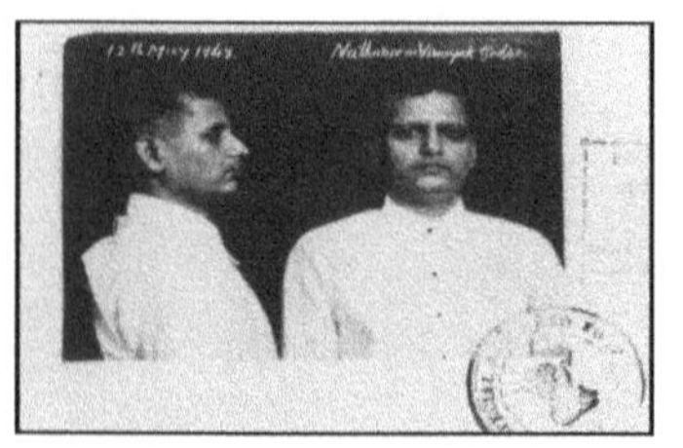

Nathuram V Godse

Death Sentence

Narayan D. Apte

Death Sentence

Vishnu R. Karkare

Transportation for Life

HONOURABLE ACQUITTAL

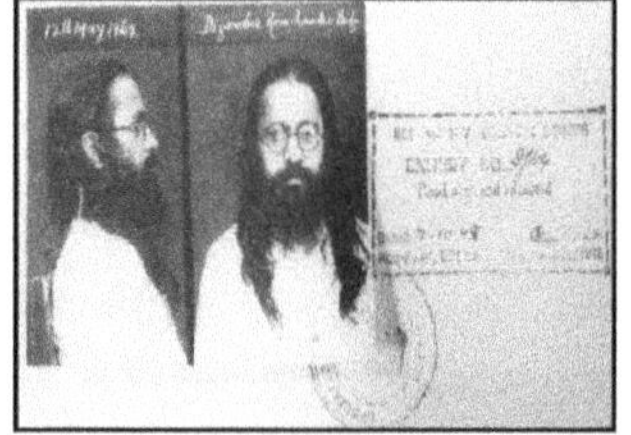

GENERAL PARDON TENDERED

APPEAL TO
PUNJAB AND HARYANA HIGH COURT, AT SIMLA

FROM THE ORDER OF CONVICTION AND SENTENCES

BYTHE TRIAL COURT, RED-FORT, DELHI[1]

Madanlal K Pawa

Transportation for Life

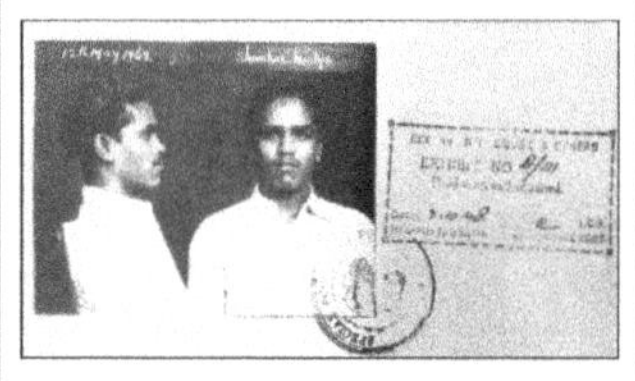

Shankar Kistayya

Transportation for Life

Gopal V Godse

Transportation for Life

Dattaraya S Parchure

Transportation for Life

---

[1] **Feeling** aggrieved from the judgment of the learned Trial Court Special Judge, the seven convicts have filed seven separate appeals in the Punjab and Haryana High Court. Of the appellants, Nathuram V Godse has not challenged his conviction under Section 302 of the Indian Penal Code for the offence of the murder of Mahatma Gandhi on the 30th January 1948 nor has he appealed from the sentence of death passed on him in respect of that offence. He has confined his appeal to the theory of conspiracy only and also his arguments at the Bar, he personally argued his appeal… The appeals of the other 6 appellants (N.D. Apte, V.R. Karkare, Madanlal Pahwa, Gopal V Godse, Dr. Parchure, and Shankar Kistayya) of course attack their conviction for all the offences of which they have been found guilty and the arguments addressed to the High Court by their learned counsel naturally cover the entire field. All the appeals are jointly taken up under Criminal Appeal No.66/1949 by the Punjab and Haryana High Court, at Simla.

TRIAL COURT FINAL ORDERS

AGAINST WHICH THE PRESENT APPEAL IN PUNJAB AND HARYANA HIGH COURT IS SOUGHT BY THE CONVICTS

ACCUSED NO.1
NATHURAM VINAYAK GODSE

DEATH SENTENCE + 19 YEARS RIGOROUS IMPRISONMENT

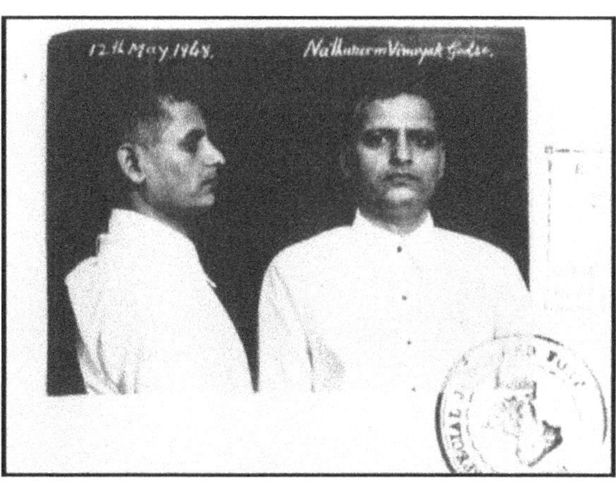

Nathuram Vinayak Godse is found guilty:

a. Under Section 120-B of the Indian Penal Code read with Section 302 of the Code.

b. Under Section 19(c) of the Indian Arms Act or in the alternative u/s 114 of the Indian Penal Code read with Section 19(c)of the Indian Arms Act.

c. Under Section 19(f) Indian Arms Act.

d. Under Section 5 of the Explosive Substances Act or in the alternative u/s 5 of the Explosive Substances Act read with Section 6 of the Act.

e. Under Section 4(b) of the Explosive Substances Act read with Section 6 of the Act.

f. Under Section 3 of the Explosive Substances Act read with Section 6 of the Act.

g. Under Section 115 of the Indian Penal Code read with Section 302 of the Code and

h. Under Section 302 of the Indian Penal Code.

is convicted thereunder and is sentenced

1. to **Two Years' RI** u/s 19(C) of the Indian Arms Act or in the alternative u/s 114 of the Indian Penal Code read with Section 19(c) of the Indian Arms Act;

2. to **Two Years' RI** u/s 19(f) of the Indian Arms Act;

3. to **Three Years' RI** u/s 5 of the Explosive Substances Act or in the alternative u/s 5 of the Explosive Substances Act read with Section 6 of the Act;

4. to **Five Years' RI** u/s 4(b) of the Explosive Substances Act read with Section 6 of the Act;

5. to **Seven Years RI** u/s **8/9** of the Explosive Substances Act read with Section 6 of the Act; and

6. to **DEATH** u/s 302 of the Indian Penal Code – **he is to be hanged by the neck till he is dead; the sentences of imprisonment shall run concurrently.**

He is **found 'not guilty'** of the remaining offences as specified in the charge, and is **acquitted** thereunder.

____

ACCUSED NO.2
NARAYAN D APTE

DEATH SENTENCE + 19 YEARS RIGOROUS IMPRISONMENT

Narayan D Apte is found guilty:

a. Under Section 120-B of the Indian Penal Code read with Section 302 of the Code.

b. Under Section 19(c) of the Indian Arms Act or in the alternative u/s 114 of the Indian Penal Code read with Section 19(c) of the Indian Arms Act.

c. Under Section 114 of the Indian Penal Code read with Under Section 19(f) Indian Arms Act.

d. Under Section 5 of the Explosive Substances Act or in the alternative u/s 5 of the Explosive Substances Act read with Section 6 of the Act.

e. Under Section 4(b) of the Explosive Substances Act read with Section 6 of the Act.

f. Under Section 3 of the Explosive Substances Act read with Section 6 of the Act.

g. Under Section 115 of the Indian Penal Code read with Section 302 of the Code and

h. Under Section 109 of the Indian Penal Code read with Section 302 of the Indian Penal Code.

is convicted thereunder and is sentenced

1. to **Two Years' RI** u/s 19(C) of the Indian Arms Act or in the alternative u/s 114 of the Indian Penal Code read with Section 19(c) of the Indian Arms Act;

2. to **Two Years' RI** u/s 114 of the Indian Penal Code read with Section 19(f) of the Indian Arms Act;

3. to **Three Years' RI** u/s 5 of the Explosive Substances Act or in the alternative u/s 5 of the Explosive Substances Act read with Section 6 of the Act;

4. to **Five Years' RI** u/s 4(b) of the Explosive Substances Act read with Section 6 of the Act;

5. to **Seven Years RI** u/s 3 of the Explosive Substances Act read with Section 6 of the Act; and

6. **to DEATH u/s 109 of Indian Penal Code read with Section 302 of the Code – he is to be hanged by the neck till he is dead; the sentences of imprisonment shall run concurrently.**

He is found "not guilty" of the remaining offences as specified in the charge and is acquitted thereunder.

ACCUSED NO.3
VISHNU RAMAKRISHNA KARKARE
TRANSPORTATION FOR LIFE + 17 YEARS R.I.

a. U/s 120-B of the Indian Penal Code r/w Section 302 of the Code.

b. Section 114 of the Indian Penal Code r/w Section 19(f) of the Indian Arms Act.

c. U/s 5 of the Explosive Substances Act or in the alternative u/s 5 of the Explosive Substances Act r/w Section 6 of the Act.

d. U/s 4(b) of the Explosive Substances ACt r/w Section 6 of the Act.

e. U/s 3 of the Explosive Substances Act r/w Section 6 of the Act.

f. U/s 115 of the Indian Penal Code r/w Section 302 of the Code and

g. U/s 109 of the Indian Penal Code r/w Section 302 of the Code

is convicted thereunder and is sentenced:

1. to **TWO YEARS' RIGOROUS IMPRISONMENT** u/s 114 of the Indian Penal Code r/w Section 19(f) of the Indian Arms Act.

2. to **THREE YEARS' R.I.** u/s 5 of the Explosive Substances Act or in the alternative u/s 5 of the Explosive Substances Act r/w Section 6 of the Act.

3. to **FIVE YEARS' R.I.** U/s 4(b) of the Explosive Substances ACt r/w Section 6 of the Act.

4. to **SEVEN YEARS' R.I.** U/s 3 of the Explosive Substances Act r/w Section 6 of the Act.

5. to **TRANSPORTATION FOR LIFE** u/s 109 of the Indian Penal Code r/w Sec.302 of the Code.

the sentences of imprisonment shall run concurrently and concurrent with the sentence of Transportation For Life.

He is found "not guilty" of the remaining offences as specified in the charge and is acquitted thereunder.

ACCUSED NO.4
MADANLAL K PAHWA

TRANSPORTATION FOR LIFE + 25 YEARS R.I.

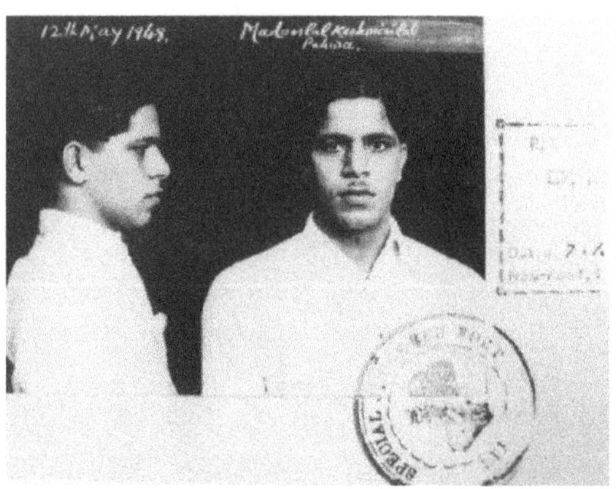

Madanlal K Pahwa is found "guilty":

a. u/s 120-B of the Indian Penal Code r/w Section 302 of the Code.

b. u/s 5 of the Explosive Substances Act or in the alternative

u/s 5 of the Explosive Substances Act r/w Section 6 of the Act.

c. u/s 4(b) of the Explosive Substances Act r/w Section 6 of the Act.

d. u/s 3 of the Explosive Substances Act r/w Section 6 of the Act.

e. u/s 115 of the India Penal Code r/w Section 302 of the Code.

f. u/s 109 of the Indian Penal Code read with Section 302 of the Code.

is convicted thereunder and is sentenced

1. to **TRANSPORTATION FOR LIFE** u/s 120-B of the Indian Penal Code r/w Section 302 of the Code.

2. to **THREE YEARS' R.I.** u/s 5 of the Explosive Substances Act or in the alternative u/s 5 of the Explosive Substances Act r/w Section 6 of the Act.

3. to **FOUR YEARS' R.I.** u/s 4(b) of the Explosive Substances Act

r/w Section 6 of the Act.

4. to **TEN YEARS' R.I.** u/s 3 of the Explosive Substances Act.

5. to **SEVEN YEARS' R.I.** u/s 115 of the India Penal Code

r/w Section 302 of the Code.

the sentences of imprisonment shall run concurrently and concurrent with the sentence of Transportation For Life.

Madanlal K Pahwa is found **"not guilty"** of the remaining offences as specified in the charge, and is **acquitted** thereunder.

ACCUSED NO.5
SHANKAR KISTAYYA

TRANSPORTATION FOR LIFE + 25 YEARS R.I.

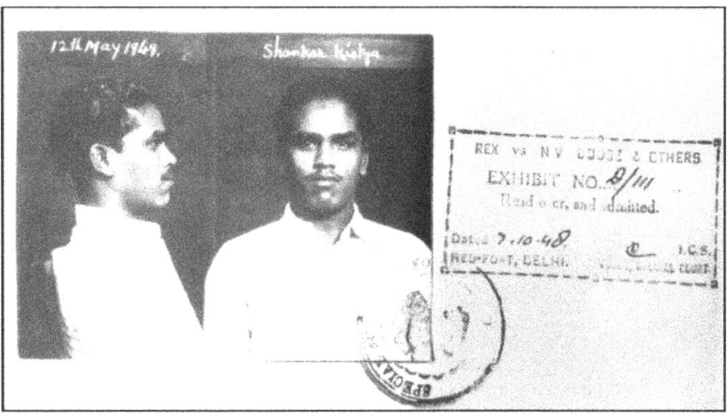

Shankar Kistayya is found **"guilty"**:

a. u/s 120-B of the Indian Penal Code r/w Section 302 of the Code.

b. u/s 5 of the Explosive Substances Act or in the alternative

    u/s 5 of the Explosive Substances Act r/w Section 6 of the Act.

c. u/s 4(b) of the Explosive Substances Act r/w Section 6 of the Act.

d. u/s 3 of the Explosive Substances Act r/w Section 6 of the Act.

e. u/s 115 of the India Penal Code r/w Section 302 of the Code.

is convicted thereunder and is sentenced:

1. to **TRANSPORTATION FOR LIFE** u/s 120-B of the Indian Penal Code r/w Section 302 of the Code.

2. to **THREE YEARS' R.I.** u/s 5 of the Explosive Substances Act or in the alternative u/s 5 of the Explosive Substances Act r/w Section 6 of the Act.

3. to **FIVE YEARS' R.I.** u/s 4(b) of the Explosive Substances Act

    r/w Section 6 of the Act.

4. to **SEVEN YEARS' R.I.** u/s 3 of the Explosive Substances Act

    r/w Section 6 of the Act.

5. to **TEN YEARS' R.I.** u/s 115 of the India Penal Code r/w Section 302 of the Code **with recommendation** that the sentence of Transportation For Life u/s 120-B of the Indian Penal Code r/w Section 302 of the Code may be commuted to Seven Years' R.I. u/s 401 and 402 of the Code of Criminal Procedure Code.

THE SENTENCE OF IMPRISONMENT SHALL RUN CONCURRENTLY AND CONRURRENT WITH THE SENTENCE OF TRANSPORTATION FOR LIFE.

Shankar Kistayya is found **"not guilty"** of the remaining offences as specified in the charge, and is **acquitted thereunder.**

———

ACCUSED NO.6
GOPAL V GODSE

TRANSPORTATION FOR LIFE + 15 YEARS R.I.

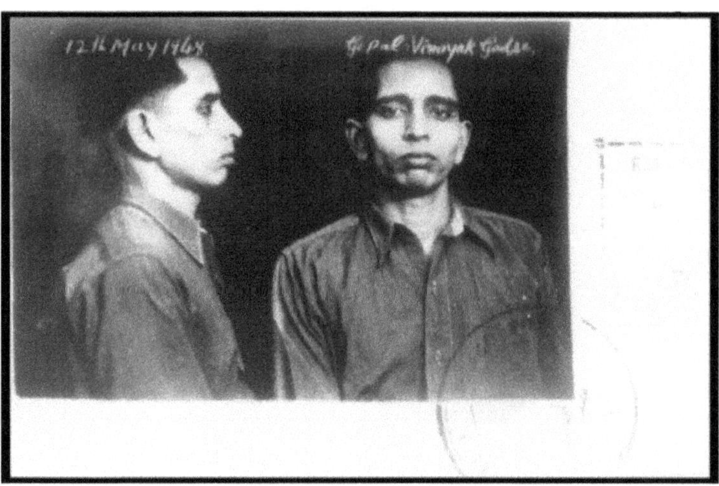

Gopal V Godse is found 'guilty':

1. u/s 120-B of the Indian Penal Code r/w Section 302 of the Code.

2. u/s 5 of the Explosive Substances Act or in the alternative

u/s 5 of the Explosive Substances Act r/w Section 6 of the Act.

3. u/s 4(b) of the Explosive Substances Act r/w Section 6 of the Act.

4. u/s 3 of the Explosive Substances Act r/w Section 6 of the Act.

5. u/s 115 of the India Penal Code r/w Section 302 of the Code.

6. u/s 109 of the Indian Penal Code read with Section 302 of the Code.

is convicted thereunder and sentenced

1. to **THREE YEARS' R.I.** u/s 5 of the Explosive Substances Act or in the alternative u/s 5 of the Explosive Substances Act r/w Section 6 of the Act.

2. to **FIVE YEARS' R.I.** u/s 4(b) of the Explosive Substances Act

   r/w Section 6 of the Act.

3. to **SEVEN YEARS' R.I.** u/s 3 of the Explosive Substances Act

   r/w Section 6 of the Act.

4. to **TRANSPORTATION FOR LIFE** u/s 109 of the Indian Penal Code r/w Section 302 of the Code.

   the sentences of imprisonment shall run concurrently and concurrent with the sentence of TRANSPORTATION FOR LIFE.

He is found **"not guilty"** of the remaining offences as specified in the charge, and is acquitted thereunder.

ACCUSED NO.7
VINAYAK D SAVARKAR
HONOURABLY ACQUITTED

Vinayak Damodar Savarkar is found **'NOT GUILTY'** of the offences as specified in the charge, and is acquitted thereunder, if he is in custody; He be released forthwith unless required otherwise.

ACCUSED NO.8
Dr. DATTATRAYA PARCHURE
TRANSPORTATION FOR LIFE

Dattatraya Parchure is found "guilty"

a. **u/s 120-B of the Indian Penal Code read with Section 302 of the Code.**

b. **u/s 109 of the Indian Penal Code read with Section 302 of the Code.**

is convicted thereunder and is sentenced to **TRANSPORTATION FOR LIFE** u/s 109 of the Indian Penal Code read with Section 302 of the Code.

Dattatraya Parchure is found **"not guilty"** of the remaining offences as specified in the charge, and is acquitted thereunder.

APPROVER
DIGAMBAR R BADGE

TENDERED PARDON AND BE RELEASED

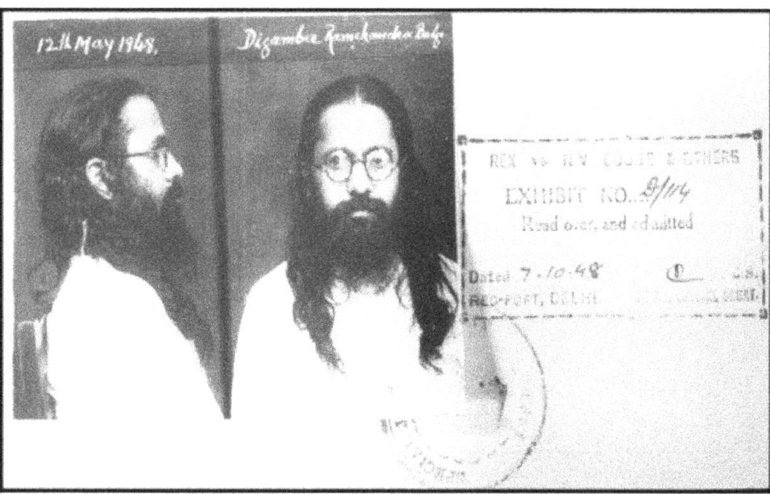

"Digambar R Badge has fulfilled the condition of his pardon and he be releasedfrom custody forthwith unless required otherwise."

APPEAL TO HIGH COURT

Nathuram V Godse, Narayan D Apte, Vishnu R Karkare, Madanlal K Pahwa, Shankar Kistayya, Gopal V Godse, Dattatraya S Parcurer are informed that, if they want to appeal from the order, they should do so within **FIFTEEN DAYS** from today (ie 10th February 1949).. Copies of the judgment are ready and may be had on application just now.

IN THE HIGH COURT OF JUDICATURE
FOR THE PROVINCE OF EAST PUNJAB AT SIMLA

CRIMINAL APPELLATE SIDE

CRIMINAL APPEAL NO.66 of 1949

Mr. Justice ACHHRU RAM	Mr. Justice BHANDARI	Mr. Justice G.D. KHOSLA

PRESENT:	**MR. JUSTICE BHANDARI**
	MR. JUSTICE ACHURU RAM and
	MR. JUSTICE KHOSLA

Appeal from the order of

Atma Charan, Esquire, Judge, Special Court, Red Fort, Delhi,

dated the 10th February, 1949 convicting the appellant

Nathu Ram V. Godse	...Convict-Appellant
Versus	
Rex	...Respondent

CHARGE:

Under Section 120-B of the Indian Penal Code read with Section 302 of the Code, under Section 19(c) of the Indian Arms Act or in the alternative under Section 114 of the Indian Penal Code read with Section 19(c) of the Indian Arms Act, under Section 19(f) of the Indian Arms Act, under Section 5 of the Explosive Substances Act or in the alternative under Section 5 of the Explosive Substances Act read with Section 6 of the Act, under Section 4(b) of the Explosive Substances Act read with Section 6 of the Act, under Section 3 of the Explosive Substances Act read with Section 6 of the Act, under Section 115 of the Indian Penal Code read with Section 302 of the Code and under Section 302 of the Indian penal Code.

Nathuram V Godse

(APPEAL AGAINST CONSPIRACY ONLY)[2]
by
NATHURAM VINAYAK GODSE

Sentence: (to Nathuram Vinayak Godse)

(1) to **TWO YEARS' RIGOROUS IMPRISONMENT** under Section 19(C) of the Indian Arms Act or in the alternative under Section 114 of the Indian Penal Code read with Section 19(c) of the Indian Arms Act;

(2) to **TWO YEARS' RIGOROUS IMPRISONMENT** under Section 19(f) of the Indian Arms Act;

(3) to **THREE YEARS' RIGOROUS IMPRISONMENT** under Section 5 of the Explosive Substances Act or in the alternative under Section 5 of the Explosive Substances Act read with Section 6 of the Act;

(4) to **FIVE YEARS' RIGOROUS IMPRISONMENT** under Section 4(b) of the Explosive Substances Act read with Section 6 of the Act;

(5) to **SEVEN YEARS' RIGOROUS IMPRISONMENT** under Section 3 of the Explosive Substances Act read with Section 6 of the Act; and

(6) to **DEATH** under Section 302 of the Indian Penal Code – to be hanged by the neck till dead: the sentences of imprisonment shall run concurrently;

Appellant:	**In person under Police Custody.**[3]
Respondent:	By M/s.
	C.K. Daphtary, Advocate-General, Bombay;
	N.K. Petigara, Public Prosecutor, Bombay; and
	Shri M.G. Vyavaharkar, Advocate, Bombay.

---

[2] **Accused Nathuram Vinayak Godse has appealed to theHigh Court of Judicature for the Province of East Punjab at Simla "Against the Theory Conpiracy". He has not appealed against his conviction of Death Sentence.: Editors.**

[3] (Mr. Bannerji appeared for Apte and Madanlal) (Mr. N.D. Dange for Karkare) (Mr. Inamdar for Gopal Godse and Dr. Parchure) and (Mr. D.N. Avasthy for Shankar Kistayya). **and (**Mr. Daphtary who was assisted by Mr. M.K. Petigara, Mr. Kartar Singh Chawla, and Mr. M.C.Vyavaharkar appeared for the Crown)

Chapter 1

JUDGMENT

Delivered on 21/06/1949 Tuesday

Mr. Justice A.N. Bhandari

Judgment of

A.N. BHANDARI, Judge

Chapter 1

Judgment of A.N. BHANDARI, Judge

At about 5 o'clock on the afternoon of the 30th January, 1948 Mahatma Gandhi had just ascended the steps of the prayer platform when a person sprang out of the crowd and fired three shots at him at point blank range. The Mahatma sank to the ground with three pistol wounds in his chest and a cry of **"Hey Ram"** on his lips. He was carried hastily into his room but he was past human aid and a long life of simplicity, service and sacrifice came rapidly to a close. While the corpse of the injured innocent lay weltering in its blood the shocking and unexpected news of his assassination was broadcast to the nation and the world. The life of a great seer, saint, and statesman, considered by many to be one of the greatest men of the world, had passed into history.

The assassin was secured at the spot along with the pistol with which the fatal shots had been fired. On the .... following[4] day the police were able to apprehend Badge of the principal figures in this crime. The events now moved with dramatic rapidity and in a short space of time the police were able to examine some startling evidence, the effect of which was to disclose the deliberate manufacture of a very cunning plot to assassinate the "Father of the Nation". Eight persons were brought to trial, upon charges of murder, conspiracy to murder, abetment to murder and of offences under the Indian Arms Act and the Indian Explosives Act.

The trial opened in the historic Red Fort of Delhi on the 27th May 1948. The recording of evidence commenced on the 24th June and continued till the 6th November. Arguments were heard from the 1st to the 30th December and orders were pronounced on the 10th January 1949. During the course of the trial the Court recorded the statements of as many as 149 witnesses covering 326 pages and of eight accused persons covering 223 pages. 638 documentary exhibits and 72 material exhibits were examined and considered. After a laborious trial of unprecedented length conducted, as I hope, with patience and fidelity, the Trial Court proceeded to deliver its judgment consisting of 110 printed pages. Out of the.........[5] only one name by, Mr. Savarkar, was......................................[6] were ....[7] there was a conspiracy to murder Mahatma Gandhi and that he was a member of the said conspiracy. The other prisoners have appealed against the findings of the leaned Special Judge and the sentences awarded to them. Mr. Bannerji appeared for Apte and Madanlal,

____

[4] Nearly"one line" is faded away.:Editors.

[5] Some three words are missing. Eds.

[6] About a line is missing. Eds.

[7] About a line is missing. Eds.

Mr. N.D. Dange for Karkare, Mr. Inamdar for Gopal Godse and Dr. Parchure and Mr. D.N. Avasthy for Shankar Kistayya. Mr. Godse argued his own appeal. Mr. Daphtary who was assisted by Mr. M.K. Petigara, Mr. Kartar Singh Chawla, and Mr. M.C.Vyavaharkar appeared for the Crown. The cases for the appellants and the Crown were argued with conspicuous ability and I take this opportunity of expressing the gratitude of this Court for the help that has been rendered to us in the decision of this difficult case. I must also acknowledge the fair, the temperate and the humane way in which Mr. Daphtary has discharged his stern, imperative but painful duty.

To trace various sequences of events which combined to bring the illustrious victim to his doom it is necessary to go back to the year 1914 when Mahatma Gandhi returned triumphantly to his native country after a sojourn of several years in South Africa. He brought with him a very high reputation for courageous leadership of Indians in that alien soil. His simplicity of life, his selfless devotion to the cause which he had made his own, his sincerity, his self ....[8] Muslims by the policy of divide and rule and that there was little or no chance of his leading a united host to the battle for freedom unless he was able to cement fellow feeling and common devotion to the Motherland. He accordingly made Hindu-Muslim unity the foundation stone of his politics. He promised a 'blank cheque' to the Muslims; he backed the **Khilafat Movement**[9] in this country, he placed the Ali Brothers on a high pedestal. His real and genuine sympathy for the Muslims does not appear to have struck a sympathetic chord in the Muslim heart, for the **Moplah Rebellion**[10] which broke out shortly afterwards showed that the Muslims were not responding to the friendly approaches that were made by the Hindu leaders. They spurned the offer of friendship and brotherhood which was extended to them and continued to demand special rights and privileges. The Government of India Act, 1919 enlarged separate electorates and continued communal representation. Mahatma Gandhi, however, did not relent. On the other hand he lived in the hope of being able to weld the Hindus and Muslims into a single entity known as the Indian nation. He was always prepared to concede the claims of the Muslims even at the risk of incurring the displeasure of his own followers. He agreed to the separation of Sind and to the creation of a separate Province of the North West Frontier. He went on conceding one demand after another in the hope no doubt of enlisting the support of the Muslim League in the final encounter with British Imperialism. Notwithstanding these concessions, the Muslim demands continued to increase; and when the Hindu and Muslim representatives sat together t the Round Table Conference in London. Mahatma

---

[8] About two lines are missing. Eds.

[9] Khilafat Movement was organised by the Ali brothers (Shaukat Ali 1873-1938 and Muhammad Ali 1878-1931) erstwhile students of Aligarh Muslim University to protest against the injustice done to Turkey. It was an agitation by Indian Muslims to pressure the British Government to preserve the authority of the Ottoman Sultan as Caliph of Islam after the First World War. Khilafat Movement finally collapsed when Ataturk abolished the Caliphate altogether in 1924. Mahatma Gandhi had supported the Khilafat Movement as part of his opposition to the British Empire and he also advocated for a wider non-co-operation movement at the same time. Valllabhbhai Patel, Bal Gangadhar Tilak and other Hindu and Congress leaders also supported the movement. The Ali Brothers served a prison sentence for inciting Indian Muslims against the British to protect the Khalifat in Turkey. They were released from prison in 1919.

[10] Moplahs were the Islam believers who were said to be exploited day by day by the Hindu landlords and British officials. Moplahs became frustrated with the British Raj. Due to their economic vulnerability, they became the neglected people under the rule of the colonial government. The Moplah Rebellion, also known as the Moplah Riots of 1921 was the culmination of a series of riots by Mappila Muslims of Kerala in the 19th and early 20th centuries against the British and the Hindu landlords in Malabar (Northern Kerala). It was an armed revolt. It was led by Variyamkunnath K Haji. From August 1921till the end of the year, the rebels completely controlled larger parts of Malabar. By the end of the same year, the rebellion was crushed by the British through its newly raised Special Battalion named The Malabar Special Force For the Riot. In November 1921, nearly 70 Moplah prisoners were killed during transit in a closed freight wagon from Tirur to the Central Prison in Podanur. Death occurred due to suffocation. This tragedy is called as the Wagon Tragedy.

Gandhi was reluctantly ....[11] compelled to ask the British Prime Minister to come to their rescue. The communal award was given and the **seeds of antipathy, dissention, and discord were sown.** Shortly after the Second World War had broken out in the western hemisphere, Mr. Jinnah came out with his demand for the creation of Pakistan on the basis of the two nation theory which is well known to everyone in this country.

At least two persons in this country were dissatisfied with the pro-Muslim policy followed by Mahatma Gandhi, for they appear to have entertained the opinion that the teachings of ahimsa advocated by Mahatma Gandhi were likely to result in the emasculation of the Hindu community and make it incapable of bearing the stresses and strains of the modern world. These two persons were Nathuram and Apte, the two principal offenders in this case. In order to counteract this Policy of Appeasement, they resolved to enter public life and to form a group of persons who held views similar to their own. They started a daily newspaper known as the 'Agrani' and later as the 'Hindu Rashtra'. In this paper they criticised the policies and programmes of Mahatma Gandhi and particularly the methods adopted by him for achieving his ends. They objected particularly to fasts and hunger strikes undertaken by him. At about this time Mahatma Gandhi started reciting the Koran[12] at meetings which were attended by almost exclusively by members of the Hindu community. Apte decided to stage a peaceful demonstration with the object of registering his protest against the policy which appeared to him to be prejudicial and determined to the interests of the community as a whole. ...[13] number of such demonstration are said to have been staged at various places such as ....[14] Panchgani, Poona, Bombay, and Delhi. These demonstrations, however, do not appear to have deflected Mahatma Gandhi from the programme which he had chalked out for himself, and the policy of Mahatma Gandhi was fully endorsed by the Congress.

On the 15th August, 1947 the sub-continent of India was split up into the two rival dominions of India and Pakistan. Independence came and brought it changes to the lives of the people. Large populations from the Punjab and Bengal were uprooted from the soil in which they had nurtured and grown. Blood flowed like water. Mass murder on a .....[15] colossal scale was committed to shock humanity. It is said that despite the misery and the suffering which had been brought to the people of this country and despite the brutality of Muslims, Mahatma Gandhi did not consider it necessary to alter his policy of appeasement. On the other hand, he continued reciting the Quran at the prayer meetings attended by Hindus with **Mr. Suhrawardy** by his side. Towards the middle of January 1948 Mahatma Gandhi decided to undertake a fast with the object of promoting Hindu-Muslim unity in the dominion of India. Nathuram and Apte were of the opinion that the real motive behind the fast was not to promote the cause of Hindu-Muslim unity but to compel the dominion Government to pay a sum of 55 crores of rupees to Pakistan. It is said that as soon as Apte heard of this fast he suggested that a strong but peaceful demonstration should be staged at one of the prayer meetings at Delhi. In the absence of a better alternative, Nathuram agreed to the proposal although he was almost certain that no useful purpose was likely to be served. The prisoners state that they or some of them assembled at Delhi between the 17th and the 20th January with the object of staging a strong but peaceful demonstration in the presence of Mahatma Gandhi. The prosecution on the other hand allege that between the period commencing with the 1st December, 1947 and ending with the 30th January, 1948 Nathuram, Apte, and some of

---

[11] One word is missing.: Eds.

[12] In the "True Copy" is typed as 'Woran'. Eds.

[13] One word is missing. Eds.

[14] Some two or three words are missing. Eds.

[15] One word is missing. Eds.

their companions conspired among themselves to commit the murder of Mahatma Gandhi and that the same act, namely, the murder of Mahatma Gandhi was done in pursuance of the said agreement and conspiracy at Delhi on the 30th January, 1948. The Trial Court was required to adjudicate upon the correctness or otherwise of those two rival versions. The Trial Court has found in favour of the Crown and the question for this Court is whether the Court below has come to a **correct determination in points of fact and law.**

No points of law really arise in this case for the question whether a conspiracy to assassinate Mahatma Gandhi has or has not been established is question of fact which must be determined on the evidence on record. The points of law raised by Mr. Bannerji have been ably dealt with by my learned brother. They are so simple and straightforward that Mr. Daphtary did not consider it necessary to cite a single authority in refutation of the authorities cited by Mr. Bannerjee.

The prisoners in this case belong to different places and different walks of life.

Who is Nathuram V. Godse?

Nathuram V. Godse is the Editor of newspaper. He was born in a devotional Brahman family of the Bombay Presidency. He worked for several years in the R.S.S. and subsequently jointed the Hindu Mahasabha of which Mr. Savarkar was the President.

Who is Narayan D Apte?

Narayan D Apte, aged 34, is the Manager of a newspaper. He is a graduate of the Bombay University. He worked as a teacher in the American Mission High School at Ahmednagar. In or about the year 1941 he came to know Nathuram as a Hindu Mahasabha worker of Poona and in or about the year 1944 both Nathuram and Apte started the Marhatti Newspaper known as the daily **"Agrani"** with the object of propagating political views of the Hindu Mahasabha and of publishing the political programme of what is called the ideology of **Hindu Sanghatan.** The views which the "Agrani" and later the "Hindu Rashtra" propagated as regards the then current political problems were that India should not be divided, that the pro-Muslim policy or the **Policy of Appeasement** which was being pursued by Mahatma Gandhi and the Congress was detrimental not only to the cause of Hindus but also to the welfare of India as a whole. The Hindu Rashtra Dal was started in or about the year 1941-42 to propagate and publicize the **Hindu Sanghatan** ideology. From time to time demonstrations were held at Gandhiji's prayer meetings to disseminate their feelings and to express their opposition to some of the Gandhian and Congress views which the prisoners thought were detrimental to the interests of the Hindu Society.

Who is Vishnu Ramkrishna Karkare?

Vishnu Ramkrishna Karkare is a businessman of Ahmednagar. He was born in a Brahman family of the Bombay Presidency in or about the year 1910. He lost his father in his childhood and was brought up by his mother. In or about the year 1935, he started a tea shop at Ahmednagar. He states that in 1937 he helped in the election of certain candidates who stood on the Hindu Mahasabha ticket, that he was elected unopposed to the Municipal Corporation at Ahmednagar in 1942 and was elected Chairman of the Sanitary Committee in the year 1944, and that in 1946 he proceeded to Noakhali in order to render social service to the Hindus who were victims of Muslims aggression. In December 1947, he started giving assistance to the Hindu refugees who had flocked to Ahmadnagar and were in need of help and shelter. In November 1947 a **Detention Order** was passed against him under the Bombay Public Security Measures Act.

Who is Madanlal Pahwa?

Madanlal Pahwa hails from the Montgomery district which was a part of the United Punjab at **that** time and which is now a part of Pakistan. He passed his Matriculation Examination in 1945. He served in the Army for two years and on release from the Army in 1947, he started preparing for the **Parohakar Examination.** The Punjab was partitioned in the same year and communal disturbances broke out all over the province. The atrocities which were committed by the rioters spread terror and consternation all over the country and held the horrified attention of the world. Madanlal left his native village in a caravan of 60,000 persons in **circumstances** of indescribable terror and hardship and touched the soil of Indian Dominion after walking day and night a distance of 65 miles. He left for Bombay in the last week of September and started working as a Congress Volunteer in the Chembur Refugee-Camp at Bombay. In due course he was introduced to Dr. Jagdish Chandar Jain, a Professor of a local College, who gave him some of his own books to sell. The income which was **produced** by the sale of books was not sufficient to maintain his body and soul together, and he accordingly proceeded to Ahmadnagar in the hope of being able to earn a comfortable living by dealing in fruit. He took interest in the welfare of refugees many of whom had migrated from the Punjab. He came into contact with Karkare and a deep and abiding friendship sprang up between them.

Who is Mr. Gopal V Godse?

Gopal V Godse, aged 27, is a younger brother of Nathuram V Godse. He joined the I.A.O.C. as a temporary store man on the 28th October 1940. He was posted to the Kirkee Arsenal on the same date and was posted to Ferozepore in August 1941. He went overseas in October 1941 and came back to India on the 13th April 1994. He joined the Reinforcement Camp at Ferozepore on 2nd May

1944 and was posted to the M.T.S. Sub-Depot at Kirkee on10th May 1944. He was serving in the Motor Transport Spares Sub-Depot at Kirkee on the 30th January when Mahatma Gandhi was assassinated.

Who is Shankar Kistayya?

Shankar Kistayya is a young man of about 20 years or 22 years of age. He was an apprentice in a carpenter's shop. **Digambar R. Badge (Approver)** took him on, in his own employment in order that he should prepare handles for the daggers that Badge wanted to sell. Shankar, however, made himself so useful hat before long it was impossible for Badge to carry on without him. He was a jack of all trades. He looked after the domestic work of his employer. He dug large holes in the ground and buried arms and ammunition which needed to be kept away from the prying eyes of the police and he repeated the operation when he wanted to take out the arms and ammunition from the place of concealment when a customer was at the door. He used to carry the stuff for Badge from place to place without being found out by the officers of the law. He used to wheel his master about in a cycle rickshaw without any extra payment and I his spare time he used to manufacture handles for hid daggers and he did all this willingly and cheerfully for a paltry sum of Rs. 30/- per mensem plus food and clothing. He never grumbled or complained and never refused to do the task that was assigned to him.

Who is Dr. Parchure?

Dr. Parchure, aged 49, is a medical practitioner at Gwalior. In the year 1939 he established the Gwalior Raj Hindu Sabha of which he became the Secretary and Principal Organiser. Six months later he established another association named Hindu Rashtra Sean which was constitutionally separate from the Hindu Sabha. Upto 1942 he was the dictator of the Hindu Rashtra Sena which was formed to regenerate the Hindu nation and of which the strength was three thousand in the year 1942. Dr. Parchure became the President of the Gwalior State Hindu Sabha three years ago and when a question arose whether the power should be transferred from the Maharaja of Gwalior to the people of Gwalior he made it clear that the Hindu Sabha should be given a share in the administration of the State. The Ruler is said to have agreed that the representatives of the Hindu Sabha should be allowed to participate in the Government of the State but later to have changed his mind and to have transferred the entire power to the Congress Party. Dr. Parchure and the organisation which he represents protested against the decision of the Maharaja and staged a demonstration on the 24th January. It is said that Dr. Parchure has been falsely implicated in this case as he was opposing the party in power.

Who is Digambar R. Badge?

Another central figure in this case is **Digambar R. Badge** a Marhatta of about 30 or 40 years of age. He established a **Shastar Bhandar** in Poona in the year 1942 and dealt extensively in the sale of arms and ammunition which he had obtained from unauthorised sources. In the year 1943 he set out on a propaganda tour in some of the more important towns of Bombay and Madras Presidencies and sold weapons of the value of Rs. 10,000/- or more by visiting houses and shops. Nathuram and Apte were two of his numerous customers. They would take Badge about in their car, introduce him to prospective purchasers and help him to realise the price of the stuff sold by him. They paid him gratuities of Rs. 5/-Rs. 10/- Rs. 50/- or even Rs. 100/- at a time without demanding anything in return. He was a frequent visitor to the office of the daily **'Agrani'** where he often asked for financial assistance. When the paper required him to furnish security in a sum of Rs. Six thousand and a fund was started to meet such security, Badge contented

himself by paying a sum of Rs. 4/- or Rs. 5/- as his contribution. He became a member of the Hindu Rashtra Dal in 1946 or 1947 but did not attend any session of the Dal, although he sold a number of weapons to the people who had assembled at the camp place. **Penny-catching meannesses of mind is one of his important characteristics.** Even when he set out to collect funds for the Hind Maha Sabha of which he professes to be a member he did not refrain from charging a commission on the amount that he collected. He says that he has been dealing in arms and ammunition for the benefit of the Hyderabad State Congress but there can be little doubt that these transactions could not have been entered into for altruistic purposes alone. He used to sell the stuff to the Congress for cash and charged a sum of Rs. 50/- per revolver and Rs. 25/- per gun-cotton-slab over and above the price paid by him.

When he left Bombay for Poona along with Shankar in the middle of January 1948 he was confronted with the problem of having to purchase inter class tickets for himself and his servant. His active and fertile brain rose to the occasion. He purchased two platform tickets for himself and his servant, got into the train, alighted at Poona and crossed the barrier by paying a small bribe to the clerk at the gate. On the 24th November, 1946 he was arrested by the police for the contravention of a provision of the Indian Arms Act. He filed a complaint under Sec.420 of the Indian Penal Code against Shankar who was alleged to have taken a sum of Rs. 200/- from his sister and had run away out of fear. He explains that he has lodged the complaint against Shankar so that he might not be blamed by the police for making Shankar run away. He had taken no steps to withdraw the case against his servant although he led no evidence whatsoever in support of the complaint. One of his brothers is stated to be an employee in the police department at Poona.

The history of this remarkable case commence on a certain date in a month of November 1947, when Apte met badge accidentally at Yerandawane and expressed a desire to purchase some arms and ammunition. Badge told him that he was on his way to a pilgrimage to the Bhor State but that on his return from the pilgrimage he would be in a position to supply the stuff required by him.

In the last week of December 1947 Apte asked Badge whether the stuff was ready and on his reply in the affirmative stated that it would be collected by Karkare in 2 or 3 days' time. Apte went to Badge on the 9th January 1948 at about 6 or 6.30 p.m. and asked Badge to show the stuff to Karkare and certain other persons who were expected shortly. About two hours later Karkare and three other persons who were introduced to Badge as Madanlal, Om Parkash and Chopra arrived. Karkare asked Badge to show the stuff to them and Badge accordingly instructed his servant Shankar to fetch the stuff from the place where it had been kept. Shankar brought the stuff which consisted of gun-cotton slabs, hand-grenades, cartridges, pistols, and fuse wires. Madanlal and his companions had a look at the stuff and went away.

Apte took Badge with him to the Hindu Rashtra Office at 10 o'clock on the morning of the 10th January 1948 and asked him to supply two gun-cotton-slabs, two revolvers, and five hand-grenades. Badge agreed to supply the slabs and the grenades but stated that he was not in a position to supply any revolvers. He further agreed to supply the stuff to them at Bombay on his return from his village Chalisgaon where he wanted to sell his house. In the meantime Nathuram who was working in a tent nearby arrived at the spot. Apte told him that Badge was willing to deliver the "stuff" at Bombay and that their one work was complete. Both Nathuram and Apte asked Badge to make certain that the "stuff" reached the Hindu Mahasabha Office at Dadar by the evening of the 14th January.

Badge left for his village the same evening i.e. on the 11th January 1948, disposed of his house on the 12th January and returned to Poona on the 13th January. He told Shankar that certain "stuff"

had to be delivered to Nathuram and Apte by the evening of the 4th January and asked him to keep it in readiness for being taken to Bombay. Shankar packed the stuff in a cloth bag of Khaki colour.

Poona 13/01/1948:

On the same day, i.e., the 13th January Nathuram effected a nomination on his Life Policy in a sum of Rs. 2,000/- in favour of Mrs. Champutai wife of Narain Apte and on the following day he effected a similar nomination in respect of his policy for Rs. 3,000/- in favour of Mrs. Sindhutai wife of Gopal Godse.

Poona to Bombay: 14/01/1948:

Badge and Shankar left Poona for Bombay on the afternoon of the 14th January and alighted at Dadar at about 7 o'clock the same evening.

Bombay (Dadar): 14/01/1948

On arrival at the office they were somewhat disappointed to discover that Apte and Nathuram whom they expected were not there to meet them. Badge's enquiries revealed the fact that Apte and Nathuram were expected at any moment. Badge and Shankar waited for half-an-hour and then left the place with the **khaki** bag. As they were getting down they saw Apte coming from the road. On seeing Badge, Apte said that it was good that he had come, and that arrangements would have to be made for keeping the stuff. Badge took the bag from the hand of Shankar and started accompanying Apte. They had covered only four or five paces when they met Nathuram on the pavement and Nathuram, Apte and Badge proceeded to the **Savarkar Sadan,** Shankar having been left in the office of the Hindu Mahasabha. On reaching Savarkar-Sadan, Apte took the bag from the hands of Badge and went inside the house accompanied by Nathuram. They returned with the bag five or 10 minutes later. Nathuram, Apte, and Badge went back to the Hindu

Mahasabha Office, called out to Shankar and all four of them proceeded in a car brought by Apte to the house of Dixitji Maharaj at Bhuleshwar. They got down from the car at about 10 or 10.30 pm asked Shankar to wait inside the hall while they went into the interior of the house. Dixitji Maharaj had retired for the nigh and they accordingly asked one of the servants to keep the bag with him until the following morning. Badge said that the bag would be taken back by Apte, Nathuram and himself. On return to the Hindu Mahasabha Office at Dadar, badge and Shankar were asked to get down.

"Badge kab aye?"

Apte paid some money to Nathuram and the latter paid a sum of Rs. 50/- to Badge stating that, that was not the price of the stuff supplied but was intended to cover the travelling expenses incurred by Badge and Shankar. As soon as Badge entered the office he was greeted by Madanlal who said **"Badge kab aye?".** Badge at first did not recognise him but on being reminded of the meeting at Poona on the 9th, Badge enquired after Karkare and was told by Madanlal that the latter was at Thana but was likely to return that night or the next morning.

All the preparations were now complete. Nathuram and Apte had arrived, Madanlal was already in Bombay and Karkare was expected any moment. The "stuff" had arrived and was deposited in the house of Dixitji Maharaj where it could not attract the attention of the police. All that needed to be done was to examine the "stuff", to see that it was good and effective and capable of giving the performance that was claimed for it, and to transfer the men and the material to the capital of India where the final act was to be staged.

Apte was up early on the morning of the 15th January at 7.20 A.M., he purchased two tickets through Air India Ltd., for journey to Delhi by air on the 17th January under the assumed names of D.M. Karmarkar and S. Marathe.

Mr. Badge, Meet at Bori-Bunder on 17th January Morning:

At 8.30 a.m. Apte and Nathuram went to the Hindu Mahasabha and found Badge, Shankar and Madanlal sitting with two or three persons connected with the Hindu Mahasabha Office. Badge and Shankar left the office with Apte and Nathuram as Madanlal was not dressed. When they were in the vicinity of the **Agrani Printing Press** otherwise known as the **Shivaji Press** they met Karkare. Apte, Nathuram, Karkare, Badge, and Shankar entered the press of which Mr. G.M. Joshi is the Proprietor. Shankar was asked to sit down on the planks in front of the press, while Apte, Nathuram, Karkare and Badge entered the press where they met Mr. Joshi. Badge was left in the press, while the others entered the office of the press. They came out of that office after about an hour or so. Apte, Nathuram, Karkare, badge, and Shankar left for the Mahasabha office at Dadar. On reaching the office, Karkare asked Madanlal to take his bedding and put it in the car which Apte had brought ________ [16] Nathuram, Karkare, Madanlal and Badge entered the taxi with the bedding of Madanlal and proceeded to the house of Dixitji Maharaj at Bhuleshwar. Madanlal kept his bedding in the Hall and all of them went further into the interior of the house. They greeted Dixitji Maharaj and Badge asked for the bag that he had left there the preceding evening. After an hour or so, the bag was produced by a servant of Dixitji Maharaj. Badge opened the bag and showed the "stuff" contained in the bag to Apte. After contents had been examined by Dixitji Maharaj and the other persons who were present in the room, Badge put the contents back into the bag, closed the bag and handed it over to Apte who passed it on to Karkare. Apte asked Karkare to leave for Delhi by the Frontier or the Punjab Mail along with Madanlal. Karkare handed over the bag to Madanlal and asked him to tie it up in the bedding which was

---

[16] One word is not discernible.: Editors

lying in the Hall. Karkare and Madanlal then left the place and went away. When these two persons had gone away, Apte told Dixitji Maharaj that they were proceeding on some "important work" and asked for the loan of one or two revolvers. Dixitji Maharaj stated that he had no revolver but that he had a ______[17] pistol which he was unable to spare. Apte then asked Dixitji Maharaj to do all that he could to obtain a revolver for him. Apte, Nathuram and Badge came out of the house of Dixitji Maharaj and stood in the compound of the temple in which the house is situated. Apte then asked Badge if he was prepared to go with them to Delhi. Badge asked Apte to indicate the nature of the work that was to be done in Delhi and Apte replied that Tatyarao Savarkar had decided that Gandhiji, Pandit Jawahar Lal Nehru, and Mr. Suhrawardi should be "finished" and had entrusted the work to Apte and Nathuram. He asked Badge to accompany them to Delhi and told him that they would find funds for meeting his travelling expenses. Badge expressed his willingness to proceed to Delhi but stated that he could do so after paying a visit to Poona and after making arrangements regarding his household affairs. Nathuram thereupon said that he also wanted to go to Poona to meet his brother Gopal Godse who had undertaken to make arrangements for producing a revolver and to bring him down to Bombay for accompanying them to Delhi. After this conversation had taken place in the compound of the temple Apte, Nathuram and Badge left the premises and entered taxi. They proceeded to the Cotton Exchange Building where Apte and Godse wanted to transact some business. On their return after 20 or 25 minutes, the party proceeded to the Hindu Mahasabha Office at Dadar. Badge got down from the taxi in front of the office and Apte asked Badge to meet him (Apte) at Bori-Bunder (Victoria Terminus) on the morning of the 17th January. Badge entered the Mahasabha Office and met Madanlal at about 6 or 6.30 p.m. in front of the

said office. Madanlal told Badge that he had missed the train and that Karkare was waiting with his bedding at the Victoria Terminus Railway Station. He stated further that they would be leaving the same evening for Delhi. Bade and Shankar left the Victoria Terminus Station for Poona by the night train reaching Poona at about 2 o'clock in the early hours of the 16th January. Nathuram also returned to Poona the same day.

Poona 16/01/1948:

At about 7 or 7.30 p.m. on the 16th January 1948 Badge went to the house of Amdar Kharat, a member of the Legislative Assembly, and deposited some arms and ammunition with him in order that the latter should sell the stuff to the Hyderabad State Congress. He was anxious to sell the stuff that very day and asked Mr. Kharat to receive the money for the stuff and hand it over to him. On his return from the house of Mr. Kharat, Shankar informed Badge that Nathuram had called at his house on two occasions. Badge accordingly went to the Hindu Rashtra Office to see Nathuram. Nathuram asked Badge if he was ready to go to Delhi and Badge replied in the affirmative. Nathuram then took out a small pistol and gave it to Badge asking him to exchange it for a big revolver and in case he could not get a big revolver to take the pistol with him to Bombay. Badge accordingly went to see one Sharma, a worker of Hyderabad State Congress whom he had sold a .32 revolver and gave this pistol in exchange for the revolver and some cartridges.

Badge and Shankar left Poona for Bombay with the revolver and 4 cartridges by the 2.40 a.m. train on the 17th January 1948, Shankar getting down at Dadar and Badge at Bori-Bunder (Victoria Terminus Station). As soon as Badge crossed the ticket barrier, he met Apte and Nathuram who had promised to meet him at the Victoria Terminus Station on the morning of the 17th January. They had travelled only a few paces when Apte suggested that

---

[17] One word is not discernible.: Editors

they should collect some funds before proceeding to Delhi. Apte brought a taxi and the three of them, namely, Nathuram, Apte, and Badge got into it and proceeded to the Bombay Dyeing House where Badge introduced the Proprietor Seth Charandas Meghji Mathuradas to Apte and Nathuram. After having a conversation with the Seth for sometime Apte, Nathuram and Badge proceeded to the Hindu Mahasabha Office at Dadar in order to pick up Shankar. After Shankar had taken his seat in the car, the party proceeded to Savarkar-Sadan at Shiv Ji Park to take the last darshan of Tatyarao. Shankar was asked to wait outside the compound while Apte, Nathuram and badge entered the compound. Apte asked Badge to wait in the room on the ground floor. Nathuram and Apte went up and came down 5 to 10 minutes later. They were followed immediately by Tatyarao who gave them his blessings and wished them all success in their enterprise. The party then got into the taxi and proceeded to the Ruia College. Apte said in the taxi that Tatyarao had predicted that Gandhiji's hundred years were over and that there was no doubt that their work would be successfully finished. They then proceeded to the house of Afjulpurkar where some discussion took place between Afjulpurkar and Apte and Nathuram about the affairs in the Hyderabad State. Afjulpurka gave a sum of Rs. 100/- to Badge.

From Afjulpurkar's house the party proceeded to Kurla, picked up Mr. R.M. Patankar (P.W.87) and went to the House of Mahadeo Ganesh Kale (P.W.86), Proprietor Kale's Inks.[18] Shankar was left behind in the taxi. Patankar introduced Nathuram and Apte to Kale and thereafter left the place. Nathuram and Apte entered into conversation in English with Kale, as a result of which Kale went upstairs and came back with a bundle of notes and handed them over to Godse. The party then proceeded to the taxi to the Bombay Dyeing works as arranged but Mr. Charandas Meghji

Mathura Dass was not to be found. Nathuram told Apte that he had some work and should be taken to the taxi-stand. Nathuram and Apte went away in the taxi and Nathuram was dropped at the taxi-stand. Apte came back in the taxi shortly afterwards. The proprietor had not come till then. Apte told Badge that he and Shankar should wait at the works for some time and that he wanted to see Nathuram before 12 noon. Apte went away in the taxi and came back after about an hour or so. Mathura Dass had returned by this time and Apte had a talk with him in English for a few minutes. Mathura Das gave him sum of Rs. 1,000/- by way of donation.

Apte, Shankar and Badge next proceeded in the taxi to the house of Dixitji Maharaj at Bhuleshwar. They got down from the taxi. Shankar sat down in the hall while Apte and Badge went into the interior of the house and met Dixitji Maharaj. Apte asked Dixitji Maharaj for a revolver, whereupon the latter showed him a small pistol. Apte asked him for it but Dixitji Maharaj said that he was not prepared to part with it without consideration. Badge, Apte and Shankar then drove in the same taxi to the Juhu[19] Aerodrome, from where they proceeded to Santa Cruz Aerodrome. Apte got down at Santa Cruz, handed over a sum of Rs. 350/- to Badge and asked him to leave for Delhi along with Shankar the same day by the night train. Badge and Shankar then drove back from Santa Cruz [20]Aerodrome by same taxi and went to Kurla. Badge proceeded to Kurla because he wanted to see R.K. Patwardhan. Patwardhan was not at his house but was expected to return at about 4 or 4.30

---

[18] Inc. is an abbreviation for incorporated company that are legally established. It is in vogue in US.

[19] Juhu Aerodrome is located in Juhu, Mumbai. Juhu is a residential suburb of Mumbai.Juhu Aerodrome in Mumbai is the first and oldest airport in India, established in 1928.

[20] Santacruz Airport was built during the 1930s It was a larger airfield than nearby Juhu Aerodrome. It had covered approximately 1500 acres. It was renamed in 1999 from the previous "Sahar Airport" to"Chhatrapati Shivaji Maharaj International Airport" in 1999. The title "Maharaj" was inserted in 2018. Actually the Airport is situated across the suburbs of Santacruz and Sahar Village in Vile Parle East, Mumbai, India.

p.m. Badge thereupon decided to wait for him. He discharged the taxi paid a sum of Rs. 55/10/- to driver and took a receipt from him. Patwardhan did not turn up for sometimes and Badge and Shankar accordingly left the Kurla Railway Station for Dadar by a local train. They again went back to the house of Patwardhan at about 3.30 pm and met Patwardhan, had a conversation with him and remained at his house till 9 or 9.30 p.m. because Badge wanted some money from him. Patwardhan borrowed Rs. 200/- from Patankar and Rs. 200/- from Acharya Master and paid it to Badge. They returned from Kurla to Dadar and slept that night the Asra Hotel. Badge states that on the morning of the 18th January he went to the house of Dixitji Maharaj with Shankar and had a conversation with him. Badge and Shankar picked up their luggage from Dadar, proceeded to the Victoria Terminus Railway Station and left Bombay for Delhi by the Punjab Mail.

Karkare and Madanlal who had left Bombay on the height of the 15th January reached Delhi at about 12.30 **a.m.** on the 17th. A fellow passenger by the name of Angchekar (P.W.5) was also travelling with them. All three of them, namely, Karkare, Madanlal, and Angchekar drove from the Delhi Railway Station to the Hindu Mahasabha office where unfortunately they were unable to obtain any accommodation. So they went to the Birla Mandir where also no accommodation was available. Thereupon they came back to Chandni Chowk and engaged a room in the Sharif Hotel. The hotel register shows that Karkare stayed there under the assumed name of B.M. Bias.

On arrival at Delhi, Nathuram and Apte proceeded to the Marina Hotel and stayed in Room No.40 from the 17th to the 20th January under the assumed names of S. Deshpande and N. Deshpande.

On the afternoon of the 19th January Gopal Godse paid a visit to Karkare and Madanlal in the Shariff Hotel.

Badge and Shankar arrived in Delhi at about 9.30 or 10 p.m. on 19th January. No one met them at the Railway Station and they accordingly took a *Tonga* and proceeded to the Hindu Mahasabha Office at New Delhi. They went inside the office and "enquired as to where they could stay. The office boy directed them to a hall behind the office where they met Madanlal who introduced them to Gopal. Nathuram, Apte and Karkare came there shortly afterwards. They said that they had been to the railway station to see Badge and Shankar but had not been able to find them there. They then asked Badge and Shankar to sleep in the hall and said that they would look them up on the following morning. Badge, Shankar, Madanlal and Gopal slept the night in the same hall. It will be seen from the above that Karkare and Madanlal arrived in Delhi on the afternoon of the 17th January, Nathuram and Apte on the evening of the 17th, Gopal on the 18th or 19th, and Badge and Shankar on the night of the 19th.

At 8.30 a.m. on the 20th January 1948 Apte and Karkare came to the Hindu Mahasabha Office to see Badge. Karkare paid some money to Madanlal for purchasing fuel for getting the bath-water heated. Apte and Karkare left the place stating that they would come back later. They came back after about half-an-hour and Apte asked Badge and Shankar to accompany him to the Birla House. Apte, Badge and Shankar took a car and stopped it in front of the main gate of the Birla House. They got down from the car and were about to enter the main gate when the gatekeeper stopped them and asked them where they wanted to go. Apte said that he wanted to see the Secretary and the gatekeeper asked them for a chit. Apte wrote something on a piece of paper and the gatekeeper took the piece of paper and went into the bungalow. There came out of the bungalow a stoutish gentleman dressed in a black suit. Apte pointed him out and said "This is that Suhrawardy" and further said that he used to sit with Gandhiji at the time of prayers.

Badge, Apte and Shankar left the place and proceeded towards the back of the Birla House by taking the road that passes by its side. They came to a place enclosed by a red brick wall where there is a gate through which they entered. They passed the **chawl** and proceeded to the place where Badge was told by Apte that prayers used to be held. Apte then pointed out a spot and said that Gandhiji and Suhrawardy used to sit there. Apte also showed Badge a window with trellis work behind that spot. Apte took measurements of the opening in the trellis work with a piece of string and said that a revolver-shot could be fired and a hand-grenade thrown through that opening. Apte said that the window opened from a room behind. He also said that so far as possible Gandhiji and Suhrawardy should be finished and if it was not possible to finish both of them, then at least one of them should be finished. Badge and Apte then came back to the chawl[21] and came out of the gate and at some distance therefrom and said that one gun-cotton-slab could be exploded from each place for diverting the attention of the people. Badge and Apte then entered the gate and stood in front of the **chawl.** Apte pointed out a room as the room in which the trellis work existed and said that it was possible to enter the room as a photographer. They did not enter the room that had been pointed out by Apte. After having surveyed the locality they left the Birla House at about 11 or 11.30 a.m.

Badge, Shankar and Apte returned to the Hindu Mahasabha Office. Apte left the place saying that he would come back after some time. He returned after about 20 or 25 minutes and told Gopal who was in the Mahasabha building that they all should go to the jungle to try out the two revolvers that had been brought by Gopal and Badge. Apte, Gopal, Badge, and Shankar then proceeded to the jungle behind the Hindu Mahasabha Office, one revolver being carried by Gopal and the other by Shankar. The revolver of Gopal was a service revolver of .38 bore. The revolver carried by Shankar was a .22 or .32 bore revolver. On reaching the jungle Apte asked Gopal to take out his revolver and on pressing the catch, it was found that the revolver-chamber did not come out. Apte thereon asked Badge to take out his revolver and Badge in his turn asked Shankar to take out the revolver. Apte loaded the revolver with four cartridges and asked Shankar to shoot at a tree with it. Shankar fired a shot which did not reach the tree but fell down in between. Apte thereon said that the revolver would be of no use and Gopal said that he would repair his own revolver. Gopal asked Shankar to go back to the Hindu Mahasabha Office and to bring a bottle of oil and a penknife from his bag which Shankar did. They then moved on a short distance and sat down and Gopal began repairing his revolver. While this was being done three Forest Guards came out that way. Apte and his companions hid the revolvers under the show. The Forest Guards enquired as to what they were doing. Apte, Gopal, Badge, and Shankar stood up and Gopal spoke to them in Punjabi. The explanation given by him appears to have satisfied the Guards and they went away. Apte thereafter suggested that it was no use sitting there and that they should go back to the Hindu Mahasabha Office. All of them went back to the Hindu Mahasabha Office and found Karkare and Madanlal sitting there. Apte asked Karkare to go ahead with Madanlal to the Marina Hotel and told him that he and the others would follow. After Karkare and Madanlal had gone, Apte asked Gopal to accompany him to the Marina Hotel with the bag containing the stuff. Apte, Gopal, Badge and Shankar left for the Marina Hotel, Gopal Godse carrying the bag which had been brought by Madanlal from Bombay and which contained the stuff supplied by Badge.

---

[21] A chawl is a type of low quality housing residential building found in Western India, similar to a tenement. Chawls are generally associated with poverty. The first chawls were constructed in the early 1700s, as housing for industrial workers.

Mr. Badge, this is our Last Effort!

On reaching the Marina Hotel Apte, Gopal, Badge and Shankar went up to the second floor and found Nathuram lying on a bed in a room. Badge and Shankar went down to the first floor to take their meals, while Apte, Karkare, Madanlal and Gopal remained in the room with Nathuram. When they returned they found Gopal repairing a revolver. They then closed the doors of the room from inside, and Apte, Karkare, Madanlal and Badge went into the bathroom where Nathuram and Shankar also came and stood. Apte, Karkare, Madanlal and Badge began fixing the primers and fuse-wires in the gun-cotton-slabs and detonators in the hand-grenades. Nathuram addressed Badge and said "Badge, this is our last effort – the work must be accomplished – see to it that everything is arranged properly."

Deshpande-Bias-Karmarkar-Tukaram-Bandopant:

After the gun-cotton-slabs and the hand-grenades had been fitted properly they came back to the room, and found that Gopal had repaired his revolver. Apte then said that they should decide as to what articles should be carried by whom. Nathuram, Apte, Karkare, Madanlal, Gopal, Badge and Shankar were all in the room at the time. Apte said that Madanlal should have one gun-cotton-slab and one hand-grenade, Shankar one gun-cotton-slab and one hand-grenade, Nathuram, Gopal, and Karkare should have one hand-grenade each and that he (Apte) and Badge should have one revolver each. Badge thereon said that one gun-cotton-slab was enough to create commotion by explosion and asked as to why two gun-cotton slabs were required for the purpose. He then said that his (Badge's) suggestion was that one gun-cotton-slab and one hand-grenade should be given to Madanlal, that one hand-grenade should be given to Gopal, that one hand-grenade should be given to Karkare, that one hand-grenade and one revolver should be given to Shankar, and that one hand-grenade and one revolver should be given to Badge. He further suggested that Nathuram and Apte should remain there to give signals. This suggestion of Badge was accepted. Karkare then suggested that as soon as Madanlal exploded the gun-cotton-slab, all of them should shoot and throw the hand-grenades on Gandhiji. Apte then said that Madanlal should explode the gun-cotton-slab near the wall and that Badge should enter the room posing as a photographer and that he should shoot and throw the hand-grenade through the trellis work of the window of that room. Apte then said that he would stand and give signals to Madanlal and that Nathuram would stand and give the signal to Badge. The others were to mix themselves up with those in the prayer-ground. **Apte then suggested that they should assume false names. Nathuram assumed the name of 'Deshpande', Karkare that of 'Bias',Apte that of 'Karmarkar', Shankar that of 'Tukaram' and Badge that of 'Bandopant'. Appropriate names were also assumed by Madanlal and Gopal. It was also decided that they should change their clothes, Godse put on a half-sleeve shirt, shorts, stockings and shoes of khaki colour like those worn by soldiers, Apte put on a coat and trousers of dark blue colour like that worn by officers of the Air Force, Karkare put on a Nehru Shirt, a dhoti and a Gandhi cap; Madanlal put on a coat, trousers, etc., Gopal put on a coat, a shirt, and shorts. Badge put on a Nehru shirt and a dhoti, and Shankar put on a white coat, a shirt, a dhoti and a cap.** Karkare painted false moustaches and darkened his eyebrow and place a red mark on his forehead. Apte handed over the gun-cotton slab and one-hand-grenade to Karkare to be handed over to Madanlal; he gave one hand-grenade and one revolver to Shankar, and one hand-grenade and one revolver to Badge. Karkare and Gopal took one hand-grenade each. Badge put the revolver and the hand-grenades handed over to him at the Marina Hotel in the bag which Madanlal had brought with him from Bombay. Madanlal and Karkare then left the place for the Birla House with one grenade each. Apte, Gopal, Badge, and Shankar left the place 15 or 20 minutes later. Nathuram stayed behind stating that he would follow later.

Shoot and finish:

In the Marina Hotel conference, the prisoners had spoken in Marhati. When the discussions took place as to show the stuff was to be distributed and as to how it was to be used none of them told Shankar anything, but going down from the Marina Hotel Badge suggested to Shankar as to the part that he had to play. Shankar had taken no part in fixing the detonators in the room. He was just standing there. Even on the morning of the 20th January when they went to the Birla House, Badge did not issue any instructions to him. At no stage had Shankar asked Badge as to what the matter was all about. It was only when they were getting out of the Marina Hotel that Badge told Shankar that he was to throw the hand-grenade on the person at whom he throw the hand-grenade and that he was to shoot the person at whom Badge would shoot, and that the person concerned was an old man known as Gandhiji and that he was to be finished.

"Tyayyar hai kiya?" (Are you ready?).

The four of them viz., Apte, Gopal, Badge, and Shankar engaged a taxi near the Marina hotel and proceeded to the Hindu Mahasabha Office. They carried two bags with them. Badge's bag contained the revolver and the hand-grenade which were made over to him, while Gopal's bag contained a gun-cotton-slab, some fuse wire and some cartridges. Gopal and Badge got down from the taxi and proceeded to the hall of the Hindu Mahasabha Bhawan. Gopal kept the bag that he had brought with him in the cupboard. Badge took a towel. Both of them came out, got into the taxi and went to the Birla House along with Apte and Shankar. They went to the back of the Birla House near the **chawl** by the same road that Apte had shown them that morning. The taxi was stopped in the circular space on the left hand side. All four get out and met Madanlal when they had proceeded three or four paces. There were two or three persons at the place form where Madanlal had come. All five then proceeded towards the gate leading to the chawl. Apte then asked Madanlal *"Tyayyar hai kiya?"*(Are you ready?). Madanlal said that he was ready, that he had placed the slab and that it was only to be ignited. Apte thereon said that as soon as he gave the signal Madanlal was to light a match and ignite it. This conversation took place when they were proceeding towards the gate leading to the **chawl.** As they reached the gate Karkare came out from towards the prayer-ground side and proceeded towards the room that had been shown to Badge in the morning by Apte. He was seen talking to somebody there. He also saw Apte, Badge, Gopal, Shankar, and Madanlal and both he and Apte proceeded towards each other and met.

Madanlal Challo!

Karkare told Apte that much time had passed, that Mahatmaji had come and that the prayer had begun. He stated further that he had made arrangements with the occupant of the room to allow someone to enter the room as a photographer. When Apte said this to Badge, Nathuram arrived. Badge looked towards the room and found two persons near the room. There was also a one-eyed man sitting on a cot outside the room. Badge got frightened because he thought that if he went into the room and something happened, he would get trapped inside the room. Nathuram told him that he should not get frightened as arrangements had been made for all of them to escape. Nathuram, Apte, and Karkare went on pressing Badge to go into the room and told him that he should not get frightened. Badge told them that rather than strike from inside the room he would prefer to strike from the front. He said that he would shoot from the open opposite where Mahatmaji sat and Apte accepted this suggestion. Badge signalled to Shankar and Apte and Shankar then went to the taxi. Nathuram, Apte, Karkare, Madanlal, and Gopal were moving about and talking among themselves in the compound of the chawl. Badge took out his revolver and also got Shankar's revolver taken out. He wrapped the two revolvers in the towel, kept the package in the bag and placed the bag in the taxi. Badge handed over his hand-grenade to Shankar and asked him not to do anything with the grenade unless he gave the word. They then left the taxi and went towards Nathuram and others. Badge placed both his hands in the outer pockets of his shirt in order to show Godse and Apte that he was ready. When he approached Apte, he asked him whether Badge was ready. He told Apte that he was ready and started proceeding towards the prayer-ground. Shankar was with Badge. Apte placed his hand on Madanlal's back and said *'challo'*. Madanlal proceeded towards the place where the slab had been kept. Karkare also followed them towards the prayer-ground.

There was a good gathering at the prayer meeting which was being presided over by Mahatma Gandhi. Badge took his place towards the right of Mahatmaji, Karkare stood towards the right of Badge, and Shankar took his position further towards the right of Karkare. About three or four minutes later there was a big explosion. About 5 or 6 persons ran in the direction from which the smoke was coming. Mahatmaji raised his hand signifying to the people to keep calm. Madanlal was arrested at the spot and was led in custody towards a tent. Badge and Shankar got mixed up in the people who were leaving the prayer grounds and left by the main gate. They engaged a *Tonga* and reached the Hindu Mahasabha Bhawan.

As soon as Badge and Shankar reached the Hindu Mahasabha Office, Badge asked Shankar to go into the jungle behind the office and throw away the hand-grenades that Shankar had with him. Shankar went out to throw away the hand-grenades, and Badge started tying up the bedding. At this time Nathuram and Apte also arrived. Apte asked Badge what had happened. Badge abused both of them and asked them to get out. They went away. Shankar buried the explosives and returned to the Sabha. Badge suddenly recollected that Gopal had left his bag in the cupboard and be accordingly asked Shankar to throw away that bag as well. Shankar went out with the bag and came back after emptying the bag and concealing its contents. They left the empty bag in the room, came out of the Mahasabha office with the bedding, engaged a *Tonga* near the Birla Mandir and proceeded to the New Delhi Railway Station. Badge purchased two third class tickets to Bombay. The police were moving about and there was commotion at the Station. Badge got suspicious. He took a *Tonga* and left with Shankar for the main Railway Station at Delhi. They took train at 9.30 or 10 p.m. on the 20th and got down at the Kalyan Railway Station at 11.30 p.m. on the 22nd. They then purchased tickets for Poona and reached Poona Railway Station at about 4 or 4.30 p.m. the same day. Gopal and Karkare are said to have spent the night of the 20th January at the Frontier Hindu hotel near the Delhi Railway Station.

There is nothing on the record to indicate the date on or the time at or the manner in which Gopal left Delhi or the manner in which he occupied himself from the 21st to the 24thJanuary. It is surmised that during this period he returned to Bombay for we hear of him next at the Elphinstone Hotel Annexe on the 24th at C.M. Joshi's place and at Thane on the 25th January 1948.

20/01/1948: Retiring Room No.1 Kanpur Railway Station:

There is no doubt, however, in regard to the movements of Nathuram and Apte. Shortly after the explosion on the 20th they proceeded to the Railway Station at Delhi and purchased two first class tickets for Kanpur Central Station. On reaching Kanpur, Nathuram and Apte went to Retiring Room No.1 at the Kanpur Railway station and engaged it for the night after making appropriate entries in the appropriate register.

22/01/1948: Room No.6 Elphinstone Hotel Annexe, Bombay:

They left Kanpur on the 22nd January, and reached Bombay on the 23rd. They went to the Arya Pathik Ashram at about 9 p.m. and Apte asked for a room with two beds under the name of D. Narayan. No room with double beds was available, but they were allotted two beds in a room containing eight beds. They left their luggage in the Ashram, went out of the building and returned at 1 a.m. Early next morning (at 6 a.m.) the Manager (P.W.63) asked Nathuram to register his name. The latter began looking towards Apte and Apte told the Manager that person was his own man, that he was going to leave him at the Railway Station and that he would make a full entry on his return. Apte returned at about 1.15 a.m. was given a separate room (No.30) and made the entry Ex.P.110 (The previous entry is Ex.P.109). Apte returned with a lady who stayed with Apte throughout the day on the 24th January and the night between the 24th and the 25th January. Apte and the lady left the hotel in the early morning of the 25th January while it was still dark.

Nathuram and Apte do not appear to have been satisfied with accommodation provided for them in the Arya Pathik Ashram and they accordingly went and engaged Room No.6 Elphinstone Hotel Annexe. They stayed there from 2.15 p.m. on the 24th January to 6.30 am on the 27th January. The names of the passengers as given to the Manager (P.W.61) were N. Vinayak Rao and a friend. It is said that Gopal came to visit the two passengers on the 24th or 25th January 1948.

25/01/1948: Viking Service Bombay to Delhi:

On the 25th January 1948 Apte and Godse went to the Air India Office in the morning and reserved two seats for Delhi on the 27th January 1948 by the Viking Service under the assumed names of **D. Narayan Rao** and **N. Vinayake Rao.**

Nathuram, Apte, Karkare and Gopal are said have met each other in the house of Mr. G.M. Joshi at Thana on Sunday, the 25th January.

26/01/1948: Dada Maharaj and Dixit Maharaj:

Karkare left Thana sometime on the 26th January. On the morning of the 26th January Nathuram and Apte went and saw Dixitji Maharaj and his elder brother Dada Maharaj. They repeated their request for a revolver. Dixitji Maharaj put them off by stating that he would consider the matter only if they told him the object for which the revolver was required. Dada Maharaj also asked them as to why they were so anxious to obtain a revolver. They replied that he (Dada Maharaj) would see in due course what they were about to achieve.

27/01/1948: D, Narayan Rao and N. Vinayaka Rao by air to Delhi:

On the 27th January, Nathuram and Apte left Bombay for Delhi by the morning plane travelling under the assumed names of D. Narayan Rao and N. Vinayaka Rao. They are said to have left Delhi the same afternoon by train and to have reached Gwalior at about 10.30 p.m. They proceeded to the house of Dr. Parchure and stayed there for the night. The prosecution allege that on the following day they told Dr. Parchure that they were "going to do some terrible feat" before the 2nd February 1948. This terrible feat was the "assassination of Mahatma Gandhi" at Delhi. They showed a revolver to Dr. Parchure and asked him to get a better one for them from someone at Gwalior. Dr. Parchure introduced them to Dandwate who brought a pistol belonging to one Jagdish Prasad Goel (P.W.39). The purpose of their visit to Gwalior having been accomplished they returned to Delhi by train.

At about 12 o'clock on the 29th January Nathuram appeared at the Booking Office at Delhi and engaged a Retiring Room at the Delhi railway Station under the assumed name of N. Vinayak Rao. Apte and Karkare are said to have been with Nathuram at the Railway Station on the 29th and 30th February 1948.

Thees January 1948: Delhi Birla House: Avaben and Manuben:Impending Doom:

At about 5 o'clock on the afternoon of the 30th January S. Gurbachan Singh (P.W.82) signalled to Mahatma Gandhi that it was the time for prayer. Mahatma Gandhi came out of the room and the witness told him that he was a little late that day but Gandhiji laughingly replied that those who are late receive punishment. He then began his last walk from his room upto the prayer ground with no premonition. He was resting his hands on the shoulders of two girls Avaben and Manuben of the impending doom. A big congregation was waiting at the prayer ground as this was the first day after the fast that Mahatma Gandhi was about to address a prayer meeting. Mahatma Gandhi climbed up the steps leading to the prayer ground and had gone only six or seven paces from the steps when the crowd opened up into a lane to enable him to pass through. When Mahatmaji had gone about three paces into the opening made by the crowd, Mahatmaji folded his hands to the crowd according to his usual practice. Then Nathuram stepped out of the crowd took his pistol between the palms of his two hands bowed his head before the Mahatmaji and fired thrice at point blank range. Mahatmaji uttered the words **"Hey Ram'** and sank to the ground

with folded hands. The assassin was seized by the persons who had collected at the spot and when his pistol was snatched from his hand the smoke was still coming out of the barrel. The infuriated crowed began assaulting the assassin who received an injury on his head and started bleeding. Assistant Sub Inspector Amar Nath assisted by a Constable and Sergeant Devraj Singh took the assailant on the other side of the platform and away from the crowd. He was taken down from the platform and four cartridges were removed from the pistol. The assassin was removed to the Tughlak Road Police Station and a number of articles were recovered from his person.

Efforts were made to apprehend the persons who were suspected of having had a hand in the crime. Badge was arrested at Poona on the 31st January 1948. Gopal was arrested at Uksan on the 5th February. Shankar was arrested at Bombay on the 6th February. On the 11th February Shankar took certain respectable persons to a place behind the "Hindu Mahasabha Bhawan" New Delhi, and dug out a live hand-grenade, a gun-cotton slab and twenty-five cartridges from one place and two live hand-grenades from another place.

Beretta for Mahatma Gandhi:

On the 18th February Dr. Parchure made a Confession before Mr. R.B. Atal, Magistrate First Class, Laskhar,[22] in which he admitted that he was aware that the pistol was required for killing Mahatma Gandhi.

On the 26th February, Apte took certain respectable persons behind the Hindu Mahasabha Bhawan where he said they had tried out a pistol. A tree with four bullet marks thereon was shown by him. The branches of the tree containing the bullet marks were cut and taken into possession. Apte also

---

[22] Laskhar Court in Gwalior, Madhya Pradesh. Dr. Parchure was native of Gwalior.

pointed out a place from where he said the pistol had been fired. An empty cartridge-case found lying there and was taken into possession.

The Bombay Public Security Measures Act was made applicable to the Province of Delhi on the 2nd June 1947 under the provisions of the Delhi Laws Act, 1912, and came into force with effect from the 13th June 1947. A Special Court was constituted under Sections 10 and 11 of the statute on the 4th May 1948. Charges under Sections 120-B, 109, 114 and 115 of the Indian penal Code read with charges under Section 302 of the Indian Penal Code and charges under Sections 3,4,5, and 6 of the Indian Explosives Substances Act, and under Section 19 of the Indian Arms Act were framed against all the prisoners as well as against Badge who was later granted a pardon. A summary of the main prosecution evidence was then supplied to the prisoners. Badge was tendered a pardon on the 21st June and evidence connected on the 24th June.

Such are the tragic and sordid circumstances of the crime which has led to this conviction against which the prisoners appeal; but before the Court **proceedings** to apply itself to the consideration of the question whether these circumstances have been established it would be desirable to set out the version given by Nathuram and Apte, the principal offenders in this case.

They state that on the 15th January they happened to go to the office of the Hindu Mahasabha at Dadar on one of their usual visits when they came across Badge who asked them what they were doing there. They told him that they wanted to wastage a peaceful demonstration at one of the prayer meetings at Delhi. He enquired if he could accompany them to Delhi and join the demonstration as that would enable him to sell his stuff in the capital of India. Nathuram and Apte told him that they had no objection to his accompanying them to Delhi but they objected to his carrying the stuff with him as it would get them into trouble. Nathuram and Apte reached Delhi o0n the 17th and went to the various refugee camps with the object of enrolling volunteers for the demonstration on the 20th or the 21st January.

Badge happened to turn up at the Marina Hotel on the morning of the 20th and Apte asked him to proceed to the Birla House that evening and meet him there so that it might be found out if it was possible to stage a demonstration there that evening. At about 4.30 p.m. Apte left the Marina Hotel for the Birla House as arranged but Nathuram could not go as he had a slight headache. Badge and Shankar met Apte as he came out of the Birla House and he took them to the Birla House in a car. They alighted from the car at the back of the Birla House and proceeded to the prayer grounds. Unfortunately, none of the volunteers with whom they had fixed up had arrived. When the prayers began they found that loud speakers had failed. Some of the volunteers arrived thereafter but Apte thought that it was a fit occasion to stage a demonstration at the Birla House. Apte and Shankar then returned by car to the Marina Hotel. Badge arrived at the Hotel about half an hour later and saw Apte. He looked terribly frightened and said that a refugee by the name of Madanlal had been caught hold of at the Birla House in connection with the explosion that had taken place there. He further said that he had sold some stuff to the refugee and expressed regret for having brought the stuff to Delhi in spite of directions to the contrary. He then said that he was proceeding direct to Poona as it was unsafe to stay any more in Delhi. Apte conveyed the information to Nathuram who was still in bed and decided to leave Delhi forthwith. They thought that Madanlal would give up the name of Badge and Badge would give up their names as the three had come to Bombay for the purpose of staging demonstration.[23]

---

[23] One page ie Page 62 was blank in the Original Judgment. This remark is available in "True Copy" on page No.41.

Approver Evidence and the Prosecution Story:

The prosecution story outlined above in so far as it relates to the incidents commencing with the year 1947 and ending with the 20th January 1948, is based principally on the evidence of Badge who, as I have said above, was granted a pardon on the 21st June 1948. An accomplice is a competent witness against a prisoner but as he can escape the consequences of his own acts by helping the prosecution to secure the conviction of others, a practice has come to be established that the testimony of an accomplice cannot be acted upon unless it is corroborated in material particulars. If the necessary corroboration is available and if the Court is satisfied that the story narrated by him is substantially correct, it is open to the Court to believe one part of his story as well as another. In Tidd's Trial, 33 How. St. Tr. 1483 Garrow B., charging the jury, observed as follows:

"It may not be unfit to observe to you're here that the confirmation to be derived to an accomplice is not a repetition by others of the whole story of the accomplice and a confirmation of every part of it; that would be either impossible or unnecessary and absurd *** and therefore you are to look to the circumstances to see whether there are such a number of important facts confirmed as to give you reason to be persuaded that the main body of the story is correct. ***** You are each of you, to ask yourselves this question: Now that I have heard the accomplice and have heard other circumstances which are said to confirm the story he has told, does he appear to me to be so confirmed by unimpeachable evidence, as to some of the persons affected by his story or with respect to some of the facts stated by him, as to afford me good ground to believe that he also speaks the truth with regard to other prisoners or other facts with regard to which there may be no confirmation? Do I, upon the whole, feel convinced in my conscience that his evidence is true and such as I may safely act upon?"

The kind of corroboration required is not confirmation by independent evidence of everything the accomplice relates, as his evidence would be unnecessary if that were so. *R. v. Mullins* (3 Cox 526, 531). What is required is some independent testimony which affects the prisoner by tending to connect him with the crime; that is, evidence, direct or circumstantial, which implicates the prisoner which confirms in some material particular not only the evidence given by accomplice that the crime has been committed, but also the evidence that the prisoner committed it *R. v. Baskerville* (12 Cr.A.Reports 81). The prisoner's own evidence may afford the necessary corroboration, as may also his conduct in the circumstances of the case, *R. v. Modraft* (23 Cr.A.R.116) see also *R. V. Blatherwick* (6 Cr.A.R. 281).

Badge has given a very full and detailed account of the circumstances leading to the occurrence and the occurrence itself. Although the narration of facts covers several printed pages I have not been able to discern any obvious falsehood or a desire to suppress the true facts. He has made certain admissions which are damaging to his own character and reputation and which affect his own credibility, but he has not faltered or prevaricated as far as the facts of this case are concerned. It is his interest to tell the truth and so far as I can judge he has told it. I am of the opinion that the story narrated by him is substantially correct.

Let us now see whether the necessary amount of corroboration is available in this case.[24]

It is scarcely necessary to reproduce Badge's story in regard to the incidents which took place between the 9th and 20th January, for it has been set out in detail in the preceding paragraphs which are based principally on the evidence given by Badge. He himself states that on the 9th January Karkare,

---

[24] Page No.66 is blank in the Original Judgment. This remark can be found in the scanned copy of"True Copy Type Version" in Page No.43.

Madanlal, Om Parkash and Chopra saw the stuff at his house in Poona; that on the 10th January he went to the office of the Hindu Rashtra and promised to deliver two gun-cotton-slabs and five hand-grenades to Nathuram and Apte at Bombay on the evening of the 14th January; that Badge and Shankar met Nathuram and Apte near the office of the Hindu Mahasabha on the evening of the 14th and deposited the bag containing the stuff in the house of Dixitji Maharaj; that Nathuram, Apte, Karkare, Madanlal and Badge went to the house of Dixitji Maharaj on the morning of the 15th January; that they examined the stuff and told him that they were proceeding on an important mission; and that they requested him for the loan of one or two revolvers. The prisoners have challenged the correctness of this story. It is contended that even if the prosecution could not produce any independent evidence in regard to the incident of the 9th, they could certainly produce Om Parkash and Chopra who actually went to see the "stuff" that night and who did not figure in the list of prisoners who were arraigned before the Trial Court. It is said that the testimony of Badge in regard to this incident has been categorically denied by Apte, Karkare, and Madanlal and that the statements of these three persons should in fairness to the prisoners be allowed to outweigh the state of Badge. The Trial Court expressed the view that the prosecution were unable to trace Om Parkash and Chopra and that even if they had appeared in Court, it is somewhat doubtful if their evidence could have amounted to more than that of accomplices.

Again it is contended that the evidence in regard to the story that Badge was taken to the Hindu Rashtra Office on the morning of the 10th January and was asked to supply certain arms and ammunition stands uncorroborated and alone. It is contended that if that incident were true the prosecution could have had no difficulty in producing evidence in support thereof particularly as Badge paid his visit under the broad glare of the sun and must have been seen by a number of clerks and other employees who were working in the office of the Hindu Rashtra. Nor can it be said that the police could not have found a number of persons willing to state the truth. If the prosecution could examine persons like Mr. P.V. Godbole (P.W.85) who was the manager of an engineering firm of which a brother of Nathuram was a proprietor and if they could produce Mr. G.V. Kale (P.W.88) a friend of Mr. Godbole they could have had no difficulty in producing some member or employee of the press or even an outsider to support the assertion that Badge did in fact visit the office of Nathuram on the morning of the 10th January.

Again, it is said that corroborative evidence is conspicuous by its absence in regard to Badge's arrival in the office of the Hindu Mahasabha on the evening of the 14th January, in regard to his meeting Nathuram and Apte on the road near the said office and in regard to the deposit of the bag containing arms and ammunition in the house of Dixitji Maharaj. It is argued that if the facts to which he deposes are true it was not beyond the resources of the States to examine witnesses from the Hindu Mahasabha or at least to produce the servant with whom the bag was left.

Badge's statement to the effect that Nathuram and Apte met Badge and Shankar near the Hindu Mahasabha Office at Dadar on the 14th January, that they later accompanied them to the house of Dixitji Maharaj where the bag containing the stuff was deposited and that Nathuram paid a sum of Rs. 50/- to Badge on account of the travelling expenses incurred by him is said to be corroborated by two facts, namely, (a) that on the afternoon of the 14th January Nathuram and Apte travelled from Poona to Delhi and (b) that on the said date Nathuram did in fact pay a sum of Rs. 50/- to Badge. The evidence of P.W.60 Miss. Shantabai B. Modak makes it quite clear that these two persons did undertake the journey from Poona to Dadar on the afternoon of the 14th January, Miss. Modak who is a film actress of some repute deposes that she took the Poona Express at 3.20 or 3.30 p.m. on the 14th January and entered a second class compartment. While she was looking for a seat for herself, Apte who happened to be travelling in the same compartment stood up and offered his seat near the window to her, while he himself went and occupied a seat opposite that of Miss. Modak. In the meantime another gentleman whom the witness later identified as Nathuram arrived and took his seat by the side of Apte. Miss Modak and Apte conversed with each other on general topics. During the course of the conversation she happened to mention the fact that she was alighting at Dadar and Apte chivalrously offered to see her home. On arrival at Dadar Miss Modak told Apte that her brother had arrived with a car and offered to give a lift to the two male passengers to Shivaji Park. This offer was readily accepted. Both Nathuram and Apte admit that they travelled by train from Poona to Dadar and that Miss. Modak dropped them opposite the Savarkar Sadan. The evidence of Miss. Modak which is supposed by the admission of the two prisoners corroborates to an extent the statement of Badge that he was to deliver the stuff to Nathuram and Apte at Bombay and that they had travelled from Poona to Bombay to receive it.

But can the statement of Badge to the effect that both he and Shankar also travelled from Poona to Bombay the same day be accepted without demur? It is said that if Badge, Shankar, Nathuram and Apte travelled by the same train, they must have met each other either at Poona or at Dadar or at an intermediate station. I agree that if a number of persons travel by the same train, they are almost certain to meet each other at some stage of the journey; but the circumstances of this case are somewhat different. In the first place, there is nothing on the record to indicate that these two sets of passengers were travelling by the same train. It is true that both of them left Poona in the afternoon, but it has not been established that only one train left Poona for Dadar in the afternoon. Secondly, it must be remembered that we are dealing with at least one set of

passengers who were particularly anxious to avoid the public gaze. Badge and Shankar were travelling with a bag containing arms and explosives and were particularly anxious to appear as inconspicuous as possible. Again, it is possible that both he and his employee stayed inside their compartment as both of them are in the habit of travelling without ticket. The allegation, therefore, that Badge and Shankar could not have undertaken the journey from Poona to Dadar on the afternoon of the 14th January cannot thus be said to carry much force

The second piece of evidence which has been relied upon in support of the contention that Nathuram, Apte and Badge met on the 14th January is an entry Ex. P.323 in a diary Ex.P.218 which was recovered from the possession of Nathuram. This entry shows that on the 14th January Nathuram paid a sum of Rs. 50/- to a person of the name of Bandopant. The prosecution allege that this entry supports the statement of Badge that a sum of Rs. 50/- was paid to him on account of the travelling expenses incurred by him and his servant Shankar but that the name of Bandopant has been wrongly mentioned in order that the police should be prevented from establishing a connection between Nathuram and Badge. It is significant that the payment was made out of a joint fund of Rs. 2,000/- kept by Nathuram and Apte for carrying out the purposes of the conspiracy and that the name of Bandopant was assigned to Badge at the conference which took place at the Marina Hotel on the afternoon of the 20th January, Nathuram admits having paid a sum of Rs. 50/- to one Bandopant but he states that this Bandopant is an employee of his and a completely different person from Badge. It is unfortunate that Nathuram did not consider it desirable to put Bandopant into the witness-box in support of his assertion. The inevitable result, therefore, is that the statement of Badge, supported as it is by that of the entry, holds the field.

No evidence has been produced by the prosecution in support of the story narrated by

Badge that Nathuram, Apte and Badge went to the house of Dixitji Maharaj at 10 o'clock on the night of the 14th January and left the bag containing the stuff with a servant of the said Dixitji Maharaj. The prisoners allege that the servant should have been produced and that the non-prosecution of a witness who was available and who was actually examined by the police entitles the Court to presume that if the said witness had come to Court his evidence would have been unfavourable to the prosecution. *Prima facie* there is force in this contention, but the events which took place subsequently make it quite clear that the story narrated by Badge is substantially true.

Let us now examine the events which took place in Bombay on the 15th January which constitutes an important land-mark in the history of this case. Badge's statement to the effect that he accompanied Nathuram, Apte, Karkare and Madanlal to the house of Dixitji Maharaj for examining the contents of the bag which had been left in his house on the preceding evening has been corroborated by P.W.77 Goswami Dixitji Maharaj who resides within the precincts of the Mota Mandir at Bombay. This witness deposes that on the morning of the 15th January, Badge came to his house accompanied by Nathuram, Apte, Karkare, and Madanlal and asked for the bag that he had left with his servant on the preceding night. The witness asked Badge the name of the servant with whom the bag had been left and Badge immediately pointed towards **Angre** as the person to whom the bag had been given. Angre was asked to bring the bag but as he took some time in coming, the witness who had been ailing for a few days went to have a bath. On his return to the room, 20 or 25 minutes later he saw Badge showing the contents of the bag to his companions and talking to them. Amongst the articles which were being shown were two hand-grenades and two gun-cotton-slabs. Badge was trying to explain the manner in which the grenades should be used. The witness thought that the way Badge was trying to work the grenade was wrong and he actually demonstrated to the visitors the manner in which the grenade should be worked. After the explosives had been examined by those present they were put back into the bag and three of the persons, namely, Nathuram, and Madanlal left the room. The witness asked Badge and Apte who were still in the room as to the object of their coming to his house and exhibiting those articles in his room. They replied that they were proceeding on an important mission and asked for the loan of a revolver or a pistol. The witness asked them to tell him the nature of the mission on which they were proceeding, but they were not willing to divulge the secret at the stage. As they started to leave the room, the witness asked Badge to stay on but the latter replied that he would come and see the witness after a short while. Badge came back 15 or 20 minutes later, but was still unwilling to give any further information in regard to the mission on which they were proceeding. On being further pressed Badge ultimately agreed to visit the witness that day in the evening and to throw further light on the matter which had excited the curiosity of Dixitji Maharaj. Nathuram saw the witness again on the evening of the 15th or the morning of the 16th January or possibly a day or two later. Badge showed a revolver to the witness and told him that he had purchased that revolver for a sum ofRs. 325/- He requested the witness that even if he was not prepared to part with the revolver of his own, he might be good enough to pay him the price of the weapon which Nathuram, Apte, and Badge had paid for the same. The witness asked Badge to tell him the object for which the revolver was required and Badge replied that they had collected arms and ammunition worth thirty or forty thousand rupees and that they were proceeding to Kashmir with the arms to help the native population against the raiders and for the purpose of sabotage. The witness, however, expressed his inability to be of any help to them. On the 17th January the witness met with an accident.

The witness was taken to an identification parade where he identified Nathuram, Apte, and Madanlal. He gave a description of Karkare to the police but was unable topic him out of at the identification parade.

Our attention has been invited to a number of discrepancies between the statements in the testimony of the approver and that of Dixitji Maharaj. The first is that according to the approver he handed the bag over to Apte who gave it to Karkare who passed it on to Madanlal. Dixitji Maharaj makes no reference whatsoever to this incident, though he admits that Karkare and Madanlal had come to his house. The second contradiction is in regard to the date on which the approver saw Dixitji Maharaj after he had paid a visit to him on the morning of the 15th January. Badge states that he was in Poona on the 16th and visited the house of Dixitji Maharaj on the morning of the 18th. Dixitji Maharaj on the other hand deposes that this visit took place either on the evening of the 15 January or on the morning of the 16th although he does not rule out the possibility of there being a difference of one or two days between his visit on the morning of the 15th and his last visit. While referring to the incidents of the 26th January he states that Badge saw him 7 or 8 days before (that is on the 18th or19th January) and showed him a revolver which he had presumably purchased in Poona. He is hopelessly vague in regard to his dates and I am inclined to think that Badge is telling the truth when he states that in accordance with the arrangement that had been made between himself and Nathuram and Apte, he reached Bombay on the 17th and saw Dixitji Maharaj on the 18th. The fact that Badge showed him a revolver goes to prove that Badge must have gone to Poona as alleged by him

There is yet another contradiction between the statements of Badge and Dixitji Maharaj. Badge stated that after the stuff had been shown to the conspirators and after Karkare and Madanlal had left, Apte asked Dixitji Maharaj to lend them a revolver or two as they were proceeding on an important mission. According to him, therefore, Nathuram was present when the talk about the revolvers took place. Dixitji Maharaj on the other hand states that this talk took place after Nathuram, Karkare, and Madanlal had left the room.

Two other criticisms have also been made. It is said, in the first place, that the bag in which the stuff was brought from Poona to Bombay and which was later recovered from the possession of Gopal could not be identified by Dixitji Maharaj and consequently that the story about the meeting on the 15th, and the contents of the bag being shown must be characterised as false. Again, it is said that the statement of Badge to the effect that he supplied two gun-cotton-slabs and five hand-grenades to Nathuram and Apte is contradicted by Dixitji Maharaj who admits having seen only two gun-cotton-slabs and two hand-grenades were shown to Dixitji Maharaj on the morning of the 15th January and if those articles alone were made over to Madanlal, it is contended that the story of Badge to the effect that a larger number of articles was supplied falls to the ground.

The discrepancies to which our attention has been invited are of a minor character and serve only to show that Dixitji Maharaj is not repeating a story which has been taught to him but is making a correct statement of the facts which he saw with his own eyes. He is unable to remember whether Apte handed over the bag to Karkare and whether Karkare passed it on to Madanlal but this is too minor a detail to be remembered by a person who had no particular interest in the bag. He is making a mistake in regard to the precise date on which Badge is said to have visited him after 15th January, but again his failure to remember the correct date may be due either to lapse of memory or to an honest mistake. He says he saw only two slabs and two grenades with badge but there may be others in the bag. He was not interested in the number of articles in the bag but in the manner in which a grenade should be worked.

he does not remember the names of the particular persons who were in his room when Apte asked the witness for the loan of a revolver, but again the witness may not have been able, after the lapse of so long a period, to identify the particular bag in which the articles had been brought by Badge. None of these objections appear to me to shed any doubt on the credibility of a witness who is wholly independent and disinterested, who is occupying a very prominent position in the city of Bombay and who is closely related to the head of a religious sect. He has no reason to be biased or partial to one party or the other. He has given his evidence convincingly and has not departed from the truth. His evidence furnishes very strong corroboration of the testimony of the approver.

Nathuram, Apte, Karkare, and Madanlal deny having visited the house of Dixitji Maharaj on the morning of the 15th January or having seen the stuff which is said to have been brought by Badge. Nathuram stated before us in Court, that although Apte and Madanlal had previous contacts with Dixitji Maharaj, he (Nathuram) had none. He contends that although he was picked up by this witness at the identification parade that fact does not necessarily prove that he had gone to the house of the witness on the 15th January. He had paid a visit to him on the 26th January **when** he went to the Mota Mandir in connection with the affairs of the Jaiselmer State and the witness had seen him there. It is accordingly contended that the witness must have identified Nathuram merely because he had seen him on the 26th January.

I have gone carefully through the evidence of this witness and am satisfied that he is telling nothing but the truth. He has no reason for making the statement that they visited his house on the morning of the 15th January if they did not go there on that date. If he had been a tutored witness, he could have made his statement conform to the statement of Badge and obviated the possibility of discrepancies occurring. It may be that he has

been purchasing arms and ammunition for himself and for his friends' relations but that fact would not show that he is making this statement under the pressure of the police. His evidence establishes beyond reasonable doubt **(a)** that a bag containing arms and explosives was left at his house on the night of the 14th January; **(b)** that it was left with his servant Narayan Vithal Angre; **(c)** that Nathuram, Apte, Karkare, Madanlal, and Badge came to his house on the morning of the 15th;**(d)** that Badge showed the contents of the bag to his companions; **(e)** that Badge told him that they were proceedings on an important mission; **(f)** that neither Badge nor the other visitors would disclose to him the nature of the mission; **(g)** that they were anxious to obtain one or two revolvers from him; and **(h)** that they allowed him to live in the belief that the arms and ammunition were required either in connection with the agitation against the Hyderabad State or in connection with the trouble in the Kashmir State. There can be little doubt that the bag containing the stuff was left in the house of Dixitji Maharaj as the police were not likely to visit that place. The Hindu Mahasabha building was not regarded as safe. it is also clear that Nathuram, Apte, Karkare, and Madanlal went to the house of Dixitji Maharaj on the following morning with the object of examining the stuff prior to its being sent to Delhi with Karkare and Madanlal. Badge states that Madanlal had taken his bedding from the Hindu Mahasabha office to the house of Dixitji Maharaj and that as soon as the bag containing the stuff was handed over to him, he packed the bag along with the stuff into his bedding. This statement is fully in accord with the probabilities of the case. It is common ground that Karkare and Madanlal left Bombay for Delhi the same night.

The story narrated by Dixitji Maharaj to the effect that Nathuram and his companions came to his house on the morning of the 15th January and examined the contents of the bag, strongly supports the statement of Badge that he had brought the stuff to Bombay as a result of the order placed with him by Nathuram and Apte. Badge states that a definite order had been placed with him by Nathuram and Apte for the delivery of the two gun-cotton-slabs and five hand-grenades to them at Dadar on the evening of the 14th January. The evidence of Dixitji Maharaj substantially corroborates that statement.

It may perhaps be convenient at this stage to deal with an objection which has been taken. It is contended on behalf of the prisoners that if Angre produced the bag containing the stuff before Dixitji Maharaj on the morning of the 15th January and if he was examined by the police shortly afterwards and if he was actually taken to the identification parade where he identified the persons whom he had seen including Karkare, and if he was available for examination before the Trial Court, the prosecution should have produced him before the Trial Court particularly as Dixitji Maharaj did not identify Karkare at the identification parade. There is in my opinion considerable force in this argument. I am clearly of the opinion that prosecution have failed in their duty in not examining an essential witness. This does not mean, however, that the entire story must break down merely because one of the witnesses has not been produced. Even after raising the necessary presumptions against the prosecution, I am of the opinion that Badge's story to the effect that an order was placed with him for the supply of explosives and that he brought the explosives in compliance with that order has been corroborated in material particulars. [25]

Taxi No:BMT-110: Driver: Aitappa Kotian:

Badge states that in accordance with the arrangement which had been arrived at between Nathuram and Apte on the one hand and Badge on the other, he arrived at the Victoria Terminus Railway Station on the morning of the 17th January. Nathuram and Apte met him outside the barrier when Apte suggested that before proceeding to Delhi, they should collect some funds for the purposes of the conspiracy. They engaged Tax No. BMT-110 belonging to **Aitappa Kotian** (P.W.80) and visited the Bombay Dyeing House where they met Seth Mathuradas (P.W.74), the Hindu Mahasabha Office where they picked up Shankar, the Savarkar Sadan where Mr. Savarkar blessed their mission, the house of Afjulpurkar (P.W.73) where Mr. Afjulpurkar gave them a donation of Rs. 100/-, the house of Mr. M.G. Kale (P.W.86) where Mr. Kale advanced them a loan of Rs. 1,000/- and again the Bombay Dyeing Works where Mr. Mathuradas paid Apte a sum of Rs. 1,000/- by way of a donation, the house of Dixitji Maharaj where Apte asked for a revolver and the Santa Cruz Aerodrome where Apte paid a sum of Rs. 250/- to Badge and asked him to leave for Delhi the same day left for Delhi by air from the Santa Cruz Aerodrome, badge and Shankar then drove back from Santa Cruz in the same taxi and went to the house of Mr. R.K. Patwardhan in Kurla. Patwardhan was________ but Badge told Rs. 55_____ to the taxi-driver and awaited the arrival of Patwardhan. The latter did not turn up and Badge and Shankar accordingly left by train from Kurla Railway Station to Dadar Railway Station. They returned to the house of Patwardan at 3.30 p.m. and stayed with him till 9 or 9.30 p.m. Patwardhan advanced a sum of Rs. 400/- by way of **loan** to Badge. They returned to Dadar and spent the night at Asra Hotel.[26]

_____ **Both** Nathuram and Apte admit that they engaged a taxi on the morning of the 17th January for collecting funds for the Hindu Rashtra and for proceeding to Delhi. This part of Badge's story thus stands corroborated.[27]

---

[25] Page No.86 is blank in the Original Judgment. This remark can be found in the scanned copy of 'True Copy Type Version" in Page No.55.

[26] Words are undecipherable for the underlined places. Eds.

[27] Words are undecipherable for the underlined places. Eds.

Agreement to assassinate Mahatma Gandhi:

The story narrated by Badge to the effect that the **"prisoners had entered into an agreement to assassinate Mahatma Gandhi"** receives general corroboration from the fact that between the 17th and the 20th January all six prisoners namely, Nathuram, Apte, Madanlal, Karkare, Badge and Shankar happened to be in Delhi. Karkare and Madanlal left Victoria Terminus at about 9.15 p.m. on the 15th January and travelled by the Peshawar Express. Karkare and Madanlal took the 9.15 p.m. train from Delhi on the 15th January and travelled in a 3rd Class compartment. P.W. Angchekar who happened to be travelling in the same compartment states that on the morning of the 16th he heard one of the passengers talking to another in Marhatti. Taking him to be a man of his own country, the witness entered into conversation with him (Karkare). He told Karkare that he was a refugee from Karachi and was proceeding to Delhi for getting his services transferred to the Government of India. He stated further that he was anxious to leave Delhi the same day but was somewhat doubtful of his being able to do so if the train was running late. Karkare told him that he would make arrangements for his stay at the Birla Mandir in case the train reached Delhi and he was unable to finish his work in time. When the train stopped at Delhi at 12.30 p.m. on the 17th and the passengers alighted at the platform,. Angchekar noticed for the first time that Madanlal had also travelled in the same compartment. Karkare, Madanlal, and Angchekar engaged a *Tonga* and proceeded to the Hindu Mahasabha Office. No accommodation was available there. They then proceeded to the Birla Mandir where also no accommodation could be secured. The *Tongawala* then took them to the Sharif Hotel in Chandni Chowk where Karkare, Madanlal, and Angchekar engaged a room on the first floor. Within two hours of their arrival in the hotel, Karkare left the room saying that he was going to the Hindu Mahasabha Office.

Madanlal also expressed a desire to go out, for he said that he wanted to see his uncle in the Chandni Chowk. Both Madanlal and the witness went to the Chandni Chowk. On the following morning i.e., the 18th January the witness accompanied Madanlal to Sabzimandi as Madanlal wanted to see a relation of his in connection with his marriage. At about midday Madanlal and the witness went to the house of Madanlal's maternal uncle. Karkare did not return to the hotel for dinner or until the witness went to bed on the night of the 18th January. He had not returned when the witness got up from his bed on the following morning. The witness left for the Transfer Bureau on the morning of the 19th. When he returned from the Bureau at about 3 or 3.30 p.m. he saw Karkare and Madanlal talking to a person when the witness later identified as Gopal. As soon as he entered the room, Karkare told him that Madanlal and he were going to vacate the room as they were spending the night in the Maharashtar Niwas and were proceeding to Jullundur in connection with the wedding of Madanlal. Angchekar told Karkare that he had finished his work and was returning to Bombay the very same day. The witness asked Karkare his permanent address in Bombay but Karkare replied that it was not necessary to supply him his permanent address. Madanlal, however, appeared to be more friendly. He said that he was residing at the Chembur Refugee Camp at Bombay. Angchekar stayed in the room till about 5 p.m. except for a short period when he went to the Town Hall to receive a free ticket to Bombay. Karkare and Madanlal had not left by 5 p.m., for the clothes which they had given for washing had not arrived. The witness paid a sum of Rs. 20/- to Karkare as his share of the bill which had been submitted in respect of Karkare, Madanlal, and the witness. The evidence of this witness shows that Karkare and Madanlal left Bombay on the 15th January and reached Delhi at about midday on the 17th; that they put up together in a room in the Sharif Hotel; that Karkare left the hotel within two hours of his arrival stating that he was going to the Hindu Mahasabha; that he did not return to the hotel either on the night of the 18th or till after breakfast on the morning of the 19th, that when the witness returned to the hotel at about 3 o'clock on the afternoon of the 19th he found a stranger whom he later identified as Gopal sitting with Karkare and Madanlal; and that Karkare told the witness that they were leaving the room the same day, spending the night in the Maharashtar Niwas and proceeding to Jullundur the following morning in connection with the wedding of Madanlal. An effort was made on behalf of the prisoners to impugn the credibility of this witness on the ground that as he was a refugee from Sind (who had lost everything as a result of the political upheaval) he should be regarded as a man of straw whose evidence should not be accepted at its_________ value.[28] A perusal of Exhibit P.12 makes it quite clear that the witness is not a person whose evidence should be viewed with suspicion. He is poor but respectable. The witness who is about 30 years of age passed the Matriculation Examination of the Bombay University in the year 1936 and was working as a Rationing Enquiry Inspector immediately before the 15th August, 1947, when Sind became a part and parcel of Pakistan. He can read, speak, and write Marhatti and English and can read and speak Hindi and Gujarati. He was drawing an aggregate salary of Rs. 163/- *per mensem*. He has no reason to be hostile either to Madanlal or to Gopal. The statement made by him does not betray any anxiety on his party to implicate Gopal. He identified Gopal in an identification parade which was held on the 30th March. Knowledge, intelligence, quality of memory and all other attributes which constitute ability together with those moral qualities which constitute credibility are united in this witness. His testimony is consistent with reasonable probabilities. He appears to me to be intrinsically and inherently reliable and there is no reason, therefore, why his evidence should not be accepted

at its face value against Karkare, Madanlal, and Gopal.[29]

In the arguments addressed to us by Nathuram a good deal of emphasis was laid on the fact that there was no evidence to show that either Badge or Madanlal had stayed at the office of the Hindu Mahasabha on the night of the 19th January. Mr. Daphtary admits that he has not been able to produce any witness from the Hindu Maha Sabha or from any other place with the object of establishing that Madanlal and Badge did in fact stay in the Hindu Maha Sabha on the night in question. But he contends that the allegation made by Badge in his evidence to the effect that he had spent the night of the 19th January in the Hindu Maha Sabha was not challenged in the Court below. In that Court the prisoners appear to have proceeded on the assumption that Badge and Madanlal had in fact stayed in the Hindu Maha Sabha, for no questions whatsoever were directed to the witnesses appearing for the prosecution with the object of challenging this allegation. On the other hand the questions which were put in cross-examination make it quite clear that the presence of Badge and Madanlal in the Hindu Maha Sabha on the day in question was assumed. At one place he states:

> **"It** is not a fact that on return from the Birla House I had gone to the jungle behind the Hindu Mahasabha office to answer the call of nature when I was challenged by the forest guards."

Again at another place a question was put to Badge on behalf of one of the defence counsel. The question is as follows:

> **"I** put it to you that you held discussions in regard to the distribution of the 'stuff' and in regard as to how the 'stuff' was to be used in the room in which Nathuram Godse was

---

[28] Word is undecipherable for the underlined place. Eds.

[29] Page No.94 is blank in the Original Judgment. This remark can be found in the scanned copy of "True Copy Type Version" in Page No.60.

lying ill and that Nathuram Godse asked you not to discuss things there but to go to the bath room. Is it true?"

Then follows a note which is in the following terms:

"**The** counsel at this stage after consulting Mr. Bhopatkar does not press the question and withdraws it saying that this is not the sense that he intended to convey to the witness."

It may be that this question was later withdrawn but the fact remains that the question was actually put to Badge. The language of the question makes it quite clear that the prisoners were not seriously challenging the story that there was a meeting of the prisoners in the Marina Hotel on the morning of the 20th.

Again at another place Badge made the following statement in his cross-examination:

"**When** Madanlal, Om Parkash and Chopra along with Karkare came to see me on 9th January 1948, I knew that those were the persons who had been referred to by Apte."

The answer appears to show that the prisoners were not seriously challenging the visit of these men to Badge on the 10th January, although they wanted to establish that these persons visited Badge with some other object.

Again, at page 113 appear certain other statements. At lines 14 and 15 Badge states as follows:

"**It** is not a fact that I had gone with Madanlal to the Gole-Market to take meals in the evening of 19th January 1948. It is not a fact that I had gone to the Gole-Market to take tea on the morning of the 20th January 1948."

These questions show that the allegation that Madanlal and Badge were together on the evening

of the 19th January and the morning of the 20th January was not denied. At lines 42 to 46 of the same page appear the following:

"**It** is not a fact that when I reached the Hindu Mahasabha office on the night of 19th January 1948 Apte rebuked me for having come late and for not having brought with me volunteers although he had left money with me for that purpose."

This answer also goes to indicate that the prisoners admitted that Badge came to the Hindu Mahasabha on the night of the 19th. Certain other statements appear at page 117. At lines 18 to 20 Badge stated as follows:

"**It** is not a fact that the discussion that had taken place in the room of Nathuram Godse was in regard to a demonstration that was to be held at the prayer ground. It is not a fact that the discussions were held loudly and that Nathuram Godse had asked us to shift to the bath room."

Here is a definite suggestion that a number of persons met in the room of Nathuram Godse and held a discussion. In other words these statements show that the prisoners were not challenging in the lower Court certain allegations made by the prosecution.

If Badge visited Nathuram and Apte in the Marina Hotel on the morning of the 20th, it is open to the Court to presume that Nathuram and Apte must have been aware of the place at which Badge was staying. If so they could have easily asked Badge as to whether he was not in fact staying at such and such a place. No such question was put to Badge.

Badge states that at about 11 or 11.30 a.m. on the 20th January, Apte, Gopal, Badge, and Shankar went to the jungle behind Hindu Mahasabha with the object of trying out their revolvers. Gopal took out his revolver but the revolving chamber would not come out. Shankar then took out his revolver, loaded it with 4 cartridges and tried to shoot at a tree. The shot did not reach the tree but fell down in between. Apte thereupon said that that revolver was of no use. Gopal sent Shankar to the Hindu Mahasabha office to bring a bottle of oil and a penknife, but when these articles were brought and Gopal started repairing the revolver, three Forest Guards appeared on the scene. Apte and his companions hastily concealed the revolver underneath the Chaddar[30] on which they were sitting. One of the Forest Guards came up and enquired as to what they were doing. Gopal spoke to him in Punjabi. The Forest Guards were apparently satisfied and went away. In consequence of the information given by Badge the police got into touch the Forest Guard Mehar Singh (P.W.9) in March 1949. He was taken to identification parade held on the 24th March and identified Apte, Gopal, Badge and Shankar as the persons whom he had seen on the morning of the 20th January. The statement of this witness cannot, in my opinion, be relied upon for it is difficult to believe that a person who sees another casually for a short time and who does not connect him with any unusual or extraordinary incident should be able to identify him after the lapse of over two months. It is possible that this witness did see four persons on or about the 20th January, but his evidence cannot be taken any further and it cannot be said that the four persons he saw were Apte, Gopal, Badge, and Shankar.

A number of witnesses have come from the Marina Hotel to testify the fact that while Nathuram and Apte were staying in the said Hotel from the 17th to the 20th January a number of persons came to see them. P.W.8, Nain Singh who is a head bearer in the Marina Hotel deposes that on a certain day which he is unable to remember he served tea to Karkare and Shankar in Room No.40 of the Marina Hotel. He served two teas to start with but it was later asked to supply three more. The hotel registers Exhibits P.17 and P.24 show that three extra teas were served on

the 20th January. Nain Singh's statement, therefore, to the effect that he served tea to the occupants of Room No.40 and in particular to Karkare and Shankar is thus corroborated by the entries in the hotel registers relating to Room NO.40. These entries are further corroborated by Bill No.7859 which was issued to the occupants of this room on the 20th January 1948 and which is reproduced as Exhibit P.17. The fact that this witness served tea to Shankar who was a menial servant must have left a deep impression on the mind of the witness. The identification memo relating to the parade which was held on the 30th March shows that this witness identified Karkare and Shankar along with a wrong person as occupying Room No.40. It is argued that **the** fact that he referred to Karkare and Shankar as occupants of Room No.40 whereas the real occupants were Nathuram and Apte detracts considerably from the value of the evidence given by him. I regret I am unable to concur in this contention. The statement which has been attributed to Nain Singh was not put to him when he was being examined in the Court below and he was not confronted with the said statement. That statement cannot, therefore, be used against the witness. It has been held repeatedly that statements appearing in identification parades can at best be regarded as being memoranda of the officer who supervises an identification parade and cannot be treated on the same footing as statements made by a witness to a police officer. In any case this particular witness was not confronted with the statement which has been attributed to him and he was not afforded a reasonable opportunity of explaining the discrepancy between what he stated to the Magistrate and what he stated before the trial Court.

The next witness is Gobind Ram (P.W.11). A bearer of the Marina Hotel, whose duty is to serve drinks in the bar. He states that he saw Nathuram, Karkare, Gopal, and Badge in his hotel three days before the explosion of the bomb i.e. on the 17th January. He served one peg on the first day and two

---

[30] Chaddar: A large cloth used as a head covering or veil.

pegs on the second day. He took the drinks to Room No.40 himself and served them to Karkare on both occasions. The police came to him two months later and asked him to produce the chits signed for the drinks. He had seen the four persons mentioned above first in the hotel and then before a Magistrate in Bombay and had not seen them in between. He identified them before a Magistrate on the 30th March 1948. His evidence in this behalf is fully corroborated by the vouchers issued by the hotel and the entries in the hotel registers vide Exhibits P.17, P.18 and P.19. The principal objection which has been taken to the evidence of this witness is that he could not have been either Gopal or Karkare or Badge three days before the explosion i.e. on the 17th January. Gopal proceeded on leave on the afternoon of the 16th and even if he caught the first train from Kirkee on the afternoon of the 16th he could not reach Delhi much before the morning of the 18th when Karkare is said to have gone to the railway station to receive him. Badge did not reach Delhi before the evening of the 19th. If, therefore, this witness states that he saw Badge and Gopal in the Marina Hotel three days before the explosion i.e. on the 17th January his evidence cannot be accepted as true. Mr. Daphtary contends that the statement made by Gobindram to the effect that he had seen the prisoners three days before the explosion ought not to be taken too literally. The witness appears to mean that he saw the prisoners within a period of three days immediately preceding the explosion in the Birla House. This is clear from the fact that he states that on the first day he served one drink and on the second day he served two drinks. The chits which have been produced show that one drink was supplied to Room No.40 on the 17th January and another two drinks on the 18th January.

Again, it was contended that as this witness is charged with the duty of serving drinks in the bar and as it is only on rare occasions that he is required to serve drinks in the rooms, it is improbable that he could have remembered the faces of the prisoners or could have been able to identify them correctly after the lapse of two months and ten days. In an ordinary case this contention may perhaps carry some weight but in the present case it must be remembered that most of the prisoners had peculiar features which could not be forgotten e.g., it was difficult for a person who saw Badge with his long flowing beard and long hair not to be able to identify him even after the lapse of a considerable period. Similarly, Gopal had distinctive features such as high cheek bones. Karkare was the person to whom drinks were actually served on two successive days. I am not surprised in the circumstances that this witness was able to identify Karkare, Badge, and Gopal.

The next criticism is that considerable delay was occasioned in getting into touch with this witness. The explosion took place on the 20th January and the police visited the Marina Hotel on the following day. Thaddous and Gobind Ram appear to have been interrogated but no question were put to Gobind Ram presumably because it was his duty to serve drinks in the bar and not in the rooms occupied by visitors. He was examined on a later date when a requisition was sent by the police to Bombay. The statement of Karkare to the effect that he is a pious Hindu and that as such he does not take liquor cannot be accepted in view of the testimony which has been led in the Trial Court.

P.W.12 C. Pacheco, Manager of the Marina Hotel, deposes simply that at about 11 o'clock on the night of the 20th January Madanlal brought some police officers to the hotel and showed them Room No.40 where his friends were **stopping**[31] and which he had visited earlier in the evening.

The evidence of Nain Singh, Gobind Ram and C. Pacheco strongly supports the story of Badge that Nathuram and Apte who were staying in the Marina Hotel were being visited by Karkare, Gopal, Badge, and Shankar.

---

[31] Stopping or Sleeping. It may be typographical error.

P.W.13 Martin Thaddous, who is a Receptionist Clerk in the Marina Hotel, testifies to a fact which is admitted by the prisoners, namely, that Nathuram and Apte came to him at about 6 o'clock on the 20th January and asked him to prepare their bills at once. He identified Nathuram as Mr. Deshpande who had stayed in the hotel. The statement of this witness is of some importance inasmuch as he deposes that Karkare had once come to the hotel to see Nathuram.

P.W.10 Kaliram, who is a bearer in the Marina Hotel, states that Nathuram and Apte had come to stay in the hotel three days before the bomb explosion. Nathuram gave him some clothes for washing. The witness brought them back from the *dhobi* after they had been washed but both the occupants of Room No.40 had left.[32]

Birla House:

Again, it is contended that Badge's story to the effect that immediately before proceeding to the Birla House on the afternoon of the 20th January, they went to the Hindu Mahasabha office is inherently improbable and should be disbelieved. It is said that all of the prisoners were in Room No.40 of the Marina Hotel which has been adequately provided with locks and keys and consequently that if the prisoners did not want to take all the arms and ammunitions with them to the Birla House, they could easily have kept it in the Marina Hotel and need not have gone to the trouble and expense of carrying it by taxi to the Mahasabha Bhawan the rooms of which were open. It is argued that in similar circumstances in Bomb ay, Badge deposited the bag containing the stuff at the house of Dixitji Maharaj in preference to keeping it in his possession in the Hindu Mahasabha office at Dadar. This argument is, in my

THE GRIM BLACK GRANITE HOUSE SIGN "BIRLA HOUSE" AT NO.5 THEES JANUARY MARG, NEW DELHI WHERE THE THREE FATAL PROJECTILES FROM THE MAGAZINE PISTOL – BERETTA - OF NATHURAM VINAYAK GODSE PLUCKED THE PRECIOUS LIFE OF MAHATMA GANDHIJI AT 17.17 HRS ON THE 30TH JANUARY 1948 FRIDAY

opinion, wholly devoid of force. According to the prosecution, all the prisoners, namely, Nathuram, Apte, Karkare, Madanlal, Badge, and Shankar decided to go to the Birla House. They could not accordingly run the risk of leaving any incriminating articles inside Room No.40 of the Marina Hotel which is said to be a European concern. In Bombay the "stuff" could be left in the house of Dixitji Maharaj who is a highly respectable and respected citizen of the place and whom nobody was likely to suspect of keeping unlicensed arms and ammunition. The Hindu Mahasabha office at Dadar on the other hand, was not a safe place for the storage of illicit arms. The position was reverse in Delhi. Here the Marina Hotel was undoubtedly provided with locks and keys and arms and ammunition could be placed there with safety, but in the event of any enquiry being made, Marina Hotel was not as safe a place as the Hindu Mahasabha office where the atmosphere was much more friendly. The prisoners appear to have thought that in the event of discovery, the atmosphere of the Hindu Mahasabha would be much more friendly than the atmosphere of the Marina Hotel. It may perhaps be mentioned in passing that according to the prisoners Shankar did not go to the scene of the outrage on the afternoon of the 20th January. If he was left behind at the Hindu Mahasabha Bhawan, it is obvious that the Bhawan was a much safer place for the keeping

---

[32] Page No.108 is blank in the Original Judgment. This remark can be found in the scanned copy of 'True Copy Type Version" in Page No.70.

of the surplus arms and explosives that Badge and Gopal had brought with them. The story that the prisoners did in fact go to the Mahasabha Bhawan before proceeding to the Birla House is corroborated by the testimony of Surjit Singh in whose taxi the prisoners are said to have travelled.

Let us now examine the evidence in regard to a meeting which is alleged to have taken place between Nathuram, Karkare, Apte, and Gopal at Thana on the 25th January 1948. P.W.79 Vasant Gajjanan Joshi, who is a boy of about 18 years of age, states that at about 5 or 6 o'clock on the morning of Sunday, the 25th January he was sleeping outside his house when he was awakened by Karkare whom he has been knowing since the year 1943. A couple of hours later, Mr. G.M. Joshi, father of the witness wrote out a draft telegram and asked the witness in the presence of Karkare to proceed to Bombay and to despatch the telegram from there. The witness went to the Central Telegraph Office at Bombay and despatched the following telegram at 11.20 a.m.

> **"TO**
>
> **APTE, ANANDASHRAM, POONA,**
>
> **"BOTH COME IMMEDIATELY, Vyas."**

It is not necessary for the Crown to produce every witness:

The cost of this telegram had been paid to the witness by his father. He was given a receipt by the Telegraph Office and he handed it over top his father. Gopal Godse arrived in Thana at 4 p.m. and Nathuram and Apte at 9 p.m. Nathuram, Apte, Karkare, and Gopal sat down with Mr. G.M. Joshi who was taking his meals and hold a consultation. Nathuram and Apte left shortly afterwards while Gopal took the next train for Poona. Karkare, stayed on. Mr. Daphtary states that the only assistance he seeks to derive from the evidence of this witness is that on the 25th January there was a meeting at the house of Mr. G.M. Joshi at Thana, the suggestion being that it was probably at this meeting that the plan to assassinate Mahatma Gandhi in the manner in which he was later assassinate was finally evolved. The only criticism that has been directed against the evidence of this witness is that if the prosecution wanted to give evidence of this conference, they should have produced Mr. G.M. Joshi in Court and not contents themselves with the production of his son. It is contended that the only inference that may reasonably be drawn from his non-production is that if that witness had come into Court his evidence would have been unfavourable to the prosecution. Mr. Daphtary contends that Mr. G.M. Joshi and Karkare have been known to each other for several years, that Joshi and Apte employed together as teachers in a certain school at Ahmadnagar and consequently that it would have been somewhat embarrassing for Joshi to come and give evidence against his friends. In any case, it is contended that if G.M. Joshi could have contributed anything more to this case than has been contributed by his son and the prosecution failed to produce him, they are prepared to take the risk. **It was not necessary for the Crown to produce every witness.** The son has been put in the witness-box and he has given his evidence in Court. His evidence regarding Karkare receives substantial support from the telegram which he is said to have despatched from Bombay and the evidence given by him must therefore be deemed to be substantially correct. He has not tried to magnify the case against the prisoners and has spoken nothing but the truth. If this boy was in the hands of the police and if the police wanted to fabricate false evidence against the prisoners they could have had no difficulty in obtaining a much more damaging statement against them than has been given. The boy could, for example, have said that Karkare had supplied him the draft of the telegram, or if Karkare is illiterate or is unable to write the telegram he could have said that Karkare gave him the money for the telegram. No such statement has been made and it must therefore be assumed that what has been stated is nothing more than truth. The evidence of this witness makes it quite clear that Gopal stayed for several hours in the house of Mr. G.M. Joshi at Thana on the 25th January and that Nathuram, Apte, Karkare, and Gopal had a conversation together. The general trend of cross-examination of this witness does not show that none of the prisoners was there. Apte admits in his statement that he went and stayed with Mr. G.M. Joshi at Thana for a few days in February. Karkare is connected with Mr. G.M. Joshi (a) because he is his publisher; (b) because he is a relation. When Badge met Madanlal at the Hindu Mahasabha on the 18th January and enquired about Karkare, Madanlal said that he had gone to Thana and was expected any minute. It is obvious from the statement of this witness that Karkare did not know that Nathuram and Apte were in Bombay, for if he were aware of that fact he could not have despatched the telegram to Poona.

The only other objection that was taken against the evidence of Mr. Vasant Joshi was that he was not taken to the identification parade. This objection does not appear to me to be of much substance as no question was put to the police witnesses as to the circumstances which prevented them from taking him to an identification parade. Apte had on his own showing come to stay in the house of Mr. Joshi in February that is sometime before the identification parades were held.

This witness was not cross-examined with the object of his credibility being impugned.[33]

The prosecution have endeavoured to produce evidence to show that Nathuram, Apte, and Karkare were in the vicinity of the crime shortly before the crime was committed. At about 12 noon on the 29th January 1948 Nathuram who represented himself as Vinayakrao appeared at the Railway Station of Delhi and asked the booking clerk Sundarilal (P.W.26) to reserve a Retiring Room for him. Sundarilal, told him that no room was vacant at

the time, but that if he enquired again after half-an-hour or so he might be in a position to offer him the necessary accommodation. Mr. Vinayakrao returned at about 1 p.m. accompanied by a person who was later identified as Apte. He showed two second class tickets, one from Gwalior to Delhi and the other from Poona to Delhi, and was allotted Room No.6 for a period of 24 hours. He paid a sum of Rs. 5/- for the room and was granted a receipt in respect of this sum. On the morning of the 30th January Vinayakrao and is friend (Apte) paid another visit to the booking office and asked for permission to retain the room for another day. The booking clerk was unable to accede to this request as one extension could be given without the permission of the Station Superintendent. The booking clerk did not receive the key of the room and he accordingly went upstairs to see whether the room had in fact been vacated. Nathuram and his companion (Apte) were sitting in the Room while a third person who was later identified by the booking clerk as Karkare was standing nearby. The booking clerk asked Mr. Vinajayrao to vacate the room and the latter asked Karkare to tie up the bedding. The booking clerk remained in the room for ten or fifteen minutes and Vinayakrao and his companions removed the luggage to the First Class Waiting Room on the ground floor. The statement of the booking clerk in regard to the incidents which took place on the 29th and 30th January has been corroborated by the testimony of Hari Kishan (P.W.27), bearer in charge of the Retiring Room and Jannu (P.W.28), Boot Polisher, at the Delhi Junction Railway Station. Hari Kishan states that on the 29th January, Nathuram gave some clothes to Jannu for being washed within 24 hours. The clothes were washed within the prescribed period and Nathuram paid a sum of Rs. 2/- to Hari Kishan for being paid to Jannu.

Nathuram admitted before the Trial Court that he had booked a retiring room at the Delhi main station under the assumed name of Vinayakrao on the 29th January 1948, but he denied that Apte had

---

33 Page No.116 is blank in the Original Judgment. This remark can be found in the scanned copy of 'True Copy Type Version" in Page No.75 Eds..

accompanied him at the time or that he gave any clothes to Hari Kishan for being washed or that he asked for extension of time to stay in the retiring room or that he got his shoes polished by Jannu. He stated that he had no polishable shoes with him as he was wearing canvas shoes on the dates in question. He did not see Apte or Karkare at the Delhi Main Railway Station on the 29th or 30th January as Apte and he had parted company at Gwalior. While arguing his appeal before us, Nathuram explained that he had reserved a full room for himself at the railway station of Delhi as he was on the threshold of a great venture and did not *********[34]

******** **passengers** are accommodated in a room, a sum of Rs. 2/- for every extra passengers beyond two is charged. No extra amount was charged from Godse in this case and the theory that three passengers occupied the room must be rejected.

Thirdly, it was said that two tickets were shown to the bedding clerk, one from Gwalior to Delhi and the other from Poona to Delhi. The receipt however belies this allegation, for against the entry relating to tickets held appear the words **"Nos. II Gwalior Station"**.This shows that only a ticket from Gwalior to Delhi was shown and none from Poona to Delhi. The booking clerk made no entry in regard to the ticket from Poona and may well be making a mistake when he states from his recollection that his ticket was shown to him.

Fourthly, it was said that assuming for the sake of argument that two tickets were shown it would merely establish that two persons had occupied room No.6. Who were these two persons? Apte had travelled from Gwalior to Delhi and could not be in possession of a ticket from Poona to Delhi. The only person to whom the ticket could relate could be Karkare but there was no evidence to show that he travelled from Poona to Delhi by train. It is certainly open to the prosecution to allege that the ticket was in respect of the journey performed by Karkare from Poona to Delhi but there is not an iota of evidence on the record to justify the conclusion that Karkare did in fact travel from Poona to Delhi. Moreover, Karkare generally travelled by third class and not by second class. No one is in a position to state as to how and when Karkare came to Delhi and how and when Karkare left Delhi for Bombay.

Fifthly, it is said that Sundarilal stated before the Trial Court that he went to the Retiring Room at about 1 o'clock on the afternoon of the 30th January in order to make certain that the passengers had vacated the room. This statement appears to be at variance with the statement made by him to the police for he never stated to the police that he had paid a visit to Room No.6 on the 30th January 1948. Moreover, the bearer of the room who is said to have been present when Nathuram and his companions were preparing to go does not state that Sundarilal ever came to the room on the 30th January.

Sixthly, it is said that when Sundarilal visited the Retiring Room on the 30th January he found two persons, namely Vinayakrao (Nathuram) and Apte, talking to a third person who was identified by him to be Karkare. As soon as he asked them to vacate the room, they asked Karkare to tie up the bedding. He promptly proceeded to carry out the instructions. Instructions of this kind, it is argued, could be given only to a servant and not a colleague. Hari Kishan bearer states that the third person (namely Karkare) who was carrying the luggage was putting on a dirty *dhoti* and probably a shirt or a *Kurta*. He was bareheaded. It is contended that this third man could not be Karkare who is stated by other witnesses to be the Proprietor of a Hotel in Ahmednagar and to be known popularly as a Seth.

---

[34] Original Judgement pages from P.119 (partial) to P.121 which are parallel to Scanned TypedPages 77 and 78 were missing here. Continuity of the judgment is also affected due to this. Inspite of our strenuous efforts, we could not trace the missing pages. Hence readers are advised to search for the missing pages from the Delhi Archives original sources. Eds.

Seventhly, it was said that Sundarilal had been seen Apte on two occasions only, namely, one on the afternoon of the 29th January and the other on the afternoon of the 30th January. If the evidence given by Sundari Lal in regard to the visit of the 30th January is excluded from consideration on the ground that no mention was made to the police in respect of this visit and that Hari Kishan does not corroborate Sundarilal on this point, then the only occasion o which B. Sundarilal could have seen Apte was at 1 o'clock on the afternoon of the 29th January. B. Sundarilal states that on this occasion the person who called himself N. Vinayakrao was accompanied by another person. He admits further that when Mr. Vinayakrao presented himself at that hour the witness was mainly occupied in having a talk with him from behind the counter in the booking office which has been provided with a grille with brass rods. it is argued that there is always a great amount of rush at the Railway Station of Delhi and it is difficult to expect that in the absence of a special reason, the features of the companion of Vinayakrao were so indelibly impressed on the mind of Sudnarilal that he was able to pick him up in an identification parade which was held at Bombay on the 24th March 1948 i.e. after the expiry of two months from the date on which he had seen Apte for a few moments.

After going carefully through the judgment of the learned Special judge and after examining the arguments which have been addressed to us, I am inclined to hold that Apte was at the Railway Station at Delhi on the 29th January and the 30th January 1948, when he was seen by Sundarilal, Hari Kishan and Jannu. I am not quite certain however whether Karkare was present on either of these two dates. Sundarilal does undoubtedly testify to the fact that he was present when he (Sundarilal) went to the Retiring Room on the 30th but it is significant that Sundarilal made no mention in his statement to the police regarding the visit of the 30th.

Again, it will be seen that there is no satisfactory explanation for the assignment of policies by Nathuram to the wives of Apte and Gopal. Godse attested the Deeds of Assignment and must have been aware that one of the assignments was made in favour of his wife. The question arises as to why these assignments were made. The prosecution allege that both Apte and Gopal were helping Nathuram in the assassination of Mahatma Gandhi and it thus became necessary that some provision should be made for the wives of these two men in the event of their being prosecuted upon a charge of murder. Again, it is significant that one of the assignments was made in favour of the wife of Gopal Godse. If Gopal were not to take part in the conspiracy and if his life were not in danger as a result of his participation, it is unlikely that Nathuram would have made a nomination in favour of his wife rather than in favour of Gopal. Again, it is said that Nathuram has another brother. The defence have not been able to explain why the nomination was not made in favour of this other brother.

The question of assumed names looms large on the pages of the paper-books and the prosecution contend that the fact that these false names were assumed shows that the prisoners went to Delhi not with the object of staging a peaceful demonstration but with the object of taking the life of Mahatma Gandhi. It is said that on the 17th January Nathuram and Apte travelled by air from Bombay to Delhi under the assumed names of D.N. Karmarkar and S. Marathe; that they stayed in the Marina Hotel from the 17thto the 20th under the assumed names of M. Deshpande and S. Deshpande; that on the 23rd January Apte reserved a room in the Arya Pathik Ashram at Bombay under the assumed name of D. Narayan; that on the 24th January they reserved accommodation in the Elphinstone Hotel Annexe under the name of N. Vinayakrao and a friend; that on the 25th January they booked two seats by Air India Limited from Bombay to Delhi in the names of Mr. D. Narayanrao and Mr. N. Vinayakrao; that on the 27th January they travelled by air under these assumed names and that on the 29th January Nathuram appeared at the booking office of the Railway Station at Delhi and reserved a Retiring Room in the name of N. Vinayakrao. In his statement under Section 542 of the Criminal Procedure Code, Apte explains the reason for going about from place to place under false names. He states that the pitch of the editorial in the '**Agrani**' and the '**Hindu Rashtra**' had been rising higher and higher before the 15th January, 1948 and Government had held out a threat that if in future any articles in the paper tended to communal strife or violence they would not rest content with demanding further security but would prosecute the Editor and the Manager. Nathuram and Apte accordingly concealed until they had staged the demonstration as they intended at Delhi. The explanation appears to me to be hollow and unconvincing. If Nathuram or Apte were responsible for the publication of editorials which were critical of the policy of Government, they could have been dealt with while they were in Bombay where, however, they do not appear to have been going about under assumed names. There was in my opinion no danger of being harassed or arrested while they were in Delhi or in other places.

Again, it is in evidence that when Karkare reached Delhi, he occupied a room in the Sharif Hotel under the assumed name of B.M. Bias. He states that he found it necessary to take on this false name as a detention order had been passed against him by the Government of Bombay and he wanted to take every conceivable precaution against his identity being known to others. He states that he honestly believed that there was no legal objection to that action. Again, the explanation does not appear to carry force. There is not the slightest suggestion that at any time during his stay either at Ahmednagar or at Bombay he had taken on a name other than his own. He saw Doctor Jain after the detention order had been issued against him but he

was introduced to him by his correct name. He states that he was going about in the Chembur Refugee Camp and performing various duties in connection with the relief of refugees, but he did not have to take on an assume name. It is incredible that if the Bombay Government could not locate him while he was actually going about openly in the Bombay presidency they should have bothered to follow him to the Sharif Hotel in Delhi.

But, it is contended that the fact the some of the prisoners had taken on false names does not show that they did so with the object of carrying on the purposes of the conspiracy. It is argued that Madanlal who stayed at the Sharif Hotel, along with Karkare did not take on a false name. It must be remembered, however, that Madanlal is so common a name in the Punjab and Delhi Provinces that no person who bore only that name and nothing more could possibly be traced. I am of the opinion that the fact that these three prisoners ______ ____ [35] names which did not belong to them affords an indication to the intention that they entertained vis a vis Mahatma Gandhi.

In order to establish association between Apte on the one hand and Madanlal on the other, the prosecution have endeavoured to show that the coat which was removed from the person of Madanlal immediately after his arrest on the afternoon of the 20th January formed part of the same suit of which a pair of trousers was recovered from the possession of Apte on the 16th April 1948. The question is whether the recovery is a genuine one or whether the learned Special Judge was justified in drawing the inference that Madanlal and Apte were associated with each other and had formed a combination for the purpose of committing a crime.

The evidence of P.W.17 Bhur Sing, P.W.18 Mr. K.N. Sahaney, and P.W.11 S. Daswanda Singh makes it quite clear that a blue coat was removed

---

[35] Two words in the underlined spaces are found soiled and undecipherable.Eds.

from the person of Madanlal on the 20th January. It has also been established that this coat formed part of the suit of which the pair of trousers is said to have been recovered from the possession of Apte. I have sued[36] the words "said to have been recovered" advisedly for it is contended on behalf of the prisoners that this so-called recovery has been fabricated.

Statement of Mr. Nagarvala, Deputy Commissioner of Police:

The statement of P.W.133 Mr. Nagarvala, Deputy Commissioner of Police, is most revealing. He states that as soon as he came to know that the coat recovered from the possession of Madanlal was the property of Apte, he decided to trace the pair of trousers corresponding to the said coat and if possible to prove the association between Madanlal and Apte. He took the coat with him to Bombay and issued instructions to the police at Poona that the house of Apte should be searched at once with the object of finding the pair of trousers. The house in question was searched on the 31st January 1948 but the garment for which the police were looking was not recovered. Apte and Karkare were arrested in the Apollo Hotel at Colaba[37] on the 14th February 1948. The Police carried out a very careful search of the room which was occupied by them but was unable to lay hands on the missing article. The prisoners were conveyed to the first floor of the C.I.D. building at Bombay and guards were stationed inside the rooms in which they were kept. The door from the stairs to the western portion of the front *verandah* was throughout kept locked and was used only by Mr. Nagarvala himself. Every conceivable precaution was taken to prevent the members of the public from going to the first floor. No interviews were allowed to the friends or relations of Apte

before the first week of April 1948. After that time, the near relations were allowed to interview the prisoners but only after they had given their names, _____ stated their business and had obtained a permit from Mr. Nagarvala. Detailed instructions had been issued to the subordinate staff that no person should be allowed to carry any unauthorised or objectionable article to the prison. The clothes brought to the prison were examined with the object of ascertaining whether any objectionable articles was being brought although no garment which was intended for the use of the prisoners was objected to. This statement shows that a very strict and rigorous watch was being kept by the police in regard to the persons who came to see the prisoners and in regard to the articles which were brought for their use. It may thus be assumed that it was impossible for any friend or relation of a prisoner to delivery any articles to the prisoner without the matter coming immediately and directly to the notice of Mr. Nagarvala.[38]

Mr. V.S. Dalvi (P.W.106) and Mr. M.G. Kulkarni (P.W.107) state that on the 16th April 1948 they were taken to the room of Mr. Nagarvala in the new C.I.D. building at Bombay. Mr. Nagarvala showed them a coat Exhibit 15 and directed them to ask Apte to produce the pair of trousers corresponding to the coat. On an appropriate enquiry being made Apte took out a key-ring containing two keys from inside his pocket, opened a trunk and brought out a pair of trousers (Exhibit 67) which was lying on the top. A recovery memo (Exhibit P.221) was prepared. There can thus be no doubt that the pair trouser was in fact recovered at the instance of the prisoner.

The searches which were conducted on the 31st January, the 14th February and the 13th April 1948 show that the pair of trousers which Mr. Nagarvala was endeavouring to obtains was not in the possession of Apte. It was certainly not in his possession when he was apprehended by the police on the night of

---

[36] The word 'used' is typed as 'sued' as typographical error. Eds.

[37] Colaba is a part of the city of Mumbai. It is one of the four peninsulas of Mumbai, the other three being Worli, Bandra, and Malabar Hill. Eds.

---

[38] Words are not decipherable in the Underlined places. Eds.

the 14th February and marched off to the new C.I.D. building on the morning of the following day. Not a single witness has come forward to state that when Apte was arrested he was allowed to carry a box of clothes or in fact any clothes at all. If, therefore, a box of clothes was found inside the room occupied by Apte, it must have been taken there either by his friends or relations or by the police. Would any friend or relation have carried the very articles that the police were looking for and thereby have tied the noose tighter round the neck of the prisoner? Would any friend or relation have carried a big box of clothes through a barricade of bayonets without the fact coming immediately to the knowledge of the police? How could the bunch of keys fly into the pocket of the prisoner when a careful search was made and nothing was recovered. The Crown has not been able to make any useful contribution to the solution of this conundrum.

Apte, on the other hand, has endeavoured to explain the circumstances under which the recovery was made. He states that as soon as he was arrested by the police he was asked to carry out all the orders that were issued to him and was told that if he failed to comply with those orders, he and the members of his family would be tortured and harassed. He admits that the suit of which the coat (Exhibit 15) and the trousers (Exhibit 67) formed a part belonged to him. He explains, however, that he gave this suit ever in charity to the Chembur Refugee Camp in November or December 1947. Or the 16th April 1948 the police handed over a locked trunk to him along with two keys and asked him to open that trunk with the keys when the panchas came and to hand over the pair of trousers to them. The Panchas came shortly afterwards and Apte complied with the instructions I am not prepared to accept the statement of Apte as Gospel truth, nor am I able to accept the story narrated by the prosecution but I am of the opinion that the explanation offered by Apte to the effect that the box was given to him by the police and that he was required to take out the pair of trousers from this box and to hand it over to the Panches appears to be corroborated by the circumstances of the case.

No reasonable explanation has been given as to the circumstances in which this pair of trousers came into the possession of Apte when no such garment was recovered from his house on the 31st January 1948, when no such garment was recovered from his possession, when he was arrested in the Apollo Hotel on the 14th February, when no trunk was brought by him into the C.I.D. building and when no clothes or garments could be brought in except with the special permission of Mr. Nagarvala. It is said that no pair of trousers was recovered from his house when a search was conducted on the 13th April 1948. Mr. Daphtary has not endeavoured to support the recovery of trousers.

While there can be no doubt that mystery surrounds the recovery of the pair of trousers from Apte the fact remains that a coat which admittedly belonged to Apte was removed from the person of Madanlal. An effort has been made to state that Madanlal took this coat from the Chembur Refugee Camp to which it had been gifted by Apte by way of charity but this explanation appears to me to be hollow and unconvincing. it would indeed be a most extraordinary coincidence that a coat sent by Apte to a camp containing thousands of refugees should fall into the hands of Madanlal and be found in his possession on the date on which the explosion took place. I am inclined to believe the statement of Badge to the effect that after the arms and ammunition had been distributed to the conspirators at the Marina Hotel on the 20th, they decided to change their clothes. It is probable that the coat belonging to Apte was put on by Madanlal and was recovered from his possession later in the afternoon.

The statement of Badge to the effect that the prisoner were concerned in a conspiracy to take the life of Mahatma Gandhi receives corroboration from an entirely independent quarter. In October 1947 Dr. Jagdish Chand Jain (P.W.67) a Professor of Ram Narain Ruia College, Bombay was asked to help Madanlal who was introduced to him as a refugee from the Punjab. Dr. Jain was prepared to give all sympathy and help that he could. He tried to find a job for Madanlal but having failed to find one he asked him to sell his books on a handsome commission. Madanlal was a frequent visitor to the house of Dr. Jain and was punctual and prompt in the settlement of accounts. In November 1947 Madanlal told Dr. Jain that he was unable to obtain sufficient income from the sale of books and intimated his desire to proceed to Ahmadnagar for buying and selling fruit. Two or three days later Madanlal paid another visit to the house of Dr. Jain in the company of a friend known by the name of Sood and took some books from Dr. Jain for sale in Ahmednagar. Both Madanlal and Sood returned a few weeks later and told Dr. Jain that although Sood had sold his books, he would not be able to pay the price until a later date. Madanlal paid another visit to Dr. Jain in the second week of December 1947 and expressed regret for the delay that had occasioned in the payment of the price and promised to pay it as soon as possible. He sent two post-cards to Dr. Jain from Ahmednagar in which he again offered his apologies for the delay and requested that any communications which might be addressed to him may be redirected to Ahmednagar care of Karkare.

About the end of the first week of January 1948, i.e., about 10th January, Madanlal paid another visit to Dr. Jain. This time he was accompanied by a person (Karkare) who was introduced to Dr. Jain as a *Seth* from Ahmednagar. Madanlal told Dr. Jain that he (Madanlal) owned two fruit stalls in Ahmednagar and was carrying flourishing business. Madanlal asked the *Seth* to pay the amount due by Madanlal to Dr. Jain. Madanlal and one *seth* then left the house but Madanlal came back to Dr. Jain almost immediately afterwards leaving the *Seth* on the road and told Dr. Jain that the fruit stalls that he had spoken about actually belonged to the *Seth* and that he (Madanlal) was only looking after them. He

also said that they had driven away all the Muslim fruit stall-holders and had a monopoly of the fruit trade at Ahmednagar.

"Carry on"

Two or three days later, i.e., about the 12th or 13th January Madanlal went to the house of Jain at about 8 p.m. and found Dr. Jain and Sardar Angad Singh (P.W.72) talking to each other. He joined the conversation and started narrating his exploits at Ahmednagar. He stated that he had committed an assault on Rao Sahib Patwardhan who was preaching Hindu-Muslim unity in a meeting, that the police did nothing as they themselves were Hindu-minded, that he had been armed with a knife when he committed the assault on Patwardhan, that he had organized a volunteer corps for the benefit of the refugees and Hindus and that some Marahti newspapers which Madanlal was carrying on his person had spoken highly of his work. After Angad Singh had left the house of Dr. Jain, Madanlal told Jain that the name of the *Seth* whom he brought with him to his house was Karkare, that he had formed a party at Ahmednagar which was being financed by Karkare, that his party was collecting arms and ammunitions which had been dumped in a jungle, that Vir Savarkar had heard about Madanlal's exploits at Ahmednagar, had sent for him at his house, had had a long talk with him, had patted him on the back and had said *"carry on'*. Madanlal also told Dr. Jain that his party had plotted against the life of some great leader but when asked by Dr. Jain for the name of the leader whose life had been plotted against, he declined to supply the name saying that he did not know it. After a certain amount of pressure he mentioned the name of Mahatma Gandhi. Jain was horrified to learn this and told Madanlal not to behave like a foolish child. Madanlal then volunteered the information that he had been entrusted with the work of throwing a bomb at the prayer meeting of Gandhiji to create a confusion and that in the confusion so caused

Gandhi was to be overpowered by the members of his party. Dr. Jain warned Madanlal of the perils of following so dangerous a project and dissuaded him from his wild talk and wild plan. Madanlal listened to Dr. Jain and thanked him for his advice. While leaving the house, Madanlal promised to see Dr. Jain again and said that he was putting up with his associates at the Hindu Mahasabha Office at Dadar. He was in a hurry to go back as Karkare had an eye on him and would not allow him to move about alone. Dr. Jain did not take the story of Madanlal seriously because at that time refugees of the locality were in the habit of abusing Mahatma Gandhi and the Congress.

A day or two later, i.e., on the 13th or 14th January, Angad Singh happened to visit Jain and Jain told him what Madanlal had said. He wondered whether in view of the fact that the members of Madanlal's party were collecting arms and ammunitions at Ahmednagar and the fact that Mr. Savarkar was behind the party, it was not the duty of Dr. Jain to communicate with the authorities. Angad Singh that it was the 'tall talk of a refugee' and that no importance should be attached to the conversation. He advised Dr. Jain not to take the matter seriously.

Madanlal went to see Jain again after a couple of days, (about the 14th January) and Jain asked him if he had thought over the advice which he had given him. Madanlal replied that he was under an obligation to Dr. Jain since he had helped him much, that he considered Dr. Jain like his father and that in case he did not listen to his advice he would be doomed. He thereafter left his place and went away.

A day or two later, i.e., on or about the 15th January Madanlal went to see Dr. Jain at about 8 p.m. and said that he was leaving for Delhi as he had some work at that place. He promised to see Dr. Jain on his return to Bombay.

In spite of the assurance given by Madanlal, Dr. Jain had a vague premonition of the impending doom and wanted to communicate the information given by Madanlal to responsible quarters. Two or three days after Madanlal had left, i.e., on the 17th or 18th January, Mr. Jai Parkash Narain addressed a meeting at the Poddar College, Bombay. After the meeting was over, Dr. Jain tried to contact Jai Parkash Narain who was going to Delhi and to tell him what Madanlal had said as he thought that the information might be of use to the authorities at Delhi. He could not contact Jai Parkash Narain as he was surrounded by a large number of persons, but was just able to tell him that there might be a big conspiracy in Delhi. Dr. Jain intended to contract Jai Parkash Narain on the following day but was unable to do so as his child was ill and had to be taken to hospital. Thereafter Jain came to know that Jai Parkash Narain had left Bombay.

On the morning of the 21st January, Dr. Jain read in the "Times of India" that a bomb had exploded at the prayer-ground of Mahatma Gandhi and that Madanlal had been arrested in connection with the explosion. Angad Singh came to his house the very same day and Dr. Jain told him that what Madanlal had been talking about had come partially true and that the plot against the life of Mahatma Gandhi may also turn out to be true and that they should inform the authorities at Bombay. They decided to contact Sardar Vallabhbhai Patel who happened to be in Bombay at the time. Dr. Jain tried to ring up the Sardar at his son's residence but was unable to speak to him. He then tried to telephone Mr. S.K. Patil, President of the Bombay Provincial Congress Committee but with no better results. Dr. Jain finally got into telephonic communication with Mr. B.G. Kher, Prime Minister of Bombay,[39] and saw him at the Secretariat at 4 o'clock in the afternoon in the presence of the Home Minister Mr. Morarji

---

[39] Balasaheb Gangadhar Khare(24 August 1888 – 8 March 1957) was an Indian politician. He served as the prime minister of Bombay (1937–1939, 1946–1947) and the first Chief Minister (then called Premier) ofBombay State (1947–1952). He was awarded the Padma Vibhushanby the Government of Indiain 1954. A lawyer, solicitor and social worker by choice and politician by necessity, Khare was often described as "Sajjan", good and gentle. Khare was a scholar, an accomplished orator, and a man with no pretensions.

Desai and told him everything that he knew about Madanlal.

Mr. Morarji Desai (P.W.78) asked Dr. Jain as to why he did not tell the witness all about the plan immediately after he had come to know of it, but Jain replied that he did not do so as refugees were in the habit of talking wildly and that he believed he had dissuaded Madanlal from doing what he intended to do. He realized his mistake when he read about the explosion incident in the papers and had accordingly taken the earliest opportunity of communicating the information to the authorities. Mr. Desai took the matter seriously and sent for Mr. Nagarvala, Officer-in-Charge, Intelligence Branch, asking him to see him immediately at the Secretariat. Unfortunately, Mr. Nagarvala was busy at the time and Mr. Desai accordingly asked him to see Mr. Desai at the Railway Station at about 8.15 p.m. that day. Mr. Nagarvala arrived at the appointed hour. Mr. Desai repeated what had been narrated to him by Dr. Jain and asked him to arrest Karkare, to keep a close watch on the house and movements of Mr. Savarkar and to find out the names of the persons who were involved in the plot. He did not, however, communicate the name of Dr. Jain to Mr. Nagarvala as Dr. Jain had made a particular request that his name should not be divulged having regarded to the nature of the locality in which he lived and the character of the persons involved as otherwise his life would be in danger.

Mr. Nagarvala complied with the instructions, organized a watch over the house of Mr. Savarkar and made arrangements for arresting Karkare. He made enquiries from the Ahmednagar police to find out whether Karkare whose detention had been ordered under the Bombay Public Security Measures Act 10 or 15 days before had been arrested or not. He also issued similar instructions to the various officers under him as he was giving top-most priority to this enquiry work. He also contracted various informants with the object of apprehending Karkare and his associates.

First Criticism on Dr. Jain:

Several criticisms have been directed towards evidence of Dr. Jain. It is considered in the first place that as he was aware on or about the 12th January that a serious offence was likely to be committed and as he omitted to transmit this information to the authorities without loss of time, he must be regarded as an accomplice whose statement cannot be accepted without corroboration. I regret I am unable to concur in this view. An accomplice is *prima facie* a person who is concerned in the commission of a crime and the burden of proving a person to be an accomplice is on the person who alleges him to be one, namely, the prisoner. The burden has not been discharged in the present case. Dr. Jain did not agree to the commission of the crime and he did not facilitate the commission of one. On the other hand, it seems to me that he strained every nerve to prevent it. As soon as he heard the Madanlal and the members of his party were entertaining designs on the life of Mahatma Gandhi, he told Madanlal not to behave like a child. He told him that he was a refugee from the Punjab, that he had gone through a terrible amount of suffering and that as a result of that suffering he was incapable of viewing the things in a true perspective. He had a long talk with Madanlal and tried to dissuade him from what he said he was going to do. He warned him of the folly of pursuing a plan which was fraught with such dangerous consequences. He endeavoured to prevail upon him to halt upon the threshold of crime. Madanlal thanked Dr. Jain for his advice and gave him to understand that if he did not listen to this advice he would be doomed. When Dr. Jain saw in the papers that a bomb had exploded in the Birla House and that Madanlal had been arrested in connection with the explosion, the seriousness of the situation dawned upon him. He lost no time in communicating with the authorities and placing his services unreservedly at their disposal for bringing the offenders to book. That was not the conduct of a person who had concurred in the commission of a crime. I am clearly of the opinion that Dr. Jain is not an accomplice and his statement does not need to be corroborated.

Second Criticism on Dr. Jain:

The Second criticism was that the evidence of Dr. Jain cannot be accepted at its face value because he made a considerable delay in reporting the matter to the police or other appropriate authorities. The so-called extra-judicial confession was made to him on or about the 12th January but he did not inform either the police or any higher authority till the 21st January, i.e., a day after the bomb had exploded at Delhi. It is true that a certain amount of delay was occasioned, but the facts and circumstances of the case make it quite clear that he had reasonable grounds for not rushing to make a report against Madanlal. In the first place Dr. Jain did not attach any importance to the statement made by Madanlal, (a) because Madanlal is given to a certain amount of bragging and (b) because great deal of loose talk was going on in those days. Secondly, Angad Singh told Dr. Jain not to attach any importance to the statement. Thirdly, Madanlal himself told him on the following day that he had thought over the advice given to him, that he was under an obligation to Dr. Jain, that he regarded him as his father and that he had no intention of pursuing the plan. Fourthly, Madanlal saw Dr. Jain immediately before leaving for Delhi and did not mention anything about the design on the life of Mahatma Gandhi. Fifthly, Dr. Jain had reason to believe that Madanlal was an honest and straight-forward person and that when he had given the assurance that he had abandoned the plan he _________________ [40]._______ be as

good as his word and not let down a person who had been of such great help to him in his hour of need. He and his friend Sood had taken a number of books from Dr. Jain for purposes of sale. These books were sold by them but Sood failed to pay the money. Madanlal was distressed over the conduct of his friend and expressed his profound apology to Dr. Jain in the letter which he addressed to him from Ahmednagar. Immediately on his arrival in Bombay he went to see Dr. Jain and again apologized to him. He took Karkare along with him in the hope that the presence of Karkare would reassure Dr. Jain that his money was safe. A person who was so honest and straight-forward in his dealings with Dr. Jain and who was so deeply indebted to him could not be expected to let down his friend and benefactor/ Dr. Jain was naturally reluctant to report Madanlal to the police. Indeed, Dr. Jain appears to have believed that there was nothing in the plan which had been unfolded to him.

Third Criticism on Dr. Jain:

The third criticism was that the story narrated by Madanlal is intrinsically improbable. The prosecution allege that Madanlal went to Poona on the 9th January to examine arms and ammunition and it is accordingly argued that if it is true that he went there on the 9th and if it is true that he disclosed the entire plan to Dr. Jain on the 12th or 13th he could not have omitted to inform Dr. Jain of his visit to Poona. Madanlal made no such statement to Dr. Jain and it is accordingly contended that story narrated by Dr. Jain cannot be accepted as gospel truth. Dr. Jain

---

[40] The last line of the Type PageNo.97 of "True Copy" of the Judgment is completely undecipherable due to passage of time. In Original Judgment this come in between pages No.152 and No.153. Readers if possible can have access with the original Judgment copy from the National Archives of India **https://nationalarchives.nic.in** or abhilekh patal. What is Abhilekh Patal? **'Abhilekh'**is a Sanskrit term used in India for records since ancient times and **'Patal'**is a Sanskrit word meaning a board, platform, or a surface.Thus 'Abhilekh Patal' means "A platform for ancient or old records'.A combination of both these words has been adopted as an acronym for Portal for Access to archives and Learning Abhilekh Patal is a full-featured web-portal to access the National Archives of India's reference media and its digitized collections through the internet. It is 'work-in-progress' and both the reference media and the digital data will be regularly augmented. The National Archives of India is the repository of the non-current records of the Government of India and is holding them in trust for the use of records creators and general users. It is an 'Attached Office' of the Ministry of Culture, Government of India.

was not cross-examined in regard to Madanlal's visit to Poona, but even if he had been cross-examined and if head said that Madanlal did not refer to the visit to Poona, I should have attached no importance to the omission. Madanlal had just started the story about the conspiracy when Dr. Jain interrupted him and asked him not to behave like a child. He did not allow Madanlal to finish the story. It is possible that if Madanlal had not been interrupted, he would have given further details of the plan which he was about to execute. Again, it is argued that Madanlal could not have stated to Dr. Jain on the 12th or 13th January that he had been entrusted with the task of igniting the gun-cotton slab when the part that each particular conspirator was to play was not assigned to him till the afternoon of the 20th January. This argument does carry a certain amount of force but is it beyond the realms of probability that certain tentative decisions (which were to be finalized after the inspection of the spot) were taken early in January? The prosecution allege that as early as the 10th January Nathuram and Apte had already placed an order with Badge for the supply of two gun-cotton-slabs and five hand-grenades. This order could be placed if and only if Nathuram and Apte had evolved some sort of a plan. It is by no means improbable that the conspirators, had vaguely planned that a gun-cotton-slab should be exploded and that the explosion should be caused by Madanlal. Even if no specific part was assigned to Madanlal till the 20th January, he may well have thought that in view of his exploits at Ahmednagar and particularly in view of the manner in which he had handled the Muslims of that town, the important task of throwing the bomb would be entrusted to him.

Fourth Criticism on Dr. Jain:

The fourth objection that has been taken on behalf of the defence appears to carry much greater force. It is said that Dr. Jain has testified to at least two incidents before the Trial Court which were not mentioned either to Sardar Angad Singh on the 13th or 14th January or to Mr. Morarji Desai on the 21st January or to the Presidency Magistrate on the 26th February. he stated before the Trial Court that when Madanlal saw him on or about the 12th January he said that he had been entrusted with the work of throwing a bomb at the prayer meeting of Gandhiji to create a confusion and that in the confusion so caused, Gandhiji was to be overpowered by the members of his party. This is the statement attributed to Madanlal in the Court of the Special Judge. The statement attributed to Madanlal before S. Angad Singh, Mr. Morarji Desai and the Presidency Magistrate was the bare statement that the party to which Madanlal belonged had plotted to do away with a great leader and that the leader was Mahatma Gandhi. No mention was made of the fact that a bomb was to be thrown to create a confusion or that in the confusion so created Mahatma Gandhi was to be overpowered or the task of throwing the bomb had been entrusted to Madanlal. Indeed no mention was made of the precise method in which the object which the conspirators had in view was to be achieved. The second statement which is attributed to Madanlal is that he told Dr. Jain that his companions were staying at the Hindu Mahasabha Office at Dadar. No such statement was made either to S. Angad Singh or to Mr. Desai or to the Presidency Magistrate. Unfortunately neither S. Angad Singh nor Mr. Desai kept a record of the statement of Dr. Jain and may well have forgotten the details when they gave evidence in Court after the lapse of several months; but even so it seems highly improbable that if the statements which are attributed to Madanlal had been made by him, these two witnesses could have forgotten them. The omission of these statements from the depositions of Dr. Jain under Sec.164 Criminal Procedure Code can be readily understood. Mr. Daphtary explains that such statements, are not recorded by Magistrates in the City of Bombay and that the Magistrate who was called upon to record the statement of Dr. Jain was not conversant with the procedure which is prevalent in the Punjab. He accordingly contented himself by preparing a memorandum of the statement made by Dr. Jain and scrupulously avoided the insertion of details. This explanations fully supported by the statement Ext. D.11 which Dr. Jain is said to have made. The statement is brief, sketchy, and disjointed and contains nothing but the most important facts. It does not give even the more important details such as that Madanlal had been collecting arms and ammunition which had been dumped in a Jungle or that he had committed an assault on Rao Sahib Patwardhan or that Vir Savarkar had sent for him or that Dr. Jain had narrated the story to Angad Sing.

Arrow had been shot, could not be recalled:

Dr. Jain was in a very peculiar position owing partly to the courage and integrity of his own character. He had given every possible help and encouragement to Madanlal who had lost everything in Pakistan and Madanlal on the other hand entertained a very warm regard which almost verged on adoration for Dr. Jain. Impetuous, sentimental and boastful as he was, Madanlal happened to blurt out in a moment of weakness the secret which his companions were so anxious to preserve. This was done obviously in a spirit of bravado and possibly in the hope that his statement would be received with approbation by his patron and friend. The response was completely contrary to his expectations. Approbation was replaced by reprobation and appreciation by condemnation. Madanlal hastened to retrace his steps but the mischief had been done. **The arrow had been shot and could not be recalled.** What could Madanlal do in the circumstances? He assured Dr. Jain that in view of the regard that he entertained for him he had decided to listen to his advice and to abandon the plan. Dr. Jain did not know whether to believe him or not. He was on the horns of dilemma and the prey of conflicting emotions. Could Madanlal have meant what he had

said? If so, the matter must be reported. Jain tried to speak to Jai Parkash Narain but could not take courage to say anything more than that there might be a big conspiracy in Delhi. But Madanlal may not have meant what he said, or may have abandoned the plan. Dr. Jain did not know whether to believe him or not. He was on the horns of dilemma and the prey of conflicting emotions. Could Madanlal have meant what he had said? If so, the matter must be reported. Jain tried to speak to Jai Parkash Narain, but could not take courage to say anything more than that there might be a big conspiracy in Delhi. But Madanlal may not have meant what he said, or may have abandoned the plan. Would it then be desirable to report the matter to the police, make a mountain of a mole hill and expose the person whom he had always tried to help and befriend to the risk of an unnecessary prosecution? In this state of mind Dr. Jain allowed things to drift not knowing what to do. When the bomb exploded in Delhi on the 20th, he realised the seriousness of the mistake committed by him. He realised that the information given by Madanlal was something more than the irresponsible prattle of a refugee. He rose to the occasion. He shouldered the burden of inevitable consequences and did his duty to the Society. After the death of Mahatma Gandhi, he came openly into the field and told Mr. Desai that he was prepared to help the police regardless of the consequences to himself. He had no desire to conceal his name. He has no axes of his own to grind. He is not under the influence of the police. He had no reason to think that merely because he had been helping Madanlal he was in danger of being implicated in the crime. He has been a very staunch Congressman for he was detained in custody during the movement of 1942. I have read his statement over and over again and every time I read it the conviction grows in my mind that he is telling nothing but the truth. His statement is simple and clear, the incidents he relates are probable and consistent, the story he gives fits into the story narrated by Badge like a jigsaw puzzle. I stated in an earlier part of this judgment that the statement of Dr. Jain does not require to be corroborated. In actual fact it has been corroborated by the testimony of at least two witnesses, namely, S. Angad Singh, P.W.72, and Mr. Morarji Desai, P.W.78. Angad Singh is a neighbour and a frequent visitor to the house of Dr. Jain. He had seen Madanlal at the house of Dr. Jain on various occasions and corroborates Jain generally in regard to the statements made by Madanlal about his exploits in Ahmednagar. He saw Dr. Jain a day or two after Madanlal had been to see him and enquired about the tall talk in which the latter had indulged, Dr. Jain looked a bit worried and S. Angad Singh asked him what was weighing on his mind. Jain replied that Madanlal had told him that the party to which he belonged wanted to kill a leader, that the leader was Mahatma Gandhi that the members of his party were collecting arms and ammunitions at Ahmednagar, that Mr. Savarkar was behind his party and that Jain had dissuaded Madanlal from engaging himself in any such activities. Angad Singh agreed that the matter should be reported to the authorities but at the same time he told Dr. Jain that what Madanlal had said was the tall talk of a refugee and that no seriousness should be attached thereto as refugees in those days were in the habit of abusing Mahatma Gandhi and the Congress. He saw Dr. Jain again on the 21st January after the news of the explosion in Delhi had appeared in the Press. Dr. Jain told him that what Madanlal was talking about ha come out partially true and further that the plot against the life of Mahatma Gandhi might also turn out to be true. Dr. Jain and Angad Singh then decided to communicate the information which was in their possession to the appropriate authorities. It was in consequence of this decision that Dr. Jain met the Premier and the Home Minister on the afternoon of the 21st January. I have no reason to view the story narrated of Sardar Angad Singh with doubt or suspicion. He is a Graduate of the Bombay University. He kept his law terms for sometime but was unable to obtain the Degree in Law as he was actively engaged in politics and could not devote sufficient time to his studies. He was a member of the Congress for seven or eight years. He was a candidate for the Bombay Provincial Congress Committee in the years 1946 and 1947, but he left the Congress the following year when the Socialists seceded from the Congress. He has knowledge of the fats to which he testifies, he is disinterested, his integrity is above question and the story narrated by him is not improbable. His statement strongly supports the testimony of Dr. Jain that on or about the 13th January, i.e. a week before the explosion in the Birla House, Dr. Jain had told him that Madanlal and his party were concerned in a conspiracy to take the life of Mahatma Gandhi. Dr. Jain had no motive whatever for concocting a story either before or after the 20th January; much less had Angad Singh.

Similarly, Mr. Morarji Desai has given a very clear and straight forward account of the conversation which Dr. Jain had with him on the 21st January. It is true that he did not reduce the substance of this conversation into writing but he acted with the utmost promptitude. He communicated the information at once to Mr. Nagarvala. He asked Mr. Nagarvala to arrest Karkare, to keep a close watch on the house and movements of Mr. Savarkar, and to find out the names of the persons who were concerned in this plot. He reached Ahmdabad on the morning of the 22nd January and gave necessary information to Sardar Ballabhbhai Patel, Deputy Prime Minister of India. Nothing more could have been done by another person. It is true that he did not divulge the name of Dr. Jain to Mr. Nagarvala on the 21st January but he explains this omission by stating that Dr. Jain had made a special request to him that his name should not be disclosed, and that nothing would have been lost by not divulging it. Moreover Madanlal from whom Dr. Jain had derived his information was already in the custody of the police. The defence was unable to shake the credit of this highly independent and disinterested witness who is holding the responsible position of Home Minister in an important Province of this country.

The statements of Dr. Jain and Angad Singh make it quite clear (a) that Madanlal came into contact with Karkare at Ahmednagar; (b) that he committed an assault on a person who was preaching Hindu-Muslim Unity; (c) that he had formed a party Ahmednagar which was financed by Karkare; (d) that the party which was formed_________________________arms and ammunitions which had been dumped in a jungle; (b) that the party had plotted against the life of Mahatma Gandhi; (f) that Karkare was in Bombay on or about 10th January when he accompanied Madanlal to the house of Dr. Jain; (g) that Madanlal was putting up with his associates at the Hindu Mahasabha office at Dadar; (h) that Karkare was keeping an eye on Madanlal at Bombay, and (i) that Madanlal saw Dr. Jain at Bombay immediately before leaving for Delhi on the night of the 15thJanuary. These facts strongly corroborate the statement of Badge that Madanlal was strongly opposed to the Doctrine of Hindu-Muslim Unity and was prepared to use physical violence against a person; who was preaching that doctrine, that a party which was actively engaged in the collection of arms and ammunition had plotted against the life of Mahatma Gandhi, that both Karkare and Madanlal were well known to each other, that Madanlal was in the Hindu Maha Sabha office at Dadar on the night of the 14th January, that Karkare was expected from Thana at any time. The fact that Karkare was keeping an eye on Madanlal affords a slight indication of the intention of Karkare. If he found that Madanlal was a highly sentimental and impulsive youth and if he knew that a secret which was vital to the liberty of the prisoners was confided to his case it is not surprising that he wasted to keep an eye on Madanlal.[41]

The Trial Court came to the conclusion that the conspiracy to assassinate Mahatma Gandhi

was in existence on the 9th January 1948 and that if Nathuram was not one of the conspirators on that day he certainly became a conspirator on the 10th.

It has been contended on behalf of the prisoners that there was no occasion for them to enter into conspiracy on the 9th January to assassinate Mahatma Gandhi. The partition of India had been announced on the 3rd June 1947 and Independence was celebrated on the 15thAugust 1947. Nathuram and several other persons were endeavouring to collect arms for invading Hyderabad and for destroying the Constituent Assembly of Pakistan but they had never entertained any designs on the life of Mahatma Gandhi. It is true that Mahatma Gandhi was indulging in pro-Muslim speeches in Delhi, but this conduct on his part did not constitute a departure from his previous policy. He had done the same thing in Naokhali and in Calcutta and nobody had thought of taking his life on that account. If a conspiracy came into being at all it must have come into being after the 13th January when Mahatma Gandhi expressed his determination to undertake a fast with the object of compelling the Dominion Government to remit a sum of fifty-five crores to the Government of Pakistan. It could thus be only after the 13th January and not before that any conspiracy, if one was had could come into existence. It is accordingly suggested that in view of these facts that incident relating to the 9th and 10th January should be eliminated from consideration. I regret I am unable to concur in the submission which has been placed before us for consideration. Nathuram has admitted in his statement that he was opposed to the teachings of absolute Ahimsa as it was detrimental to the interests of the community and as long as the year 1942 he entered public life with the object of counter-acting this evil. He states further that he always criticised Gandhiji's view and had in fact made demonstrations at various places. He states further that there was a wide gulf between the two ideologies – the ideology of Mahatma Gandhi and the ideology of Nathuram and it became wider and

---

[41] Page No.166 is blank in the Original Judgment. This remark can be found in the scanned copy of 'True Copy Type Version" in Page No.106 Eds..

wider as concessions after concessions were being made to the Muslims culminating in the partition of the country on the 15th August 1947. After his return from Noakhali, Mahatma Gandhi settled down in Delhi with the object of preaching the doctrine of universal brotherhood. The stage had now reached when Nathuram and persons of his way of thinking could brook no delay. They had already tried the method of "peaceful demonstration" but that method had proved wholly ineffective. Madanlal states that on the 20th January he exploded a gun-cotton-slab with the object of staging a peaceful demonstration. Could he possibly have thought that Mahatma Gandhi who could not be persuaded by the Government of India to abandon his fast would have readily agreed to give up his life-long policy (which was really an essential article of his creed) merely because one or two or 20 persons staged a demonstration? Nathuram and the other prisoners must be given full credit for intelligence. I am of the opinion that they must have known that no useful purpose was likely to be served by making peaceful demonstrations. If the evidence of Badge, Dixitji Maharaj and Dada Maharaj are to be relied upon and if they were collecting arms and ammunition as early as 9th January, it cannot be believed that Nathuram conceived the idea of the use of violence only on the 28th or 29th January.[42]

Mr. Bannerji contends that the story to the effect that Badge and Shankar had come to Delhi in connection with the conspiracy to assassinate Mahatma Gandhi is wholly false, for their visit to Delhi is susceptible of another explanation. He contends that Badge was dealing extensively in arms and ammunition and that he came to Delhi not with the object of assassinating Mahatma Gandhi but with the object of selling the arms and ammunition to the refugees in the Punjab and to the people of the Kashmir State. In his statement

before the Trial Court, Badge admits that while he was at Poona, Shankar used to bury the unwanted stuff under a tree. Here also, ascertain amount of stuff was buried under ground and was recovered at the instance of Shankar. May it not be it is contended that Badge had brought the stuff for sale to Delhi and had buried it in the precincts of the Mahasabha Bhawan so that it might be taken out at leisure and when required. In his Written Statement before the Trial Court Madanlal stated that he met Badge in the Refugee Camp at Delhi and Badge told him that he had come to Delhi for the sale of arms and explosives to the refugees. Badge then took Madanlal to the barracks where he was putting up. He opened a huge trunk containing 20 to 25 hand-grenades, 17 or 18 gun-cotton-slabs and an unlimited supply of small pistols. He then handed over a gun-cotton-slab and a hand-grenade as samples to Madanlal for sale to the refugees. I regret I am unable to concur in this contention. It may be that when Badge was in Poona he used to conceal the stuff under a tree behind his shop and that the stuff which he had brought to Delhi was found buried near the boundary wall of the Mahasabha Bhawan, but these facts do not, in my opinion, throw doubt on the story narrated by the prosecution that Badge had really come to Delhi for the purpose of carrying out the conspiracy. Bombay has, I imagine a fairly good market for the sale of arms and ammunition and I should be reluctant to accept the story that Badge came all the way from Bombay to sell hand-grenades, etc., to the refugees in the Punjab and to the people of the Kashmir State. The Kashmir problem had certainly arises in those days but it has not been suggested that any arms or ammunition were being sold in Delhi for being transmitted to Kashmir. The Kashmir problem was tackled by the Dominion of India and it was the Dominion Government which was sending an army with the necessary explosives. Nor am I prepared to accept the suggestion that the explosives were being sold to refugees. The statement made by Madanlal to the effect that Badge gave him a gun-cotton-

---

[42] Page No.170 is blank in the Original Judgment. This remark can be found in the scanned copy of 'True Copy Type Version" in Page No.108 Eds..

slab and a hand-grenade purely by way of a sample appears to me to be **wholly** preposterous. Badge is not a person who would part with an article of any value without the payment of price. Moreover, the circumstances of the case indicate that these articles were not brought to Delhi for purposes of sale. A live hand-grenade was recovered from the possession Madanlal immediately after his arrest on the afternoon of the 20th January. He could not have carried this grenade with any object other than that of making an attempt on the life of Mahatma Gandhi. Moreover, three live hand-grenades were recovered from the premises of the Mahasabha Bhawan when Shankar took a police party to the Bhawan on or about the 14th February. It is inconceivable that live hand-grenades could have been kept by Badge with himself for purposes of sales unless Badge was anxious to exterminate himself. On the other hand, the fact that these live hand-grenades were recovered corroborates the story narrated by him that they had been distributed to the several prisoners for being used at the Birla House. They were brought back by Badge after the explosion and were buried by him as they were. Badge was at the time endeavouring to flee from Delhi to the safety of his home. Nor can I see any substance in the allegation that the stuff had been buried by Shankar on the morning of the 20th and not after the explosion had taken place on the afternoon of the said date. The fact that a live hand-grenade was found in the possession of Madanlal and that three such grenades were recovered from the premises of the Hindu Mahasabha can lead to one and only one inference namely, that the stuff which was brought from Bombay was brought in pursuance of the plan to assassinate Mahatma Gandhi.

Faint-hearted Argument

A faint-hearted argument was addressed to this Court that the stuff which was found in Delhi was the property of Badge. It may be that legally and technically the stuff was the property of Badge but if it is shown that the stuff was intended to be used in pursuance of a plan to assassinate to assassinate Mahatma Gandhi, the fact that the stuff belonged to Badge would not make the slightest difference as far as the culpability of the prisoners is concerned.

There is a remarkable series of coincidences in this case:

It is common ground that Apte, Nathuram and Karkare knew each other;

that Madanlal and Karkare were known to each other;

that Karkare, Apte, and Nathuram were known to each other; and

that Gopal was not known to Badge but

that Gopal was probably known to Karkare.

It is said on behalf of the defence

that Karkare was not known to Badge.

But this statement does not appear to be true. Ex.P.90 which appears at Page 57 of Vol.IV is a letter which purports to have been written in Marhatti by Karkare to Badge on the 29th May 1947. This letter is in the following terms:

"To Badge,

The person who has come to you is a trustworthy Gentleman. I could not come yesterday due to great difficulties. I am specially sending this man. You must have received Rs. 400/- sent by telegraphic money order. The copies of the 'pustak' which you have brought may be sent with that person, who has been instructed in regard to the arrangements made for the payment. Every time ten 'vastu' are to be handed over, and for each 'vastu' Rs. 150/- should be charged. I will come on the 2nd and settle my account. Do not worry about moneys. The gentleman from Bombay must have arrived. Confusion arose because the wire from you was received one day late.

-Yours Karkare"

Karkare did not admit as having written this letter. A handwriting expert was called and he was shown the signatures of Karkare. The Trial Court, however, did not give any definite conclusion as to whether the letter was or was not written by Karkare. The evidence on the record, however, makes it quite clear that the letter was written by Karkare. At page 92 line 39 of Vol.I Badge states:

"**Ex.P.90** is a letter to me from Karkare."

At page 110 line 31 Badge states:

"**Ex.P.90** is in 8 pieces pasted on a piece of paper."

This information was elicited from Badge in cross-examination but no question was put to him with the object of challenging authorship of the letter. On the other hand the authorship is impliedly admitted. This shows that Karkare and Badge knew each other before Badge reached Delhi on the night of the 19th January.

Reverting now to the remarkable coincidences, to which a reference has just been made it may be stated that all these persons with the exception of Dr. Parchure whose case stands on a different footing were in Bombay between the 10th and 15th January. Again, it is a coincidence that all of them happened to be in Delhi on the 19th and 20th January.

Madanlal and Karkare left Delhi for Bombay on the evening of the 15th and reached Delhi at about midday on the 17th.

Nathuram and Apte left by air on the morning of the 17th January and reached Delhi at about 5.30 p.m. on the afternoon of the 17th.

Badge and Shankar left Delhi on the afternoon of the 17th and reached Delhi on the night of the 19th.

It will thus be seen that all these six persons arrived in three different batches. They were actuated by the same purpose. They state that they went to Delhi with the object of staging a peaceful demonstration. The prosecution allege that they

went there with the object of assassinating Mahatma Gandhi. Be that as it may, the fact remains that they all went to Delhi with the object of doing something *vis a vis* Mahatma Gandhi.

Again, it is a coincidence that with the exception of Nathuram all these five persons, namely, Apte, Karkare, Madanlal, Badge, and Shankar visited the Birla House on the evening of the 20th January. They state that they went there with the object of staging a demonstration but no demonstration was in fact staged. Even after the arrest of Madanlal, he did not express a desire to be shown into the presence of Mahatma Gandhi. Madanlal could have brought his grievance to the notice of Mahatma Gandhi in several different ways. In the first place he could have created a scene at the meeting just as he had created a scene in the meetings at Ahmadnagar and in the meeting at Delhi where Pt. Jawahar Lal Nehru and Mr. J.P. Narain had spoken. Secondly he could have rushed to Mahatma Gandhi just before or just after the explosion and before the police had the opportunity of arresting him. If he had appeared before Mahatma Gandhi there can be little doubt that he would have made himself heard. He did not do anything of this kind. On the other hand he kept standing at the spot. The question is why did he keep standing where he was? The answer is that he kept standing there because he wanted his fellow conspirators to perform the parts, which had been assigned to them. Even after he had been arrested he did not request the police to permit him to go to Mahatma Gandhi.

Again, there is another remarkable coincidence and that is that when Madanlal was arrested at the prayer-ground on the afternoon of the 20th January he was found to be wearing a woollen serge coat Ex.P.15. This coat is said to be a part of the suit which admittedly belongs to Apte. It is a curious coincidence that if Madanlal was not acting in association with Apte that he should be found in possession of a coat belonging to Apte. In his statement before the Trial Court Apte admitted that the suit belonged to him but he stated that he had given it away in charity to the Chembur Refugee Camp in November or December 1947. This coat was admittedly removed from the person of Madanlal vide statements of Bhur Singh P.W.17., K.N. Sahaney, P.W.18., and Daswandha Singh S.H.O. P.W.116. The recovery memo Ex.P.32 was prepared as soon as this coat was taken into possession vide Recovery Memo Ex.P.32 at Page 13 of Vol. IV. The factum of this recovery was not challenged and no question was asked of the witnesses of the recovery as to whether the coat which is said to have been recovered was different from the coat which was actually produced in Court. Bhur Singh and K.N. Sahaney were examined before Badge was examined but they were examined after the trousers had been recovered from the possession of Apte. Apte states that those trousers were planted on him. If so it was clearly his duty to put question in cross-examination to the witnesses of recovery with the object of ascertaining whether the coat which was recovered from Madanlal was or was not the property of Apte. In any case Daswandha Singh S.H.O. was examined on the 14th September 1948 long after Badge had come into Court and made a statement. It was within the knowledge of Apte that the coat belonged to him and that it was removed from the person of Madanlal. It was thus, his duty to cross-examine this witness. In his deposition Badge states that several conspirators changed their clothes in the Marina Hotel on the afternoon of the 20th January. The word **'change'** means that clothes belonging to one person were given over to another.

Madanlal states that after his arrest, he was interrogated for full five hours by several police officers. He made repeated requests to the police to take him to Mahatma Gandhi but they would not listen to him. This statement has not been substantiated by the evidence of any independent witness or even by cross-examining the persons who were present at the time of his arrest or persons who were detailing him at the time. Neither Daswandha Singh, nor Bhur Singh nor Rattan Singh nor Sulochana nor any of the other witnesses who were present when on the was arrested was asked in cross-examination to state whether Madanlal had not in fact asked to be taken to Mahatma Gandhi. It is significant that these prisoners were represented by several counsels. Not one of the counsels put any question to any of these witnesses with the object of ascertaining whether Madanlal had in fact made a request to speak to Mahatma Gandhi. The story therefore to the effect that Madanlal had gone to the Birla House and had ignited the slab with the object of staging a demonstration must be deemed to be an after-thought. Nor is the conduct of Madanlal consistent with the story that he went there to make a demonstration. It is somewhat unreasonable to expect that Madanlal would have carried a hand-grenade with him on that occasion if his intention was merely to make a peaceful demonstration and to bring the grievances of refugees to the notice of Mahatma Gandhi.

Again, the statement as to the circumstances in which he came into possession of the grenade is somewhat strange. He states:

"On the 20th morning it was announced that Mahatma Gandhi was to attend the prayer meeting personally that evening for the first time after the fast. I thought of collecting refugees and taking them to the prayer ground in the evening to place our grievances before Mahatma Gandhi. I, therefore, went to a refugee centre where, I had come to know, a large number of middle-class Punjabi refugees were staying. On that day I happened to meet Badge. He told me that he had come to Delhi as he understood that there was a good market for selling his 'stuff' among the refugee population here. He asked me to help him in such disposal of the 'stuff' as I was a Punjabi refugee myself. He gave me a gun-cotton-slab and a hand-grenade to be sold to the refugees, who were at this time attempt to occupy Muslim localities. When I got the gun-cotton-slab, I thought that I could, as a refugee, myself make sufficient noise by exploding it near-about the prayer ground and that there was no necessity of taking a large number of refugees to the Birla House. I was greatly elated by this thought. I had told Karkare about my idea of a refugee demonstration, but I did not tell him about the change of plan and the idea of exploding the gun-cotton-slab. I wanted to have the sole credit of placing the point of view of my distressed countrymen before the "Father of the Nation". I regarded my action as another form of Satyagraha which he had taught the Nation."

This statement, suffers from two defects. In the first place it is somewhat difficult to believe that Badge, who was a hard-headed but parsimonious businessman would have readily agreed to part with a hand-grenade and a gun-cotton-slab, the value of which was about Rs. 500/-. Secondly, it is improbable that if Madanlal wanted to stage only a peaceful demonstration in order to bring the grievances of his refugee brethren to the notice of Mahatma Gandhi, he would have taken the trouble of keeping the hand-grenade with him in his pocket all day and would have had this in his possession when he was arrested by the police. A hand-grenade is a somewhat heavy weapon and could not have been carried about by Madanlal except with a certain amount of inconvenience to himself. If the grenade had been given to him as a sample, he could have kept this at the place where he was residing and not have carried it with him on his way to the Birla House.[43]

The prisoners have been at pains to prove that the story narrated by Badge in regard to the incident which took place at the Birla House on the 20th

January is a tissue of lies. They state that the story is intrinsically and inherently improbable, for if the prisoners went to the Marina Hotel on that particular afternoon with the object of assassinating Mahatma Gandhi there was nothing to prevent them from executing their plan. Mahatma Gandhi had come to the prayer ground weak and emaciated after his fast and a large congregation had collected to listen to him. With the exception of Dr. Parchure all the other conspirators were at the spot. They were equipped with all the arms and ammunition that they required. **Badge and Shankar were armed with revolvers and hand-grenades while Madanlal and Karkare were armed with grenades only.** Madanlal had placed the gun-cotton-slab near the back gate to the prayer ground and had only to apply the match. The stage was set and only a signal had to be given. The signal was given, the match was applied and the explosion was caused. Why it is asked, did the conspirators who were bent upon terminating the life of the frail person who sat in front of them, not fire a single shot or thrown a single grenade? The fact that they did nothing, it is contended, proves almost conclusively that they did not mean to do anything. Could anything be simpler? The prosecution story was false from beginning to end and had been fabricated s a great man had died and he could not have died unless a large number of persons were helping and supporting the assassins.

Safety First, Safety Always Says Badge:

This in brief was the argument which was addressed to this Court and was strongly pressed upon us. The explanation appears to be simple and plausible but it cannot bear a minute's scrutiny. The plot failed not because the prisoners did not have a sufficient number of men or a sufficient quantity of explosives or because the victim had not arrived or because the prisoners did not wish to do anything other than create a commotion but it failed because although it was elaborately planned, it did not take notice of

---

[43] Page No.184 is blank in the Original Judgment. This remark can be found in the scanned copy of 'True Copy Type Version" in Page No.118 Eds.

certain fundamental factors. The whole structure collapsed by reason of three serious miscalculations. **The first miscalculation** was that Badge was assigned the principal part. He was to pose as a photographer to enter the room of Chhotu Ram to push the grenade from the trellis window and to fire at the person sitting in front. Judging from the point of view of the prisoners, heHeH Badge was a bad choice. He is a strong believer in the motto **"Safety First".** His safety did not lie in entering the room and throwing the grenade from the trellis window, for if he did what he had agreed to do, he would have been trapped inside the room and his safety was likely to be jeopardised. His companions assured him that conspirators but Badge had made up his mind and said that he would fire in the open. His companions had no choice and they allowed him to do what he pleased. But could be fire from the open? The danger of the situation dawned upon him. He quietly retreated to the taxi outside the gate, took the revolver from his pocket and the revolver from Shankar and put these revolvers into the bag. He told Shankar not to throw the grenade unless he gave the signal which he had no intention of giving. He then returned to the prayer ground, took up his place on the right side of Mahatma Gandhi and put his hands in his pockets to show that he was ready. Apte gave the signal, Madan Lal lighted the fuse and a loud explosion was heard. But nothing further happened.

The Second Miscalculation was that only one slab was used. Ever since the 10th January the plan was that two slabs were to be employed and two slabs were in fact purchased from Badge for this purpose. In the Marina Hotel conference which took place earlier in the afternoon the plan was changed for Badge, with his experience of arms and explosives, suggested that one slab was enough to produce commotion. The slab was ignited and an explosion was produced but this explosion was not loud enough to create a commotion. Commotion was the corner-stone of the edifice which the conspirators had proposed to erect. If there was no commotion, the grenades could not be thrown for if the grenades were thrown in the presence of the congregation there was no possible escape for the conspirators. They could not mix themselves up in the crowd and they could not run away.

But there was yet **another miscalculation** and **this miscalculation** was that the intended victim would sit quiet and motionless at the spot, Mahatma Gandhi had no desire of doing so. As soon as the explosion was heard and the people started getting up, Mahatma Gandhi put out his frail hand and asked them to sit down. They obeyed in silence and even the slight commotion that was caused by the explosion subsided. Nathuram and his companions had not counted on Mahatma Gandhi acting in the way he did and the plan failed. The plan failed not because there was no plan or that they did not wish the plan to succeed but because they omitted to take account of certain factors. Madan Lal was arrested at the spot and a live hand-grenade was recovered from his possession. Why did he consider necessary to bring this grenade if he had no intention of using it? The prisoners are now trying to make virtue of necessity, and saying that they did not intend to cause any harm.[44]

"Gandhiji's 100 years were over":

The evidence which has been produced in this case makes it quite clear that Nathuram, Apte, Karkare, Madanlal, and Badge had a motive to eliminate Mahatma Gandhi; that Apte and Karkare made desperate efforts to obtain revolvers from Dadaji Maharaj; that Nathuram and Apte made similar efforts to obtain revolvers from Badge, Dixitji Maharaj and Gopal; that on the 13th and 1th January Nathuram assigned his policies in the names of the wife of Apte and the wife of Gopal; that on

---

44 Page No.190 is blank in the Original Judgment. This remark can be found in the scanned copy of "True Copy Type Version" in Page No.121 Eds.

the 14th January Nathuram and Apte left Poona for Bombay possibly for delivering the stuff that had been ordered by Nathuram and Apte; that on the same date and possibly by the same train Badge and Shankar also left Poona for Bombay possibly for receiving the stuff that had been ordered; that on or about the 10th January Madanlal took Karkare to the house of Dr. Jain and introduced Karkare as a Seth from Ahmadnagar; and that on or about the 12th Madanlal told Dr. Jain that the members of his party had decided to assassinate Mahatma Gandhi. Badge testifies to a number of statements which make it quite clear that the prisoners wanted to take the life of Mahatma Gandhi. On the 10th January Apte told Nathuram that Badge was willing to deliver the stuff at Bombay and that their one work was complete; on the 14th January Apte met Badge on the road near the Hindu Mahasabha and said that it was good that he had come and that arrangements would have to be made for keeping the stuff. On the 15th January Apte asked Badge if he was prepared to go with them to Delhi saying that Tatyarao Savarkar had decided that Gandhiji, Pandit Jawaharlal Nehru and Mr. Shurawardy should be finished and had entrusted the work to Nathuram and Apte. On the 17th January while Apte and others were in the taxi of Aitappa Kotian, Apte said that Tatyarao Savarkar had predicted that **"Gandhiji's 100 years were over"** and that there was no doubt that their work would be successfully finished.

Our Last Attempt says Nathuram V Godse:

On the 20th January when Apte had taken Badge and Shankar with him to the Birla House, Apte is reported to have said that so far as possible Gandhiji and Suhrawardy should be finished or if it was not possible to finish them both, at least one should be finished. Later the same day Nathuram is reported to have told to Badge in the Marina Hotel: **"This is our last effort. The work must be accomplished. See to it that everything is arranged properly."**

Again it is obvious that all the prisoners in this case are connected with each other. Karkare has been knowing Badge since the middle of year 1947 and been corresponding with him. Karkare and Apte have both been purchasing stuff from Badge and had purchased stuff to the value of Rs. 3,000/- or Rs,1,000/- during the period August to December 1947. Apte told Badge that some of his friends would come to see the stuff at Poona on the 9th January and amongst the persons who came to see the stuff were Karkare and Madanlal. Nathuram also knows Badge as Apte and Nathuram work in the same office and Apte admittedly knows Karkare, Dada Maharaj (P.W.69) has stated on oath that when he went to Pandharpur in the year 1947 Apte sent Karkare to him and requested him to give him two revolvers. Karkare actually travelled in the station wagon of this witness from Pandharpur to Poona. The connection between Nathuram and Apte is admitted, for one is the editor and the other the Manager of the daily 'Agrani'. They have known to each other for the last several years. They have been moving about together, both before and after the 30th January under assumed names. Similarly the friendship between Karkare and Madanlal is an admitted fact. Both of them were carrying on trade in Ahmednagar. On or about the 12th January both of them were in Delhi paying a visit to Dr. Jain. Both of them were present in the house of Dixitji Maharaj on the morning of the 15th. Both of them left Bombay for Delhi on the evening of the 15th travelling in the same compartment, reaching Delhi on the 17th January and occupying the same room in the same hotel. They were together at the Marina Hotel on the 20th and later at the prayer-ground on the same day.

The relationship of master and servant between Badge and Shankar cannot be denied. Shankar entered the service of Badge in 1946 and has been following him about from place to place.

Nor can there be any doubt in regard to the relationship between Nathuram and Gopal. Gopal is a younger brother of Nathuram.

Certain sums of money were paid by Nathuram and Apte to Badge which show that they wanted him to join the conspiracy and accompany them to Delhi. On the 14th January, Nathuram paid a sum of Rs. 50/- to Badge out of joint funds belonging to himself and Apte and made an appropriate entry in his diary. On the 15th January Apte paid a sum of Rs. 350/- to Badge for defraying the expenses which were likely to be incurred by him in taking the journey from Bombay to Delhi.

The allegation that Apte, Karkare, Madanlal, and Badge were acting in concert is supported by the fact that on the 17th Nathuram, Apte, Badge, and Shankar travelled by car from place to place with the object of collecting funds for the enterprise. They did not tell the contributors the purpose for which funds were required, but they could scarcely be expected to do so.

Another important circumstance which establishes the factum of the agreement to commit the murder of Mahatma Gandhi is that all the prisoners with the exception of Dr. Parchure left Bombay for Delhi between the 17th and the 19th January.

The prosecution allege that they did so as they wanted to put themselves in possession of the opportunity of assassinating Mahatma Gandhi. They travelled in different batches.

Karkare and **Madanlal** left Bombay by train on the night of the 15th and reached Delhi at about mid-day on the 17th; they stayed in the Sharif Hotel.

Nathuram and **Apte** left Bombay by air on the afternoon of the 17th and reached Delhi on the evening of the same day; they occupied a room in the Marina Hotel.

Badge and **Shankar** left Bombay by train on the afternoon of the 18th January and reached Delhi at about 9.30 or 9 p.m. on the following day. They went to the Hindu Mahasabha Office and spent the night of the 19th January in that office.

It is not known as to when **Gopal** left Kirkee for Delhi or whether he went there by rail, road or air. It will be seen later that he was in Delhi on the 19th and 20th January.

Again it is significant that almost all the prisoners in this case, with the exception of Dr. Parchure, were anxious to conceal their identity.

Karkare and Madanlal reached Delhi at about 12.30 p.m. on the 17th January and proceeded straight to the Sharif Hotel. Karkare signed his name in the register as B.M. Bias. Madanlal appears to have given his correct name, but there was little or no danger of his being found out, for it is a matter of common knowledge that Madanlal is a common name in the Province of the Punjab and Delhi. He did not give his correct address for in the column of "address in India" he merely wrote ***"Bhuleshwar Fariwala"*** (a hawker of Bhuleshwar). Madanlal never carried on the business of a hawker in Bhuleshwar and the address given by him to the hotel authorities must be regarded as incorrect and misleading. The mention of the word 'Bhuleshwar' incidentally supports the statement of Badge and that of Dixitji Maharaj that Madanlal had paid a visit to the house of Dixitji Maharaj at Bhuleshwar on the morning of the 15th January he enquired from Karkare as to what his permanent address in Bombay was. Karkare replied that it was not necessary to furnish his address.

Again it is said that when **Nathuram and Apte** travelled together from Delhi to Bombay on the afternoon of the 17th January, they travelled under the 'assumed names' of **D.N. Karmkar and S. Marathe.** They occupied a room in the Marina Hotel under the assumed names of **S. Deshpande and N. Deshpande** vide hotel register. The chits signed by them were signed in these names and the bills which were issued to them by the hotel on the conclusion of their visit were also issued in these names, vide Ex.P.17. Again, Nathuram and Apte reached Bombay on the 23rd January and booked accommodation in the Arya Pathik Ashram. Apte asked for a room with two beds under the name of **D. Narain** *vide* Exs.P.109 and 110. The address given by him in one case was Poona and in the other Poona Raviwar Peth. The correct address of Nathuram was **'Editor, Hindu Rashtra, Shaniwar Peth'** and that of Apte **'Director, H.R. Parkashan, Ltd.22, Budhwar Peth Poona.''** Nathuram and Apte shifted from the Arya Pathik Ashram and engaged Room No.6 at Elphinstone Hotel Annexe at Bombay. The names of the visitors as given to the Manager were **N. Vinayakrao** and his friend. On the 29th January Nathuram appeared at the Railway Station of Delhi and reserved a Retiring Room for himself under the name of N. **Vinayakrao.**

The presence of all the prisoners with the exception of Dr. Parchure in the Marina Hotel has also been established. It was also been proved that the prisoners left Marina Hotel for the Birla House in three separate batches, **Karkare and Madanlal** going in one batch, **Apte, Badge, and Gopal** in another batch, and **Nathuram** all by himself. All six of them namely Karkare, Madanlal, Apte, Badge, Gopal, and Nathuram were present at the Marina Hotel on the afternoon of the 20th January. Karkare actually endeavoured to obtain admission for Badge into the room with the trellis window. Madanlal ignited the gun-cotton-slab and was arrested at the spot with a live gun-cotton-slab in his possession.

The mass of evidence that has been produced in this case leaves no doubt in my mind that all the prisoners (with the exception of Dr. Parchure and Shankar) had entered into an agreement to take the life of Mahatma Gandhi.

The evidence against Nathuram and Apte is that they place an order with Badge for the supply of arms and ammunition; that they examined the articles which were brought by Badge in the presence of Dixitji Maharaj; that they paid various sums of money to Badge for carrying out the purpose of conspiracy; that they travelled to Delhi and stayed in the Marina Hotel under assumed names; that they held a conference in the Marina Hotel at which various details in regard to the execution of the plan were settled; that they actually sent to the Birla House on the afternoon of the 20th with the object of supervising the operations; and that what they found that the plan had failed they immediately left the Hotel and reached Bombay via Kanpur. In Bombay they stayed under assumed names. On the 27th January they again left Bombay by air under assumed names and came to Delhi from where they proceeded to Gwalior; that they obtained a pistol from Gwalior and came back to Delhi to put themselves in possession of the opportunity of assassinating Mahatma Gandhi. Nathuram admits that he went to the Birla House on the afternoon of the 30th January and fired three shots at Mahatma Gandhi. He denies, however, the existence of a conspiracy. On the other hand, he accepts the entire blame for the unfortunate incident of the 30th January and states that he alone and no one else should be punished. He states that their object throughout was to stage a peaceful demonstration but that after the failure of the plan of the 20th January he secretly decided that the only method of stopping Mahatma Gandhi from pro-Muslims policy was to assassinate him. Once his mind was made up, he came to the Railway Station at Delhi, booked a room for himself in order to ponder over the future plans. He states that he did not take Apte into confidence and that Apte was not aware of what he was about to do. It is not in my opinion necessary to go into an elaborate examination of the witnesses who have appeared in evidence against Nathuram and Apte, for I am satisfied that there was a conspiracy to kill Mahatma Gandhi. If that conspiracy was in existence, there can be little doubt that both Nathuram and Apte were members thereof.

Broadly speaking the evidence against Karkare is that on the 9th January Karkare and certain other persons saw some stuff at the shop of Badge; that on or about the 10th January Madanlal took Karkare to the house of Dr. Jagadish Chandra and introduced Karkare as a *seth* from Ahmadnagar; that on the 15th January Karkare accompanied Nathuram, Apte, Madanlal, and Badge to the house of Dixitji Maharaj and examined some arms and ammunition which had been brought by Badge and handed over the bag containing the said arms and ammunition to Madanlal for being taken to Delhi; that on the same day Karkare and Madanlal left Bombay for Delhi by the night express; that Karkare told Angchekar that he was a worker for Hindu Mahasabha and was going to Delhi for some work of the Hindu Mahasabha; that on arrival at Delhi at 12.30 p.m. on the 17th January Karkare, Madanlal, and Angchekar stayed at Sharif Hotel in Chandni Chowk where Karkare stayed under the assumed name of B.M. Bias; that on the 18th January Karkare told Angchekar that he was going to the railway station as he expected somebody; that Gopal visited Karkare and Madanlal in the Sharif Hotel on the 19th January; that Karkare told Angchekar on the 19th that he and Madanlal were leaving the hotel the same day but spending the night in the Maharashtra Niwas and were leaving for Jullundur on the following morning in connection with the marriage of Madanlal; that Karkare went to Marina Hotel on various occasions between the 17th and 20th January, visited Nathuram and Apte on more than one occasion and was served with tea and alcoholic drinks at the Marina Hotel; that on the 20th January Karkare and Apte visited the Hind Mahasabha Bhawan on more than one occasion handed over the bag containing arms and ammunition which had been brought from Bombay to Gopal for being taken to the Marina Hotel; that Karkare was present at the conference in the Marina Hotel and was given a hand-grenade for being thrown on Mahatma Gandhi; that at about 5 o'clock on the afternoon of the 20th Karkare and Madanlal reached the Birla House; that Karkare endeavoured

to obtain admission into the room containing the trellis window; that on the 25th January he went to the house of Mr. G.M. Joshi at Thana and conferred with Nathuram, Apte, and Gopal; and that on the 29th and 30th he was seen in a Retiring Room at the Delhi Railway Station along with Nathuram and Apte.

Mr. Dange, who appears for Karkare, contends that his client was involved in this case because like Mr. Savarkar, he is actively associated with the work of the Hindu Mahasabha. He contends that his client has denied that he has committed any offence, that the prosecution has failed to prove the case against him beyond reasonable doubt and that he has given a satisfactory explanation of the circumstances appearing in evidence against him. According to Mr. Dange only a few witnesses have appeared against Karkare in so far as the incidents in Delhi are concerned. These witnesses are Nain Singh p.W.8 and Gobind Ram P.W.11 who saw Karkare in the Marina Hotel on the 17th and 18th January, P.W.16 Chhotu Ram and P.W.17 Bhur Singh who saw him the Birla House on the 20th and P.W.26 Sundari Lal, P.W.27 Hari Kishan and P.W.28 Jannu who are alleged to have been seen Karkare on the Railway Station at Delhi on the 29th and 30th January. The case which he has set out to establish on behalf of his client is that Karkare went to Delhi in connection with the proposed marriage of Madanlal, that while at Delhi Madanlal induced him to give his moral support to a demonstration which the refugees of Delhi were about to stage, that Karkare expressed his willingness to go to the Birla House as he was opposed to the pro-Muslim policy of Mahatma Gandhi but that he declined to take an active part as a detention order had been issued against him; and that he was unable to reach Birla House on the 20th as he was a stranger to the town and lost his way in the confusing and bewildering net work of streets for which Delhi is known. The Trial Court has come to the conclusion that Karkare was present at the Birla House on the afternoon of the 20th but that although he was present in Delhi on the 29th and 30th January he did not go to the Birla House on the date on which Mahatma Gandhi was assassinated.

After going carefully through the evidence in the case I have come to the conclusion that Nathuram, Apte, Karkare, Madanlal, and Badge had entered into an agreement to take the life of Mahatma Gandhi and that in pursuance of this agreement they collected arms and ammunition and proceeded to Delhi. The evidence which has already been commented upon shows that Karkare, Madanlal, and certain other persons examined the stuff in the shop of Badge at Poona on the 9th January, that Karkare accompanied Nathuram, Apte, and others to the house of Dixitji Maharaj where Badge had brought the stuff for being taken to Delhi, that Karkare took the bag containing the stuff and made it over to Madanlal. Karkare admits that he accompanied him to Delhi and put up in the Sharif Hotel where the room occupied by them was shared by Angchekar. The question which requires consideration is whether he went there in pursuance of the conspiracy as alleged by the prosecution or whether he went there with the object of facilitating the marriage of Madanlal as alleged by him.

I have already stated in an earlier paragraph of this judgment that I consider Angchekar to be a highly independent and respectable witness. This witness states that on their arrival at Delhi on Saturday, the 17th January, they proceeded to the Sharif Hotel where Karkare, Madanlal, and the witness booked a room for themselves, Karkare giving his name as B.M. Bias. Some two hours later Karkare left the hotel saying that he was going to the Hindu Mahasabha Bhawan. Madanlal and the witness who were left behind went to the Chandni Chowk where Madanlal wanted to see an uncle. It is not known whether Karkare returned to the hotel for the night but he was certainly back in the hotel on Sunday morning for he told Angchekar that he was proceeding to the Railway Station as he was

expecting someone. Madanlal and the witness went to various places both on the morning and the evening of Sunday including the house of the prospective bride of Madanlal. They also went to attend a meeting which was to be addressed by Pandit Jawahar Lal Nehru and Mr. Jai Parkash Narain. Karkare does not appear to have slept the night of Sunday, the 18th January, in the hotel, for he was absent the whole day, he was absent when the witness retired for the night and he was absent when the witness left his bed on the following morning. He did not come back till after the witness had gone away in connection with his business. He appears to have returned to the hotel sometime later for when the witness returned from the Transfer Bureau at 3 p.m. on the 19th he found Karkare and Madanlal talking to a stranger (Gopal) inside the room. Karkare told the witness that both Madanlal and he were leaving the hotel at once as they had decided to spend the night in the Maharashtra Niwas and to leave for Jullundur on the following morning in connection with the marriage of Madanlal. The witness asked Karkare the latter's address in Bombay but Karkare replied that it was not necessary to furnish him with address. The witness paid his share of the hotel bill to Karkare and left the hotel at 6 p.m. It is said that Karkare and Madanlal left the hotel two hours later after taking back the clothes which they had given away for washing.

The evidence of this witness makes it quite clear that Karkare came to Delhi not with the object of facilitating the marriage of Madanlal but some other object which is stated by the prosecution to be the desire to promote the objects of the conspiracy. If Karkare had come to Delhi in connection with the marriage of Madanlal, he would have done something in connection with the marriage. He does not appear to have taken the slightest interest in the matter. As stated above, he left the hotel at about 4 o'clock on the afternoon of Saturday, the 17th January, and was away the whole afternoon and possibly also the evening. He did not accompany

Madanlal top the house of his uncle. On the following morning Karkare intimated his intention of going to the Railway Station as he was expecting someone. He did not put in appearance during the whole of Sunday, the 18th January Madanlal and Angchekar, however, went out to various places including the house of the prospective bride. Karkare did not return to the hotel at night and was not back in the hotel till the following morning. On the contrary, the evidence of the Marina Hotel witnesses proves beyond reasonable doubt that Karkare had been served a drink at the Marina Hotel on the 17th and two drinks at the said hotel on the 18th. This evidence shows that Karkare was in fact visiting the Marina Hotel. The prosecution allege that he actually spent the night of the 18th January in the said hotel.

Let us know examine the truth or falsehood of the story that Karkare and Madanlal were spending the night of the 19th in Maharashtra Niwas and were proceeding to Jullundur on the following morning in connection with the marriage of Madanlal. There is not an iota of evidence on the record to show that after Karkare and Madanlal left the Sharif Hotel at about 7 p.m. on the 19th they went to Maharashtra Niwas. On the other hand, the evidence of Badge shows that Madanlal and Gopal were in the Hindu Mahasabha Bhawan when Badge and Shankar arrived from Bombay. Badge states further that Nathuram, Apte, and Karkare came to the Bhawan at night and told him that they had been to the Railway Station but had not been able to see Badge and Shankar. Nathuram, Apte, and Karkare left shortly afterwards promising to call at the Bhawan on the following morning. Madanlal and Gopal spent the night of the 19th in the Mahasabha Bhawan along with Badge and Shankar. It has not been contended that Karkare and Madanlal left for Jullundur on the following morning. On the other hand, it has been proved conclusively that Madanlal was in Delhi on the 20th January for he ignited a gun-cotton-slab at the Birla House at 5 o'clock in the afternoon and was immediately arrested. A live hand-grenade was recovered from his possession. The only conclusion that can be drawn from the statement of Angchekar which is fully corroborated by the other circumstances of the case is that Karkare was anxious to conceal from Angchekar the real object of their visit to Delhi. Neither he nor Madanlal had any intention of spending the night of the 19th at the Maharashtra Niwas or of proceeding to Jullundur on the following morning.

The evidence of Angchekar establishes

a. **that** Karkare, Madanlal and Angchekar travelled in the same compartment from Bombay to Delhi;

b. **that** they occupied the same room at the Sharif Hotel;

c. **that** Karkare left the hotel two hours later as he stated that he wanted to go to the Mahasabha Bhawan;

d. **that** Karkare was served with a drink in the Marina Hotel;

e. **that** Madanlal and Angchekar went out together to various places;

f. **that** Karkare did not spend the night of the 18th in the Sharif Hotel or that if he spent the said night in the said hotel, he came only at a very late hour;

g. **that** Karkare announced on the morning of the 18th January that he was proceeding to the Railway Station to fetch a friend;

h. **that** Madanlal and Angchekar visited various places in Delhi including the house of the bride;

i. **that** Madanlal and Angchekar attended a public meeting which was to be addressed by Pandit Jawahar Lal Nehru and Mr. Jai Parkash Narain;

j. **that** Karkare was served with two drinks in the Marina Hotel;

k. **that** Karkare did not return to the Sharif Hotel on the night of the 18th;

l. **that** Karkare made a statement which was false to his knowledge to the effect that they were spending the night of the 19th in Maharashtra

Niwas and were leaving for Jullundur on the following morning;

m. that although Karkare states that he came to Delhi in connection with the marriage of Madanlal he did nothing in connection with the said marriage; and

n. that throughout the period commencing with the 17th January and ending with the 19th evening he was engaged in activities which had no concern with the projected marriage.

Three Extra Teas:

The prosecution allege that ever since the minute of his arrival in Delhi, Karkare was actively engaged in promoting the purposes of the conspiracy. At least three witnesses have come forward to depose that Karkare was seen in the Marina Hotel on various occasions during the period 17th January to the 20th January. P.W.11 Gobind Ram served a drink to him on the 17th and another drink to him on the 20th. PW.8 Nain Singh served tea to Karkare and Shankar on the 20th January or is clear from the fact that a bill for three extra teas was went to the occupants of the room.

Sitting on a takhtposh:

Karkare's presence in the Birla House on the afternoon of the 20th January is established by the evidence of P.W.16 Chottu Ram. On the day of the occurrence Bhur Singh was sitting on a *takhtposh*[45] in front of the room through the trellis window of which the conspirators had proposed to throw the hand-grenades. He states that a car drove into the open circular space behind the Birla House and four passengers alighted therefrom. They started talking to some persons who were standing near the gate of the Birla House. One of them (whom he later

---

[45] *Takhtposh*, in Punjabi, means Bench, that is *used for sleeping are placed in the private rooms of houses* while the ones used for sitting are located in the more public parts of a house.

identified as Karkare) went up to the witness and asked him for permission to take a photograph through the trellis work of the window. The witness told him that no useful purpose was likely to be served by taking a photograph from the back of Mahatma Gandhi. He offered a small bribe to the witness which the latter declined. An explosion took place a few minutes later.

Several objections have been taken to the evidence of this witness. It is said in the first place that Karkare could not have been the person who asked for permission to take the photograph because Karkare was not carrying a bag and because the man who talked to Chhotu Ram had alighted from the car and according to the prosecution Karkare did not come to the Birla House by car. It is said that the person who asked for permission to take the photograph was carrying a khaki bag. Only two khaki bags have been mentioned in the evidence before the Trial Court. One of these bags belonged to Badge which had been brought by him from Poona to Bombay and which was later given by him to Madanlal for being taken to Delhi. This bag is said to have been returned to Badge on the 19th or 20th January and was taken by him to the Birla House on the 20th January. Shortly before the explosion of the bomb Badge went to the taxi and placed both his own revolver and the revolver which was in possession of Shankar into this bag. The second bag belonged to Gopal Godse. That bag was left in a cupboard in the Hindu Mahasabha office before Gopal and his companions went to the Birla House. Karkare had no bag with him and it is accordingly contended that if the man who spoke to Chhotu Ram had a bag it could not be Karkare. it is said that the evidence of Chhotu Ram is manifestly false as it does not fit in with the prosecution story and as no reason has been given in regard to the circumstances in which the bag came into the possession of Karkare.

The second criticism was that there is a discrepancy in the statements made by Chhotu Ram and Mt. Sulochana. Mt. Sulochana deposes that "one of the persons who had got down from the car had a talk with Chhotu Ram" who was sitting in front of the quarters at the time. P.W.14 Surjit Singh states that he brought only four persons in his car, namely, Nathuram, Apte, Gopal Godse and Shankar. Karkare and Madanlal had reached the Birla House long before the arrival of their companions. If Karkare was not in the car and if one of the persons who talked to Chhotu Ram had alighted from the car it is obvious that it could not be Karkare.

Thirdly, it is stated that when Chhotu Ram appeared at the Identification Parade at Delhi on the 28th February, 1948 he picked up Karkare and Apte and said that on the day of the bomb explosion in the Birla House four persons including Apte and Karkare came to the Birla House at 4.30 or 5 p.m. and one of them asked him to take the photograph of Mahatmaji from his quarters. In his statement before the Trial Court on the 1st July 1948 he stated clearly that Karkare was the person who had asked for permission to take the photograph and who had offered Rs. 5/- or Rs. 10/- as a bribe. It is argued that if Chhotu Ram was not quite certain on the 28th February 1948 as to which person had spoken to him it is difficult to believe that his memory had improved so considerably by the Trial Court that he was able to state with confidence that Karkare was the person who spoke to him.

Fourthly, it is said that Chhotu Ram's memory does not appear to be reliable and consequently that no reliance should be placed on what he has stated. Mr. Oscar Brown, Chief Presidency Magistrate, states that Chhotu Ram identified Shankar (besides two wrong persons) as the person whom he had seen near the Birla House on the day of the explosion. Chhotu Ram states that he does not remember whether he told the Magistrate as to the person who had asked his permission to take a photograph. It is contended that if he picked out two wrong persons at the Identification Parade it would not be safe to place implicit reliance on the evidence given by him in regard to Karkare.

The fifth criticism was that the witness identified two wrong persons on the 30th March 1948. This fact would only establish that the Identification Parade was not a farce and that witnesses were not allowed to see the prisoners before they were asked to identify them at the parade. I am clearly of the opinion that Chhotu Ram is telling the truth. Indeed, Chhotu Ram's statement is fully corroborated by Bhur Singh Chowkidar who also states that the man who talked to Chhotu Ram was carrying a bag.

It is true that Badge does not state that Karkare was carrying a bag on the 20th January 1948 but a bag could have come into his hands in any one of several ways. For example the bag which Badge was carrying could have been handed over to Karkare temporarily. Again Karkare may have brought a bag with him from Bombay in his steel trunk or he may have purchased on in Delhi. A grenade was given to Karkare at the Marina Hotel. That grenade had to be kept. Karkare may have purchased a bag from the Connaught Circus below the Marina Hotel. Chhotu Ram is positive that the man who addressed him was Karkare and that Karkare was carrying a bag. Nor can I find any serious discrepancy in the statement made by Mt. Sulochana that one of the persons who had alighted from the car had talked to Chhotu Ram. As the person who had alighted from the car started talking to two or three others who were waiting outside the back gate of the Birla House Mt. Sulochana may well have made a mistake as to which persons got down from the car and which persons met them at the gate. It is common ground that one of these persons talked to Chhotu Ramand Chhotu Ram says that it was Karkare. Nor am I prepared to attach exaggerated importance to the statements which are attributed to this witness at the time of the Identification Parade. It is true that when the witness was invited to the parade which was held on the 28th February 1948 he picked up Karkare and Apte and said that on the day of the bomb explosion in the Birla House four persons including Karkare and Apte had come to the Birla House at 4.30 or 5 p.m. and that he stated before the Trial Court on a later date that Karkare was the person who had made the request. This discrepancy does not appear to me to be of any consequence. The statement which was recorded by the Magistrate was recorded only with the object of ascertaining the particular persons whom the witness was identifying. Again, the statement which has been attributed to the witness was not put to him in cross-examination and he was not confronted with it.

The next piece of evidence against Karkare is that on the morning of Sunday, the 25th January, he appeared at the house of his friend and relation Mr. G.K. Joshi at Thana and asked him to have a telegram despatched to Apte requiring Nathuram and Apte to see him in Thana. As stated in an earlier paragraph of this judgment Nathuram and Apte arrived in Thana in response to the telegram. Gopal also came and took part in the conference which was held at about 9 o' clock in the night. The nature of the conversations which took place had not been indicated but there can be little doubt that the prisoners surveyed the situation as a result of the arrest of Madanlal and completed their plans for the future.

The next piece of evidence against Karkare is that on the 28th and 29th January he was seen at the Railway Station of Delhi in the company of Nathuram and Apte. While discussing the evidence of Sundarilal P.W.26, Hari Kishan P.W.27 and Jannu P.W.28, I stated that there was considerable doubt in regard to the presence of this prisoner in Delhi on the 29th or 30th January.

The evidence on record satisfies me that Karkare was a member of the conspiracy to take the life of Mahatma Gandhi and that he has been rightly convicted. The case against Madanlal is that he was opposed to the Pro-Muslim policy of Mahatma Gandhi; that while at Ahmednagar he came into contact with Karkare who entertained similar views; both Karkare and Madanlal went to the shop of Badge in Poona with the object of inspecting the arms and ammunitions which were being offered for sale; that on or about the 12th January, he made an extra-judicial confession to Dr. Jain telling him that he had been entrusted with the work of throwing bomb at the prayer meeting of Mahatmaji to create a confusion and that in the confusion so created Mahatmaji was to be overpowered by the members of his party; that on the 15th January he accompanied Nathuram, Apte, Karkare, and Badge to the house of Dixitji Maharaj where Badge showed the explosives which he had brought from Poona; that the bag containing the explosives was then entrusted to his _______ with the object of being taken to Delhi; that the same night he accompanied Karkare to Delhi; that on the 19th January joined Karkare in making a false representation to Angchekar that both Karkare and Madanlal were shifting to the Maharashtra Niwas the same evening and were leaving for Jullundur on the following morning; that on the evening of the 19th January he stayed in the Hindu Mahasabha Bhawan along with Gopal, Badge, and Shankar; that on the 20th January he accompanied Karkare to the marina Hotel and joined the conference that was held there; that a gun-cotton-slab and a hand-grenade were handed over to him with the direction that on a signal being given by Nathuram and Apte he was to explode the gun-cotton-slab and to throw the hand-grenade; that he ignited the gun-cotton-slab and was immediately arrested and that a live hand-grenade was recovered from his possession.

Sample Gun-Cotton-Slab and Hand-Grenade:

Madanlal denies the correctness of a circumstances appearing in evidence against him. He admits having gone to Delhi with Karkare but he states that he went ther in connection with his marriage. He admits that he went to the Birla House on the 20th January but did so with the object of making a peaceful demonstration. On being asked to explain the circumstances in which he came into possession of a live hand-grenade Madanlal stated that Badge had given him a gun-cotton-slab and hand-grenade as samples for sale to refugees.

There can be no manner of doubt that Madanlal was a member of the conspiracy which was formed to take the life of Mahatma Gandhi. I have already discussed in detail the evidence which has been furnished by the prosecution in support of the testimony of the approver in regard to the incidents which took place at Delhi between the 9th and the 17th and the incidents which took place in Delhi between the 17th and the 20th. Madanlal took an active part in procuring arms and ammunition and transporting them from Bombay to Delhi. He made a confession to Dr. Jain which shows almost conclusively that a conspiracy was in existence and that the conspirators had planned to assassinate Mahatma Gandhi. It is true that he did not take a prominent part in connection with the conspiracy on the 17th, 18th, and 19th January but he took a leading part in the execution of the plans on the following day. He went to the Marina Hotel where he put on a coat belonging to Apte and later proceeded with Karkare to the prayer grounds where he ignited the gun-cotton-slab. He was caught red-handed with a live hand-grenade in his pocket. If his object was merely to make a peaceful demonstration his object was fully served because he had created an explosion which was just what he desired to do. If he wanted merely to make a harmless demonstration he would doubtless have run up to Mahatma Gandhi immediately after he had lighted the fuse. Even if he did not rush towards the Gandhiji then, he could have run to him as soon as the slab had exploded and could have ventilated the grievances which he was so keen to bring to the notice of Mahatma Gandhi. He did nothing of the kind. His conduct at the prayer ground is, in my opinion, wholly an inconsistent with the theory that he went to the prayer ground with the object only of making a demonstration. Again, the explanation

given by him in regard to the recovery of a live hand-grenade is hollow and unconvincing. I have given detailed reasons in an earlier portion of the judgment for holding that he went there to throw the grenade on Mahatma Gandhi and not merely to stage a demonstration before him.

Mr. Bannerji, who appears for Madanlal, contends that assuming for the sake of argument that Madanlal was a member of the conspiracy he ceased to be one as soon as he was arrested by the police on the 20th January. I regret I am unable to concur in this contention. The crime of conspiracy consists in an agreement between two or more persons to do a criminal act. If, therefore, anything is done in pursuance of that agreement, all the members who are parties to the agreement are equally liable for the acts of others. In such cases every conspirator is presumed in the eye of law to be an agent of the others. But it is open to a conspirator to withdraw from the conspiracy and thus relieve himself from a homicide committed subsequent to the said withdrawal provided he notifies his associates of such withdrawal. It is true that Madanlal was arrested on the 20th January and that it was not possible for him to give any effective help to the co-conspirators in achieving the object of the conspiracy but it is not necessary for every member of a conspiracy to take an active interest in the execution of the common purpose. Silent partners are by no means uncommon future conspiracies. If Madanlal had dissociated himself from the conspirators and had made his intention plain to his associates either by express words or by his conduct it may have been possible to argue that he was not responsible for the murder which was committed after the date of his disavowal or dissociation. But Madanlal never informed his co-conspirators that he had abandoned the common purpose. It seems to me therefore that it is impossible for him to escape liability for the criminal acts committed by his confederates which have reasonably followed in the execution of the common purpose.

Briefly summarised the evidence against Gopal is that on the 14th January his brother Nathuram effected a nomination of his life policy in a sum of Rs. 3,000/- in favour of Mrs. Sindhutai wife of Gopal; that on the same date he applied for seven days' casual leave from the 15th January to the 21st January for some immediate farm affairs at his village; that seven days' casual leave was granted to him with effect from the 17th January; that on the afternoon of the 19th January he paid a visit to Karkare and Madanlal who was putting up in the Sharif Hotel; that on the night of the 19th January he stayed with Madan Lal in a room of the Hindu Mahasabha Bhawan, Delhi; that on the morning of the 20th January Apte took Gopal, Badge and Shankar to the **jungle** behind the Mahasabha Bhawan for trying out the two revolvers which had been brought by Gopal and Badge; that after his return to the Mahasabha Bhawan he accompanied Apte, Badge, and Shankar to the Marina Hotel with the *khaki* bag in which Badge had brought the stuff from Poona to Bombay and in which Madanlal had brought the stuff from Bombay to Delhi together with the revolver which Gopal had brought with him from Kirkee; that on arriving in Room No.40 of the Marina Hotel Gopal started repairing his revolver while Apte, Karkare, Madanlal and Badge started fixing primers in the gun-cotton-slabs and detonators in the hand-grenades; that in his presence and with his hearing Nathuram told Badge that this was their 'last effort', that the work must be accomplished and that they should see that everything was done properly. While they were still in the room, the various parts which the conspirators were to take in the Birla House were assigned to them and arms and ammunition were distributed; that a hand-grenade was given to Gopal with the object that it should be thrown at Mahatma Gandhi as soon as commotion was caused by the explosion of the slab; that Gopal accompanied Apte, Badge, and Shankar in a taxi belonging to Surjit Singh from the Regal Cinema to the Hindu Mahasabha Bhawan; that Gopal got out, went inside the Bhawan and left his bag containing the ammunition in the cupboard of his room; that the party proceeded by the same taxi to the back gate of the Birla House and met Nathuram, Karkare, and Madanlal; that in the presence of Gopal, Apte asked Madanlal whether he was ready; that Madanlal replied that he was ready that he had placed the gun-cotton-slab and that it remained only to be ignited; that Karkare came and told Apte that he had made arrangements with Chhotu Ram to allow someone to enter that room as a photographer; that Badge refused to enter that room for fear of being trapped inside, and intimated his desire to shoot from the open, that after the explosion Nathuram, Apte, and Gopal entered the taxi and left immediately for the Connaught Place; that Gopal stayed the Frontier Hindu hotel, Delhi under the 'assumed name' of Rajagopalam on the night of the 20th and 21stJanuary; that Karkare also stayed in the same hotel that night under the assumed name of G.M. Joshi; that some days after the 20th January he went to the house of Mr. P.V. Godbole of Poona (P.W.85) and deposited a revolver and bullets with him; that on or about the 24th January he met Nathuram and Apte in Hotel Elphinstone Annexe, Bombay; that at about4 o'clock on the afternoon of the 25th January he went to the house of Mr. G.M. Joshi at Thana with a trunk, and met Nathuram, Apte, and Karkare that he rejoined his post on the morning of the 27th January that Mahatma Gandhi was assassinated on the 30th January, 1948 by his brother Nathuram; that when he was arrested in his native village of Uksan on the 5th February he was found to be in possession of the bag (Ex.P.54) in which Badge had taken the stuff from Poona to Bombay and which had been brought by Madanlal from Bombay to Delhi; that he was identified by Gobind Malekar on the 2nd March, Angchekar on the 16th March, Mehar Singh and Ram Parkash on the 24th March, Ram Lal Dutt, Surjit Singh, Shanti Parkash and Gobind Ram on the 30th March and Bhur Singh on 31st March.

Gopal admits that his brother Nathuram effected a nomination in favour of his wife on the 14th January but states that he was not aware of this nomination then; he admits having applied for leave but he states that his leave was spent in his native village; he denies having visited Delhi or having been there between the 17th and 21st January; he denies having visited the house of Mr. Godbole of Poona or having visited the Elphinstone Hotel annexe or having gone to Thana; he denies that a bag was recovered from his possession when he was arrested near Uksan. He admits that he was identified by various witnesses on the dates mentioned above but complains that he was shown to the witnesses prior to each identification. On being questioned as to why the witnesses had given evidence against him, he states that the witnesses had deposed against him under the pressure of the police. No evidence was produced in defence.

The first important piece of evidence against Gopal is that on the 14th January his brother Nathuram effected a nomination of his policy in favour of Mrs. Sindhutai wife of Gopal. I have already referred to this matter in an earlier part of the judgment. It is no crime on the part of a brother-in-law to assign a policy in favour of his sister-in-law, but it is a curious coincidence that this policy should be assigned on the 14th January; that a sum of Rs. 250/- should be paid to him by his brother on the same day and that he should apply for leave on the same date. The prosecution allege that Nathuram assigned his policy in favour of the wife of Gopal in order that some provision should be made for her in the event of Nathuram and Gopal being put out of the way by the decision of a judicial tribunal and that he paid a sum of Rs. 250/- to Gopal for the purchase of a revolver for the purposes of the conspiracy. It is said that Gopal applied for seven days' casual leave with effect from the 14th January in order that he should be able to accompany Karkare and Madanlal from Bombay to Delhi on the 15th January. Gopal stated in his application that he wanted to take leave for some immediate farm affairs at his village but this explanation does not apply to be plausible. If

he did proceed on leave with effect from the 17th January and did actually spend that leave in his native village he could have had no difficulty in producing witnesses of his village to the effect that he was there during the whole of his leave. No evidence whatsoever has been produced and no effort has been made to establish the plea of _alibi_.

On the other hand, convincing evidence has been produced on behalf of the prosecution to the effect that Gopal was in fact in Delhi on the afternoon of the 19th January and during the whole of the 20th January

The first set of witnesses who saw Gopal in Delhi are Ram Lal Dutt P.W.2, Shanti Parkash P.W.3 and Angechkar P.W.5. The first two are partners of the Shariff Hotel while the third is a refugee from Sind. Ram Lal Dutt states that on the 19th January a person came to enquire as to the room in which Madanlal was staying. The witness had him sent to Room No.2 through a servant. Shanti Parkash deposes that on the same day he prepared a bill for B.M. Bias and Karkare in respect of the charges payable to the hotel. Bias came to the office along with an outsider and asked the witness to furnish details of the account. He was given the necessary details and he paid the bill in full. Bias then came again to the office at about 2 p.m. and said that he would leave the hotel sometime later. The witness told him that he would be charged the rent of the room for another day but later reduced the rent at his request. Angchekar states that when he returned from the Transfer Bureau at about 3 o'clock on the afternoon of the 19th January and went to his room he found Karkare and Madanlal with a stranger whom he later identified as Gopal sitting in the room. As soon as he entered the room, he was told by Karkare that Madanlal and he were going to vacate the room and that they were going to the Maharashtra Niwas for the night and proceeding to Jullundur on the following morning. The witness told Karkare that he had finished his work and was going back to Bombay that every day and enquired from Karkare as to what his permanent address at Bombay was. Karkare replied that it was not necessary to furnish him with the address. Madanlal, however, had no hesitation in giving his own address for he told the witness that he was residing at the Chembur refugee camp in Bombay. According to Angheckar, Gopal kept sitting in the room in the hotel with Karkare and Madanlal for about two hours during the whole of which period with the exception of fifteen minutes Angchekar himself was also in the room. It is argued on behalf of the defence that Angchekar was refugee from Sind, was a man of straws and consequently that his evidence should not be accepted as gospel truth. Mr. Daphtary, however, contends that Angchekar is not an unreliable witness. A perusal of Exhibit P.12 makes it quite clear that this witness, who is about thirty years of age, passed the Matriculation Examination of the Bombay University in 1936 and was working as Rationing Enquiry Inspector before the partition. He could read, speak, and write Marathi and English and could read and speak Hindi and Gujarati. he was drawing a salary of Rs. 105/- per mensem plus allowances, his aggregate salary inclusive of allowances being Rs. 163/- per mensem. He has no reason to be hostile either to Madanlal or Gopal. If he had chosen to be hostile to either of these prisoners he could have given much stronger evidence against them. The statement actually made by him does not betray any anxiety on his part to implicate Gopal. In the identification parade which was held on the 30th March 1948 the witness picked up Gopal as the person whom he had seen in his room on the 19th January. He was, however, unable to give the name of Gopal as that name was not given to him at Delhi.

While discussing the evidence of this witness in an earlier paragraph I expressed the view that he is intrinsically and inherently reliable and that there is no reason why his evidence should not be accepted as against Gopal.

I am not quite certain, however, whether the evidence of the two partners of the Sharif Hotel is equally trustworthy. Mr. Daphtary contends that the allegation made against these witnesses that they are under the thumb of the police must be discounted. In their capacity as Hotel Managers, it was their duty to come into contact with a large number of persons and to remember their faces. Memory for purposes of identification is not a matter of education and is to some extent dependent on 1 person's calling. Again, it is said that Madanlal had brought the police to the Sharif Hotel on the 23rd January and as they were examined on that day the features of the person whom they had seen in the room of Madanlal must have been impressed on their memories. Indeed, it is stated that the allegation that Gopal came to the hotel that day is consistent with the probabilities of the case. Immediately on his arrival in Delhi, Gopal must have seen Nathuram and Apte in the Marina Hotel. Nathuram must have asked Gopal to ask Karkare and Madanlal to leave the hotel and not to stay with Angchekar who was a total stranger and who might later give evidence against them. It is said that Gopal must have gone to the Sharif Hotel with the object of asking Karkare and Madanlal to leave the room and shift to another place. It was with that object that both Karkare and Madanlal informed Angchekar as soon as he returned from the Transfer Bureau that they were leaving the hotel the same afternoon spending the night in the Maharashtra Niwas and proceeding to Jullundur on the following day. Ram Lal Dutt and Shanti Parkash are admittedly the partners of a hotel and may possibly be endowed with better memories than those of persons pursuing other callings but it must be remembered that at least one of these persons namely Ram Lal Dutt started hotel business only with effect from the 11th November 1947. His memory cannot thus be said to have been so highly developed that he should remember a person whom he had seen only for a moment or so. The police enquired from hi the description of the person who had come to see Madanlal and he told him that he would be able to identify the person if produced before him. He does not remember the description he had given of the person to the police. Shanti Parkash is more precise. He states that the police enquired from him the description of the outsider and he gave the description of the outsider to the police. These persons were undoubtedly questioned on the 23rd January and the fact that they were questioned so shortly after the 19th may possibly have made them remember that a person had actually come to see Madanlal on the 19th January. It must be remembered, however, that they were not taken to Bombay till the 30th March and it is, in my opinion, extremely difficult for any person to identify another whom he had seen for a moment or so 70 days before. While I have no reason to think that these witnesses are not talking the truth. I am of the opinion, that it would not be safe to accept their testimony without demur.

The next witness who saw Gopal in Delhi is Surjit Singh P.W.14 who carried a certain number of passengers in his taxi from the Regal Cinema to the Birla Temple and from the Birla Temple to the Birla House and later from the Birla House to the Connaught Circus. This witness clearly identifies Gopal as one of the passengers who travelled in his car on the date in question.

It will be seen from the above that the statement of Badge to the effect that Gopal came to Delhi is corroborated by at least five witnesses, namely, Ram Lal Dutt P.W.2, Shanti Parkash P.W.3, Angchekar P.W.5, Surjit Singh P.W.14 and Bhur Singh P.W.17. The evidence of these witnesses is strongly supported by the fact that Gopal took leave of absence at about the same time act which the other prisoners in this case were planning an attempt on the life of Mahatma Gandhi. He has given no explanation whatsoever in regard to the place where he spent his leave. If he was in his village from the 17th to the 25th January as he states he was, he could have had no difficulty in producing a cast iron _alibi_. No evidence was produced by him in defence.

It has been argued on behalf of Gopal that he took no part whatsoever in the crime for the bag containing his revolver and hand-grenade was left behind in the office of the Hindu Mahasabha and that so far as can be judged he came to Delhi with the object of spending his leave with his brother. It is somewhat difficult to believe that Gopal would take a long and expensive journey from Poona to Delhi with no other object than of seeing his brother. He did not state in his application that he wanted to civil Delhi.

The prosecution have, in my opinion, established beyond reasonable doubt that Nathuram effected a nomination of his life policy in favour of the wife of Gopal, that Gopal applied for leave on the same day, the Gopal had lunch with Nathuram at Poona on the 14th January and applied at once for casual leave, and that Nathuram paid a sum of Rs. 250/- to Gopal _vide_ entry in his diary Exhibit P.218 and that Gopal was seen in Delhi is corroborated by the testimony of four witnesses including P.W.5. Angchekar, P.W.14.Surjit Singh, and P.W.17 Bhur Singh whose testimony I have no reason to doubt, that Gopal has given no explanation in regard to the place where he spent his leave, and that Gopal met Nathuram, Apte and Karkare at Thana on the 25th January. **<u>These reasons satisfy me that Gopal was a member of the conspiracy which was formed to assassinate Mahatma Gandhi.</u>**

The date on which Gopal left Delhi is not known, but it appears that he visited Nathuram and Apte in Elphinstone Hotel Annexe, Bombay, on or before the 2th January. P.W.6 G.V. Malkear a bear of the Hotel states that Nathuram and Apte came to the hotel on the 24th January 1948. The witness saw them on that day as well as on the 25th January. They left the hotel on the 27th January at about 6.30 a.m. On that date he had awakened them in the morning and had served them with tea and milk. This witness states that he saw Nathuram and Apte on the 24th January when they arrived and then saw them on the 25th January 1948 at about

7 a.m. while these two passengers were staying in the hotel, one gentleman who was later identified as Gopal came to visit them. The witness stated in cross-examination that this stranger had probably come on the 25th January 1948. On the other hand Mr. Vasant Joshi P.W.79 states that Gopal was at his house visiting his father Mr. G.M. Joshi at about 4 o'clock on the afternoon of the 25th January. Much capital was made out of the fact that Gopal could not be in Bomaby and in Thana which are separated by a distance of 20 miles on one and the same day After going carefully through the depositions of these two witnesses, namely, Malkear P.W.64 and Joshi P.W.79 I have no hesitation in holding that Gopal was in Thana on the 25th January and could not be in Bombay at the same hour on the same day. On the first occasion he met Nathuram and Apte and on the second Nathuram, Apte, and Karkare. He rejoined his duties on the morning of the 26th January on the expiry of his leave. The news of Mahatma Gandhi's assassination was broadcast on the 30th January and Gopal was in imminent danger of losing his own life as he was known to be a brother of the assassin. Police protection was given to him and he was sent away to his native village Uksan. It appears that on the arrest of Badge on the 31st January and on Madanlal being brought to Bombay on or about the 4th the police came to know that Gopal was also concerned in the crime. He was arrested on the 5th February.

It has been argued on behalf of the prisoners that Gopal could not have taken part in the crime. **In the first place,** he is a Government servant who is perfectly settled in a Government post and who had no motives of the nature attributed to his brother Nathuram. **Secondly,** it is said that Nathuram could have had no object in securing the help of Gopal. He did not want to make the wife of Gopal a widow by sending her husband to the gallows. **Thirdly,** it is said that no revolver, etc., has been traced to the possession of Gopal. **Fourthly,** it is alleged that Gopal was not assigned any part at the Marina

Hotel Conference or if he was assigned any part, he did not carry it out for the left the revolver and the hand-grenade which were given to him at the Hindu Mahasabha before leaving for Birla House. It may be that he did not take a prominent part in the execution of the common plan but that fact would not exonerate him from blame and entitle him to escape from the liability which attaches to every person who agrees [46] to commit an unlawful act conjointly with others.

The circumstances appearing in evidence against Shankar briefly are that while at Poona he showed the stuff belonging to his employer Badge to various persons including Karkare and Madanlal; that on the 14th January he accompanied Nathuram, Apte and Badge to Dixitji Maharaj for the purpose of leaving the bag containing the stuff; that on the 17th January he accompanied Nathuram, Apte, and Badge to various places for the purpose of collecting subscriptions; that while they were travelling by taxi Apte stated that Savarkar had predicted that **"Gandhiji's Hundred years were over"** and that there was no doubt that their work would be successfully accomplished; that on the 18th January Shankar accompanied Badge to Delhi; that on the morning of the 20th Badge and Shankar accompanied Apte to the Birla House and took measurements of the trellis-work to see if the hand-grenade could pass through the openings therein and inspected the places on either side of the gate form where gun-cotton slabs and detonators in the hand-grenades and that he was present at the conference at which various parts were assigned to the several prisoners. The most important piece of evidence against him is that while getting down from the Marina Hotel told Shankar that he was to throw his hand-grenade on the person on whom he threw his hand-grenade and that he was to shoot at the person at whom he shot and that the person

---

[46] Page No.246is blank in the Original Judgment. This remark can be found in the scanned copy of "True Copy Type Version" in Page No.154 Eds.

concerned was an old man known as Gandhiji and that he was to be finished. On the same day Apte, Gopal, Badge, and Shankar travelled by the taxi of Surjit Singh to the Birla House. On a signal from Badge, Shankar delivered his revolver to Badge and both the revolvers, namely, the one which was carried by Badge and the other which was carried by Shankar were put into a bag. After the explosion Shankar and Badge were put into a bag. After the explosion Shankar and Badge returned by a *Tonga* to the Hindu Mahasabha Bhawan and Shankar went and buried three hand-grenades and certain other stuff near the boundary wall of the Hindu Mahasabha Bhawan.

The conduct of Shankar prior to the 20th January is fully consistent with the allegation that Shankar was employed by Badge and was carrying out faithfully all the orders which were issued to him by his employer. It may be that he showed the stuff to some of the conspirators at Poona; that he carried the stuff to Bombay; that he went about with Badge to various places both at Bombay and at Delhi and that he buried the stuff at Delhi, but it must be remembered that whatever he did under the orders of Badge and in the course of his employment. Badge was carrying on an extensive trade in arms and ammunition and it may be assumed that Shankar was aware that this was being done in contravention of the law. He used to show the stuff to prospective purchasers; he used to carry it about from place to place; he used to bury it under a tree when it was not required and he used to bring it out when a prospective purchaser arrived. He accompanied Badge whenever and wherever he went for not only was he Badge's assistant but was also Badge's personal servant. It has not been alleged or proved that at any time prior to the 20th January Shankar was aware of the dare designs which were being entertained by Badge and the other members of his party. He did accompany Badge to various places but he did so purely in his capacity as a personal servant. He never joined the inner councils of the conspirators and was never taken into confidence. On the other hand the evidence proves almost conclusively that at every crucial moment i.e. whenever any vital decision was to be taken, Shankar was deliberately kept out of the picture. Numerous instances may be cited. For example, when Nathuram, Apte, and Badge went to the house of Dixitji Maharaj at Bhuleshwar on the evening of the 14th January, Shankar was made to sit in the hall while his companions went into the interior of the house along with the bag containing the stuff. He was not taken to the house of Dixitji Maharaj on the morning of the 15th. He was not present when Badge was invited to join the conspiracy or when he met Nathuram and others at Delhi. When the party proceeded to the house of Mr. Savarkar on the morning of the 17th January, Shankar was asked to wait outside the compound of the house. It is said that when was travelling by taxi along with Nathuram, Apte, and Badge, Apte said that Mr. Savarkar had predicted that *Gandhiji's hundred years were over* and that there was no doubt that their work was to be successfully accomplished. Unless we proceed on the assumption that Shankar was in the know of the secret these remarks could have had little or no significance for him. Moreover, it must be remembered that almost all conversations were carried on in Marahti, a language in which Shankar is by no means proficient. It was for this reason that the learned Special Judge came to the conclusion that the first occasion on which he joined the conspiracy was on the 20th January when he was specifically told by Badge at the Marina Hotel that the purpose of their visit to the Birla House was to assassinate Mahatma Gandhi. Mr. Daphtary does not challenge the correctness of this finding. Badge stated quite clearly that Shankar knew nothing about the conspiracy at Bombay or Delhi until they got down from the Marina Hotel for going to the Birla House on the 20th January.

The only point for decision so far as the case against Shankar is concerned is whether Badge did in fact tell Shankar while getting down from the steps of the Marina Hotel that he was to shoot Mahatma Gandhi. If the reply to this question is in the affirmative and if Shankar accompanied Badge to the Birla House with the object of carrying out the instructions given to him, there can be little doubt that Shankar would be guilty of an offence to commit a criminal conspiracy.

Fortunately for Shankar the only evidence in regard to his complicity in the crime is the statement of Badge himself. Badge is admittedly an accomplice and the statement made by him cannot be accepted unless it is corroborated as to Shankar's actual participation in the crime or connection with the offence or as it is sometimes said as to the prisoner's identity with the participators. In *R. v Farler 8 C&P 106 Lord Aibinger* observed that *'a man who has been guilty of a crime himself would always be able to relate the facts of the case and if the confirmation be only on the truth of that history, without identifying the person, that is really no corroboration at all.'* Badge's statement in respect of the complicity of Shankar stands uncorroborated unless it could be said that it has been corroborated by the event which took place after Shankar had been invited to join the conspiracy.

Two circumstances alone can be taken into consideration against him. The first is that he is said to have been present at the Birla House on the afternoon of the 20th January when the gun-cotton-slab was exploded by Madanlal. Surjit Singh taxi-driver in whose vehicle he is stated to have travelled from the Marina Hotel to the Birla House was unable to identify him in the parade. Chhotu Ram P.W.16, however, stated that Shankar was one of the persons who were present at the Birla House. It would, in my opinion, be wholly unsafe to convict Shankar on the testimony of a single witness, particularly when the taxi-driver Surjit Singh in whose vehicle Shankar is said to have reached the Birla House was unable to identify him. The only other evidence which has been produced against

him is that on the 14th February Shankar led certain respectable persons to the grounds of the Hindu Mahasabha Bhawan at Delhi and was able to dig up two live hand-grenades from one place and one live hand-grenade from another place. The mere fact that Shankar knew of the places at which these articles were buried would not prove necessarily that he had entered into an agreement to take the life of Mahatma Gandhi.

This is the sum total of the evidence against Shankar and it is in my opinion wholly insufficient to justify his conviction upon a charge under Section 120-B read with Section 302, of the Penal Code.

The confession made by Dr. Parchure on the 18th February 1948 speaks for itself:

"**I** know Nathuram Godse since 1941. I knew him in connection with the "Hindu Rashtra Dal'. I had known Mr. Nathuram Godse's name since 1939. I had been to Poona and Bombay to have talks with the workers of the Hindu Rashtra Dal as regards amalgamating the organisation, namely, the Hindu Rashtra Dal and the Hindu Rashtra Sena. At Poona I met Mr. Nathuram Godse and had discussions with him on the subject. We did not come to any agreement. Since then, I was not on good terms with him. On the night of the 27th January, 1948 at about 11 at night, when I had just gone to bed my eldest son, Nilkant came to my room and told me that "two guests" have come. I told my son to open the door and let them come in and I shall come down immediately. I came downstairs and to my surprise I found the two guests to be Mr. Nathuram Godse and Mr. Narain Rao Apte. I asked them "how is it that you have come without any previous intimation?"My surprise was due to the fact that I did not expect Nathuram Godse to my house. Nathuram Godse said that he has come for special purpose. On the night of the 27th January, 1948, Mr. Godse and Apte told me the purpose for which they had come to me. Mr. Godse and Apte said that we are going to do some terrible fiat before the 2nd February, 1948. That terrible feat was the killing plan of Gandhiji at Delhi. Then he showed me one revolver which he had brought with him, and told me to try to get a better revolver from someone at Gwalior. The trigger of the revolver that Mr. Godse and Apte brought with them was rather hard. He had about 5-6 rounds of ammunition with him. I told him that I have one pistol with me which I cannot under any circumstances part to anyone else. I told him on the night of the 27th January, 1948 that I will try if possible, to get one revolver or pistol tomorrow. I offered Mr. Godse an Apte tea which Godse refused, and then I went and slept upstairs.

On the morning of the 28th January, 1948, I told Godse and Apte that I will call one of my workers and you have a talk with him regarding your requirements. I sent my son, Nilkant Parchure, and Roopa, my body-guard, to fetch Nana Dandvate from Chatri Bazaar. They both came back and said that he is not to be found. Then I went to my patients and to my dispensary at Patankar Bazaar. I returned home from my dispensary at 12 noon and I saw Nanna Dandvate along with Godse an Apte on the ground floor of my house. I had told Godse and Apte that in case Dandvate comes to my house during my absence, they can take (talk?) to him in confidence and he will help them in their mission. During my absence Godse and Apte had talked to Dandvate about procuring a better and reliable arm for them. When I returned home from my dispensary on the afternoon of the 28th, I found all of them examining one country-made revolver. I went upstairs to take off my clothes, etc. Godse, Apte, and Dandvate took a trial of the country-made revolver in the left hand compound of my house. I heard one fire only. I was not with them when they were having a trial. Godse and Apte did not approve of the country-made revolver. The revolver was not properly working. The revolver was then returned to Dandvate. Godse and Apte said that they are going by mail and a revolver should be arranged before that time. I said I do not think it is possible to arrange a revolver and you can go if you want to, whereupon they said that they can stay on till to-day night. We all dined together. After food, we had a talk on current political development. During the talk, both of them (Godse an Apte) said that Madan Lal who had thrown a bomb at Delhi near the Prarthana Hall knows you. I said that I had never met nor her of Madan Lal.

In the evening Dandvate came to my house with a pistol with him. From where he brought the pistol I do not know. This was an automatic pistol. Dandvate brought about 11-12 rounds of automatic pistol. Godse and Apte saw this automatic pistol and approved of it. Dandvate said that the price of this automatic pistol is Rs. 500/-. Nanna Apte paid Rs. 300/- to Dandvate and promised to pay the rest later on. Godse and Apte examined the automatic arrangement of the pistol brought by Dandvate and approved of this pistol. At 10.30 p.m. on the 28th January, 1948, Dandvate got a Tonga and Godse and Apte left my house for the Railway Station. After Godse and Apte had gone to the Railway Station, I went to my bedroom and slept. Dandvate also went to his house. Next day, i.e., on the 29th January, 1943, I mentioned to my elder brother Krishna Rao Parchure who is an Investment Secretary, Finance Department, that two gentlemen had come to me with a plan to kill Gandhiji at Delhi. I told him that I had arranged a pistol for them "to kill Gandhiji" at Delhi. He was shocked to hear this and said "Why you have bothered yourself in this affair?"[47]

Mr. Mathukar Kale told me on the 30th January, 1948 at 6 p.m. as I was going to my dispensary

---

[47] Page No.260 is blank in the Original Judgment. This remark can be found in the scanned copy of "True Copy Type Version" in Page No.161 Eds.

on foot that someone had told him that news on radio has come about Gandhiji's murder. I went to my dispensary and after 15 minutes I closed the dispensary and returned home. I gave one rupee to my servant Roopa to bring sweets from the bazaar. 10-15 members of my Sena were at my house then. I distributed the sweets to them. I don't know whether the revolver that Godse and Apte brought with them remained with Godse and Apte or was given to Dandvate.

I had broken sten-gun with me which I had kept with a friend of mine at Morar. My friend's name is Ramakant Puranik, Custom Post Gordawas, Morar.

Dr. Parchure denies the correctness of circumstances appearing in evidence against him. He admits that the signatures on the various sheets of the confession were his but he explains that Major Chhatrey came to the cell accompanied by two or three police officers and a person whom he later came to know to be Mr. R.B. Atal. After Major Chhatrey had gone away Mr. Atal took six sheets of white paper with something written on and made the prisoner to sign those sheets without his knowing as to what was written on those sheets.

Dr. Parchure explains the circumstances in which the confession is said to have been signed by him. He states that at about midnight on the night of the 2nd February certain police officials took him into custody and lodged him in a solitary cell in the Fort at Gwalior. He was orally informed that he was being detained but the grounds of detention were not indicated to him and he was not produced before any Magistrate. The police officials behaved most rudely towards him; it was intensely cold in the Fort; the cell was pitch dark. For seventeen days he lived in that stone-walled room without any human company and without any amenities. Mr. Khizar Mohammad, an official of the Gwalior C.I.D. paid daily visits to the Fort, gave him all sorts of threats of torture in an underground cell and said that he would wreak vengeance on him for his being a leader of the Hindus of Gwalior. Within three days

of his arrival in the Fort, Dr. Parchure began to have an intense pain in his joints, which got swollen. He started running temperature and pleaded for medical help, which unfortunately Mr. Khizar Mohammad refused to render. After some days the Fort Medical officer sent him a "mixture' which afforded him a slight relief.

Doses of threat and Advice:

Eight or ten days after he had been taken to the Fort, the Indian Union Police Officials began to visit the cell and started interrogating him. They asked all sorts of questions and made all sorts of insinuations. On the very next day an officer of the Bombay Police whom he later came to know as Mr. Deulkar started giving him alternate doses of threats and advice. One of the threats was that all the members of his family were already taken in the custody of the police and that the said members were placed in conditions similar to the prisoner's. This officer advised reportedly that the prisoner should sign the statement that was prepared for him. He saw that an India-wide conspiracy had come to light in which thousands of arrests were being made, and he suggested that the prisoner should sign the statement by stating that he was to make his position as well as the position of his association clear. This he added would save the prisoner and serve the object of the police. When the prisoner resisted Mr. Deulkar said: **"Think of your family. All of you will suffer".** The prisoner told him that he was prepared to admit that Nathuram visited his house on the 28th January but Mr. Deulkar said that that would not suffice. He added that the police had taken possession of the prisoner's pistol from his son Nilkanda and that they would not hesitate to substitute the pistol for the one recovered from Nathuram. This threat completely floored the prisoner. He lay awake for the whole night with his body in pain and his mind thoroughly demoralized. He thought of his wife, his children, his brother and his mother in the inhuman atmosphere of public custody. Tragically situated as he was with a number of express and implied threats held out to him, he realized the horror of his position and inability to resist. He accordingly decided to sign the statement. He complained to the Fort Commander that he was being forced to sign a 'false statement' on the threat of harassment to himself and the members of his family but the latter laconically replied that he could deny it in Court.

Mr. Inamdar who appears for Dr. Parchure contends that the confession which is said to have been made by his client on the 18th February was under such circumstances that it should be held that it was caused by inducement, threat or promise proceeding from a person in authority. Dr. Parchure was arrested at Gwalior on the 2nd February and was taken straight to the Fort at Gwalior where he was kept in detention not upon a charge of murder which has now been brought against him, but on some charge which has not been indicated. During the period of his detention in the Fort, he was subjected to all kinds of indictment to which a reference has been made in his statement before the Court on the 18th February. Mr. R.B. Atal, Magistrate 1st Class went to the Fort and asked Dr. Parchure to affix his signatures to a confession which had already been recorded. The ground having already been prepared by the police officers who had been visiting the cell of Dr. Parchure incessantly over since the date of his detention, Dr. Parchure was in such a condition of mind that he was unable to resist any suggestion that was made. It is contended that the procedure adopted by Mr. Atal in recording the confession of Dr. Parchure inside his cell in the Fort and not within the premises of the Court Room is a departure from the usual practice which has occasioned a great deal of prejudice to his client. Thirdly, it is contended that Dr. Parchure has made certain allegations in regard to the treatment which was accorded to him while he was in detention. He has not produced any evidence in support of these allegations but it is these impossible for any person tragically situated as Dr. Parchure was to have witnesses available

at hand to give evidence in his favour. According to Mr. Inamdar the only conclusion that may reasonably be drawn from the circumstances of the case is that Dr. Parchure was subjected to physical force or to such mental strain as was calculated to break his will power and to get his mind into a state in which he could readily yield to any suggestions that the officers cared to make.

Mr. Daphtary has endeavoured to reply to these arguments. He states that Dr. Parchure was undoubtedly taken to the Fort at Gwalior but that he was taken where under the force of circumstances. He was the head of the Hindu Mahasabha and it was necessary for the preservation of public peace and tranquillity that he should have been kept in military custody. In regard to the suggestion that the confession should have been recorded in the Court room of Mr. Atal, it is sated that the confession was recorded in the Fort for reasons of security, as the State of Gwalior was in a condition of turmoil and it was apprehended that demonstration would take place if Dr. Parchure was brought to the Court. It is true that he was taken to the police station a short time before and that he was taken from the police station to a certain place where a sten-gun was found, but it is explained that Dr. Parchure had been taken to the Court room the population of the town were almost certain to come to know of this fact and to make a demonstration inside or outside the premises of the Court House.

In regard to the statement of Dr. Parchure and particularly in regard to the allegations that he was not properly treated while he was in detention, **Mr. Daphtary contends that allegations of this kind are easy to make and difficult to refute.** Dr. Parchure's confession was recorded on the 18th February 1948, but he did not retract this confession till the 30th July long after the proceedings in the case had started. Dr. Parchure was represented by Counsel in Court and these Counsels must have been aware that a confession had been obtained from Dr. Parchure and was likely to be used against him. Notwithstanding this knowledge Dr. Parchure chose to keep his lips shut till after the Court had started recording evidence. It is alleged that if the confession had been retracted at the earliest possible opportunity, i.e., as soon as Dr. Parchure was produced before the Court, the prosecution would have been in a position to ascertain from the several witnesses whether the confession had or had not been made absolutely voluntarily.

In regard to the confession itself, Mr. Daphtary contends that this document was not prepared by or with the connivance of the police and presented to Dr. Parchure for his signatures; Dr. Parchure is not a timid or an ignorant person. On the other hand, he is a person of education who occupies a responsible position in the life of Gwalior. He is the President of the Gwalior State Hindu Mahasabha and must, therefore, be deemed to be a person who can defend his own legitimate rights. The words of the confession show that he wants to clear himself and to clear the other members of his party. The expression "other members of his party" does not relate to Nathuram or Apte but to persons who had been working for the Hindu Mahasabha but who had been arrested at or about the same time as he himself.[48]

Again, it was contended that the inducement, threat or promise must be in relation to the charge against an accused person. There is no evidence of any inducement or promise having been made to Dr. Parchure. Assuming for the sake of argument that the police told him that they would let his friends and relations go if he confessed that would not be a confession which could be ruled out of consideration on the ground that it had been improperly obtained. The only threat which could render the confession inadmissible in evidence is the threat that if he did not confess he would be harassed. According to Mr. Daphtary, **there**

is not an iota of evidence on the file to justify the conclusion that any inducement, threat or promise was given to Dr. Parchure and the defence have not been able to indicate the nature of the so-called inducement, threat or promise. On the other hand, a perusal of the document makes it quite clear that it tends to inculpate Dr. Parchure but tries to exculpate the others. With regard to his brother, for example, he states as follows:

> **"Next** day, i.e., on the 29th January, 1948, I mentioned to my elder brother Krishna Rao Parchure who is an Investment Secretary, Finance Department, that two gentlemen had come to me with a plan to kill Gandhiji at Delhi. I told him that I had arranged a pistol for them "to kill Gandhiji" at Delhi. He was shocked to hear this and said "Why you have bothered yourself in this affair?"

Embroidery? or Embellishment?

This statement it is contended does not show that he wanted to implicate anyone other than himself or that the police were interested in putting his relations into prison. The confession is a plain statement of facts. **It contains no embroidery and no embellishment.**

Mr. Inamdar appears to have given an adequate explanation for the delay which was occasioned in retracting the confession. He states that Dr. Parchure appeared in Court on the 7th May. Mr. Inamdar interview him and was able to elicit the information that Dr. Parchure was ill when the confession was recorded and that the confession was taken down by a Magistrate who did not exercise jurisdiction in the Fort. Mr. Inamdar was not in a position on the basis of this statement to retract the confession and he wanted to make certain of the position that he ought to take after a perusal of the confession itself. The confession had not come in Court till the 3rd June 1948 and he asked the Reader of the Court to apprise him of its

---

[48] Page No.270 is blank in the Original Judgment. This remark can be found in the scanned copy of 'True Copy Type Version' in Page No.166 Eds.

arrival as soon as it was received. On the 3rd June the case was adjourned to the 14th and on this latter date Mr. Inamdar forgot to look for the confession as evidence of the Gwalior witnesses was placed in his hands and he spent the whole day in obtaining instructions from Dr. Parchure. On the 22nd June the accused were present before the Court and the charges were read over. Dr. Parchure pleaded not guilty, and thus denied by implication the truth and voluntariness of the confession. On the 24th June, the Court inspected the spot and on the 26th June Mr. Inamdar put in a Written Application for the inspection of the record. Inspection was allowed on the 1st July. Two defects manifested themselves at once, namely, (a) that there was nothing on the face of the confession to indicate that the confession was recorded in the Fort; and (b) that there was nothing to show that Dr. Parchure was ill on the date on which the confession was made. He made enquiries from Gwalior and made an application on the 13th January in which the confession was formally retracted.

Ordinarily a statement made by a person against his own interest is admissible against him, but judicial experience makes it quite clear that under certain circumstances a person is likely to say that which is not true if he thinks it to his advantage to do so. Thus a person who is arrested under a 'capital charge' may be induced to confess himself guilty of the murder he never committed if he is assured of a pardon being granted to him. Similarly a person who is subjected to torture or to other inhuman treatment may wish to make a false acknowledgement of guilt in the hope of obtaining immediate relief from suffering which his confession may be able to procure for him. It is for this reason that the Legislature has in its wisdom has enacted that "**a Confession made by a prisoner is irrelevant if the making of the confession appears to have been caused by inducement, threat or promise.**"A confession cannot be excluded on the ground that the admission of the confession would involve a breach of confidence or of good faith or on the ground that the person to whom it was made took on an Oath of Secrecy or on the ground that the method by which it was obtained or rejected according as it is or is not entitled to credit. The use of the expression "appears" in Section 24 shows that the Legislature does not require positive proof within the definition of Section 3 of the Evidence Act of improper inducement to justify the rejection of the confession. In the well-known case of *R......* *vs. ....Thompson (1893, 2 Q.B.12)* [49]*it was held that in order that evidence of a confession by a prisoner may be admissible, it must be affirmatively proved that such confession was free and voluntary, that is, was not preceded by any inducement to the prisoner to make a statement held out by a person in authority, or that it was not made until after such inducement had clearly been removed.*

A retracted confession is always a source of great anxiety to criminal Courts all over the world and particularly to Criminal Courts in this country where the police administration has degraded itself by crude methods. In **Queen.. vs. Thompson**to which reference has already been made, Cave J observed as follows:

> "**I** would add that for my part I always suspect these confessions, which are supposed to be the offspring of penitence and remorse, and which nevertheless are repudiated by the prisoner at the trial. It is remarkable that it is of very rare occurrence for evidence of a confession to be given when the proof other prisoner's guilt is otherwise clear and satisfactory; but, when it is not clear and satisfactory, the prisoner is not infrequently alleged to have been seized with the desire born of penitence and remorse to supplement it with a confession; - a desire which vanishes as soon as he appears in a Court of Justice."

---

[49] Readers to verify this detail as they are illegible in the Original Judgment. Eds.

In R… vs. … Gobardhan (9 All. 528, 566) Brodharst J. made the following pertinent observations:

> '**Confessions** made some days after arrest may also often be true, but such confessions will, I believe, in almost every instance not have been made voluntarily, but have been extorted my maltreatment, or induced by promise of pardon on being made a witness for the Crown. Confessions obtained after illegal detention by the police must be regarded with great suspicion. Confessions in this country are often obtained by undue influence, especially by the police, and this fact has been the subject of frequent judicial and public comment."

After going carefully through the arguments which have been addressed to us by the learned counsel in the present case I am in considerable doubt as to the genuineness of the confession. If the facts mentioned by Dr. Parchure in his statement before the Trial Court are true, it seems to me that they are sufficient to have created impression on his mind that he and the members of the family were likely to be harassed. Again, if his statement is true, the police officers subjected him to the pressure of a procedure which is wholly unauthorised by the law of the land. The length of the time for which Dr. Parchure was detained, the place in which he was kept and the manner in which he was interrogated lead me to doubt the genuineness of the confession.

Even if a confession retracted, it is open to the Court, after consideration of the whole evidence in the case, to come to the conclusion that the confession is true provided the confession is corroborated in material particulars by credible independent evidence.

The prosecution allege that on the 27th January, Nathuram and Apte left Delhi by the Bombay-Amritsar Express and reached Gwalior at 11.50 p.m. They spent the night in the house of Dr. Parchure and held consultations with him and Dandwate, the absconding accused, and obtained a pistol which was used in the assassination of Mahatma Gandhi. As soon as Dr. Parchure learns about the death of Mahatma Gandhi, he expressed his jubilation at the event by distribution of sweets and by making deprecatory remarks in regard to the murdered man.

Nathuram and Apte admit having visited Dr. Parchure at Gwalior but they state that they went there by train which reached Gwalior at 5 o'clock on the morning of the 28th and not at 11.50 p.m. on the night of the 27th. They deny having stayed in the house of Dr. Parchure but they admit that they paid two visits to his house, one at 10 o'clock in the morning and the other at 4 o'clock in the afternoon. They undertook the journey to Gwalior not with the object of enlisting the aid of Dr. Parchure in the assassination of Mahatma Gandhi or for the purpose of procuring a pistol with which the crime was to be perpetrated but with the object of obtaining volunteers from Gwalior for staging a peaceful demonstration in the presence of Mahatma Gandhi.

Two witnesses have appeared in Court to testify to the fact that Nathuram and Apte did in fact arrive by the Grand Trunk Express reaching Gwalior at 22.38 p.m.

According to the testimony of Ghariba (P.W.43) a *Tonga* driver of Lashkar, two or three days before the assassination of Mahatma Gandhi two passengers go down from the Bombay-Express and came out of the first and second class gate. At about 11.30 p.m. they asked the witness to take them in his *Tonga* to the house of Dr. Parchure agreeing to pay a sum of Re.1/- by way of fare. The *Tonga* had travelled only a few yards when the straps of the harness of the horse got broken,and the witness accordingly handed over the two passengers to another *Tongawala* by the name of Jumma (P.W.44). Jumma took the passengers to the house of Dr. Parchure and was paid a sum of Rs. 1/2 /- on account of the fare. Some eight days after the assassination of Mahatma Gandhi, Inspector Mandlik happened to return from Delhi by the train which reaches Gwalior at about

5 o'clock in the morning. He engaged the Tonga of Ghariba (P.W.43). He entered into conversation with the *Tonga*-driver and was informed by him that a rumour was afloat in the town that two persons who had stayed at the house of Dr. Parchure were concerned in the assassination of Mahatma Gandhi. The *Tonga*wala stated further that the two passengers who had got down at the Railway Station were taken to the house of Dr. Parchure in the *Tonga* of Jumma. Both these witnesses, namely, Ghariba and Jumma were taken to Bombay on or about the 9th April for the identification of the passengers who had been taken to the house of Dr. Parchure. Ghariba identified both Nathuram and Apte correctly while Jumma identified only Nathuram and failed to identify Apte and picked up a wrong person instead. A considerable amount of controversy raged round the particular train by which Nathuram and Apte arrived in Gwalior. The *Tonga* drivers stated that they arrived by the Bombay Amritsar Express which reached Gwalior at 11.50 p.m. If these two prisoners arrived at 11.50 they could not have engaged the *Tonga* at 11.30 p.m. On the other hand if they arrived at 10.38 p.m. no satisfactory explanation has been given as to why they should have kept on waiting at the Railway Station for an hour or so before engaging the *Tonga*.

Both these witnesses are unanimous in stating that these two prisoners took their *Tonga*s at 11.30 p.m. and I am inclined to accept their testimony. Nathuram and Apte admit that they were in Gwalior on the 28th the police had no object in ante-dating their arrival. If they had arrived at 5 o'clock on the morning of the 28th, they would have produced witnesses to say that they arrived at that hour. The police could have had no object in ante-dating their arrival. There was a 'full-moon' in the sky and they had ample opportunity of seeing the features of the passengers.

The story in regard to the incidents which took place at Gwalior on the 28th January and subsequent dates has been narrated by Mr. M.K. Kale (P.W.50),

who is employed as a clerk in an office at Gwalior. On the 28th January 1948 he asked his official superior for permission to leave office at about 12 noon as he wanted to withdraw some money from the bank. This permission was accorded. On his way to his house he happened to pass in front of the house of Dr. Parchure at 12.33 p.m. and entered it with the object of ascertaining the steps that the Hindu Mahasabha was going to take in consequence of power having been transferred to the Congress on the 24th January 1948 in spite of the agreement arrived at between the Hindu Mahasabha and the Maharaja of Gwalior. Dr. Parchure was sitting on an easy chair in the hall of his house with three other persons, namely, Nathuram, Apte, and Dandwate. Nathuram and Apte were trying the triggers of two revolvers which had in their hands. They were unable to press the triggers and they accordingly asked Dandwate to arrange a pistol for them. Dandwate said that the revolvers were in a serviceable condition and that he could show them as to how to press the triggers. Dandwate accordingly took these persons to the courtyard and the witness accompanied them to the courtyard. Dandwate then got a cartridge from one of those two persons, loaded a revolver and fired in the sky. Nathuram and Apte then tried to fire the revolver after reloading it but the revolver failed to function. They asked Dandwate to get them a revolver as soon as possible as their party had already left and they were to leave by the 2.30 or 3 p.m. train. Dandwate said that he could arrange a revolver by the evening and that they could leave by the night train. This conversation took place in the courtyard in the absence of Dr. Parchure. The revolvers which were being tried appeared to the witness to be country made revolvers. Nathuram, Apte, Dandwate and the witness then went to the private room of Dr. Parchure on the upper storey of the house. Dandwate suggested to Dr. Parchure that he should hand over his registered pistol to the two visitors but Dr. Parchure replied that he was not such a fool as to hand over his licensed pistol to anybody. The party then came down into the hall and discussed Gwalior politics. In the course of this discussion Dr. Parchure wondered what steps ought to be taken by him as the Maharaja had disregarded the agreement that he between entered into between the Maharaja and the Hindu Mahasabha. He was opposed to the principles advocated by the Congress but did not carry his opposition to the point of violence. The witness left the house of Dr. Parchure at 1.40 p.m. proceeded to the bank (which is at a distance of about a mile from the house of Dr. Parchure) withdrew the money and went back to his house. On the 29th January he came to know from Nilakantha Parchure son of Dr. Parchure that the two persons who had come to the house of Dr. Parchure on the preceding day were Nathuram and Apte.

Mahatma Gandhi died or murdered?

The news of Mahatma Gandhi's assassination was broadcast to the world shortly after the perpetration of the outrage at about 5 o'clock on the afternoon of the 30th January. The conduct of Dr. Parchure on the receipt of this news aroused the suspicions of a number of persons, among others being M.K. Kale (P.W.50), M.B. Khire (P.W.51), Ramdayal Singh (P.W.52) and Jagannath Singh (P.W.53). Kale met Dr. Parchure at about 6 p.m. on the 30th January in front of the Marahta Boarding House. He told Dr. Parchure that it had been heard on the radio that Mahatma Gandhi had died. **The latter enquired of the witness whether Mahatma Gandhi had died or had been murdered.** The witness replied that the new received was that of his death and that it was not clear whether he had died or had been murdered. The witness then accompanied Dr. Parchure to his dispensary and while he was sitting with Dr. Parchure in the dispensary one Madhukar Khire also arrived. A rumour thereafter became afloat that Mahatma Gandhi had been assassinated. The witness asked Dr. Parchure to close his shop and the latter agreed to close it. The witness then went back to his house. On the following day the witness heard that Nathuram Vinayak was the perpetrator of the crime. ***Putting two and two together*** he told his friends that the person must be Nathuram Vinayak Godse. He narrated the entire story to his mother on the 1st February and to Gangadhar Patwardhan and Shankar Pawar on the 2nd February. Madhukar Khire also visited him at his house on the 2nd February and he narrated the entire story to him. Gangadhar Patwardhan told the witness that he knew the entire story and pressed the witness to communicate the facts to Government. Patwardhan brought a car and took Madhumkar Khire and the witness to house of the Home Minister of the Gwalior State. The witness stated the facts and was immediately put under arrest. He was taken for purposes of identification to Bombay and he identified Nathuram and Apte in an identification Parade.

The statement of M.K. Kale has been corroborated to an extent by the statements of Mr. J.P. Goel (P.W.39), a Clerk in the War Profits Tax Department and M.B. Khire (P.W.51) a student of the Gwalior State. Goel states that at about 9 o'clock on the morning of the 28th January one Rupa, a bodyguard of Dr. Parchure, went to the house of the witness and asked him to see Dr. Parchure in his dispensary as soon as possible. The witness went to Dr. Parchure's dispensary at 10.30 a.m. and saw Nathuram and Apte sitting there. Dr. Parchure was not in the dispensary at the time and the witness who was in a hurry to get to his office left the dispensary. At about 9 o'clock the same evening Dandwate went to the house of the witness and told him that Nathuram was anxious to obtain a pistol and suggested that the witness could sell his pistol to him. The witness was somewhat reluctant to part with the weapon as he had only on e pistol with him at the time but he overcame his reluctance when Dandwate told him that he could get a sum of Rs. 500/- for his pistol and could easily buy another for the amount. The witness handed over his pistol to Dandwate and went off to sleep. Dandwate, however, called again about an hour later, i.e. at about 10 p.m. He gave the witness a country made revolver and a sum of Rs. 300/-. The witness refused to accept the revolver and the money and asked Dandwate either to pay him a sum of Rs. 500/- or to give his pistol back to him. The witness met Dr. Parchure on the 2nd February 1948 after Mahatma Gandhi had been assassinated and told him that his pistol had not been put to a proper use. Dr. Parchure made no answer.

The statement of Kale has also been corroborated by that of M.B. Khire (P.W.51). On hearing of the news of the death of Mahatma Gandhi this witness proceeded to the dispensary of Dr. Parchure and had a talk with him. He told him that on account of the death of Mahatma Gandhi it would not be possible for them to continue opposing the principles held by him. **Dr. Parchure thereon asked if the witness wanted his wife to be offered to Mahatma Gandhi.** The witness asked Dr. Parchure as to who could have committed the murder of Mahatma Gandhi and Dr. Parchure replied that the person who had committed the murder must be one like themselves. The witness asked Dr. Parchure to close the dispensary and the latter closed it. Dr. Parchure and the witness then left for their respective houses. On the way he changed his mind and accompanied Dr. Parchure to the Rajput Board House. One of them called out to Ramdayal Singh, President of the Rajput Sewa Sangh and when Ramdayal Singh came, Dr. Parchure said that he had completed his work and that Ramdayal Singh was to complete the rest of the work. Dr. Parchure thereafter said that their movement must end in success. There was no further conversation between Dr. Parchure and Ramdayal Singh. Dr. Parchure came out of the Boarding House and both Dr. Parchure and the witness proceeded to the residence of Dr. Parchure. When they reached the house, the radio was on. Some sweets were brought by Rupa in the presence of the witness and these sweets were distributed amongst those present. The members of the family of Dr. Parchure were listening to the radio.

The statement of Khire finds corroboration in the testimony of Ramdayal Singh P.W.52 and Jagannath Singh P.W.53.

P.W.52 Ramdayal Singh who is President of the Rajput Sewa Sang deposes that Dr. Parchure came to the Rajput Sewa Sang at about 7 or 7.30 p.m. on the 30th January while he was having a talk with his friends prior to the holding of a condolence meeting which was to be held in the Hall of the Boarding House. Dr. Parchure came along with two persons and said that a good deed has been done, that the opponent of the Hindu religion had been killed, that the Hindu Religion would now remains safe, that the man who had killed Gandhiji was their own man, that the pistol with which the crime was committed had been sent from Gwalior and that the person had come from the South. Jagannath Singh P.W.53 who happened to be present at the time asked Dr. Parchure to keep quiet and go away. After Dr. Parchure had gone away Ramdayal Singh told Jagannath Singh that Dr. Parchure was in the habit of taking credit for himself for whatever had taken place. Jagannath Singh replied that there might be something in what Dr. Parchure had said for he had met Dr. Parchure in the morning when the latter had made a statement to him which led him to think so.**P.W.53** Jagannath Singh a Forest Contractor and a Zamindar corroborates Ramdayal Singh but attributes certain statements to Dr. Parchure which are not attributed either by Khire or Ramdayal Singh. He states:

*"**Dr. Parchure** came and said that one of his works had been completed. He further said that he (Mahatma Gandhi) was a traitor to the Hindu religion and was an 'Autar' of Aurangzeb. He further said that the assailant was his own man and had come from the South. He further said that the person had taken a pistol from there. He further said that Madan Lal who had thrown the bomb was also person from there."*

It is contended on behalf of Dr. Parchure that Kale has spun out a long yarn with the object of maintaining his position as a servant of the State, of gratifying his desire for revenge, of complying with the wishes of the police, and of saving his own skin. He passed his B.A. in 1947 and got an employment in the State on 19th May 1947. He is a petty official in the Gwalior State and cannot afford to annoy the political party in power which is antagonistic to Dr. Parchure who is the head of a rival party. As pointed out by J.P. Goyel (P.W.39) the Congress Party in Gwalior which is holding the reins of Government at present is an opposition to the Hindu Sabha of which Dr. Parchure is a leading member. Kale and the other members of his family are in straightened circumstances and can ill afford to incur the displeasure of the party in power. Kale's father who was a Medical Office in the employment of the State died at the age of 45 and the State is giving a compassionate allowance to his widow and an educational allowance to his daughter who is studying in the Lady Hardinge Medical College in Delhi. The relations between Kale on the one hand and Dr. Parchure on the other have been strained for the last several years. Kale became a member of the Hindu Rashtra Sena of which Dr. Parchure is the head in the year 1941. Later, in the same year he entered State service and was immediately warned by his official superior that his allegiance to the Hindu Rashtra Sena was incompatible with his allegiance to the State. In order to ingratiate himself with official superiors he ceased attending the parades of the Sena and started acting against the interests of the Sena. Dr. Parchure resorted this attitude on his part and as the witness himself admits made it plain to him that his presence at the parades was no longer required. It seems to be extremely improbable therefore that he would have paid a visit to the house of Dr. Parchure on that particular day when he had been distinctly warned by his official superiors and by Dr. Parchure himself not to visit Parchure's house. It is difficult to believe that a person would absent himself from office from 12 noon onwards with no other object than of being able to draw moncy from a bank. No reason has been shown why it became necessary for the witness to draw money from the bank on the very same day on which Nathuram and Apte happened to visit Gwalior.

Again it is improbable that Dr. Parchure would permit the witness to enter his house when he was seriously engaged in procuring a revolver or a pistol for the assassination of Mahatma Gandhi. It is still more improbable that Nathuram and Apte who knew the mission which had brought them to Gwalior would have talked without restraint in the presence of a stranger or had tried out their revolvers in the courtyard of the house. The fact that the witness gives the precise hour and minute of his arrival in the house of Dr. Parchure (12.33 p.m.) and the precise hour and minute of his departure from the said house, namely, 1.40 p.m. appears to show that the story narrated by him is a fabricated one. it is difficult to believe that if this witness did actually take leave of absence from his office with the object of withdrawing money from the bank, he would have spent one hour and ten minutes in the house of Dr. Parchure and thus run the risk of the bank closing down for the day. Moreover he had told his official superiors that he would not be able to return to office as he did not know how much time was likely to be taken at the bank. It must be remembered that the house of Dr. Parchure is not on the way to the Bank and that the Bank is at a distance of a mile and a half from the said house. The witness went to the house of Dr. Parchure with the ostensible object of making an enquiry as to the action the Hindu Mahasabha were proposing to take in connection with the Maharaja's decision to hand over power to the Congress in contravention of the assurance given to the Hindu Mahasabha. If the Mahasabha had already staged a demonstration against the State on the 24th January the purpose with which this witness went to the house of Dr. Parchure cannot be easily understood. It is significant that Gangadhar Patwardhan with whom the witness is said to have had a talk is a police informer who stands to gain considerably by procuring the conviction of Dr. Parchure. The witness admits that when Gangadhar Patwardhan came to the house of the witness he indicated his belief to the witness that he, the witness knew the whole story. Again, iota is significant that another witness who has been produced to support the story of this witness is M.B. Khire (P.W.51) who lives in the upper storey of the house in which Patwardhan resides. The witness was arrested at 2.30 a.m. on the 3rd February within a few hours of his having made a statement to the Home Minister of the Gwalior State. He was detained in custody at the Police Station of Girid from 3rd February to the 11th March. He was taken to Bombay while he was in police custody and was kept in the Police Station at Worli under the supervision of Sub-Inspector Mandalik who has played an important part in connection with this case. It is argued with a considerable amount of justification that this witness was detained in order that he should be coerced into making a statement which the police wanted him to make.

Apart from the fact that the story narrated by Kale is inherently improbable it seems to be that it is at variance with the story narrated by Khire, Kale states that on the evening of the 30th January he met Dr. Parchure in front of the Marahta Boarding House and accompanied him to the dispensary. It is said that while Dr. Parchure and Kale were talking to each other in the dispensary Khire also arrived. Dr. Parchure, Kale and Khire then went to the petrol pump. Kale states that Khire left at this stage. Khire, however, states that Kale left while Dr. Parchure and Khire went to the Rajput Boarding House, where they had a talk with Ramdayal Singh and Jagannath Singh. If Kale was in the company of Dr. Parchure and Khire on the evening of the 30th January and if he accompanied Dr. Parchure to his house that day he could not possibly have said that Khire left them at the petrol pump. Khire states that Dr. Parchure went to the Rajput Boarding House and had a talk with Ramdayal Singh and Jagannath Singh and he is supported in this by these two witnesses. It is obvious in the circumstances that either Kale or Khire, Ramdayal Singh and Jagannath Singh are making incorrect statements. Kale's name does not appear in the confession of Dr. Parchure.

The fact that Kale is a Government servant, the fact that his mother and sister are the recipients of the bounty of the State, the fact that it is improbable in view of the relations between Dr. Parchure on the one hand and Kale on the other than Kale visited the house of dr. Parchure, the fact that he was arrested on the 3rd February and kept in detention till the 11th March and the fact that the police extorted an improper confession from Dr. Parchure throw a considerable doubt on the veracity of this witness. If his statement is eliminated from consideration there is no corroboration whatsoever of the confession so far as the incident of the 28th January is concerned.

It is true that Kale was able to identify Nathuram and Apte in an identification parade which was held at Bombay, but this fact alone would not show that Kale saw these two prisoners in the house of Dr. Parchure in the manner and in the circumstances alleged by him. Both Nathuram and Apte admit having gone to Gwalior and Kale may well have seen them there. The identification by this witness cannot, therefore, be regarded as a circumstance supporting the confession.

And what about the evidence of the other witnesses from Gwalior who were examined to corroborate the confession? Dandwate is said to have procured a pistol from J.F. Goyel (P.W.39) and to have given him a revolver and a sum of Rs. 200/- in exchange. The revolver has not been produced in court and the explanation that has been given for its non-production is that Goyel declined to accept a revolver and the money in exchange for this pistol. The Police visited his house on 3rd February 1948, but he ran away by the back door and remained absconding till 11th April 1948. He remained in custody till 6th May 1948. The fact that this witness ran away from his house as soon as the police arrived appears to indicate that there may be some truth in the story that the pistol with which Mahatma Gandhi was assassinated belonged to him and was taken away from him by Dandwate or someone else. Even if that pistol was taken away it would prove only that Nathuram and Apte came to Gwalior to look for a weapon; it would not show that they disclosed their secret to Dr. Parchure. In my opinion it was entirely unnecessary to do so. There is no evidence to show that the pistol which is said to have been taken belongs to Goyel. He does not give any identification marks of the weapon which he claims to be his own property. The charge under Section 302 was hanging like a **Sword of Damocles** over his head and could have induced him to manufacture as many falsehoods as were required for the success of the case.

When the confession made by Dr. Parchure has been found to have been induced by threat or coercion and when the statement of Kale has been found to be false and fabricated, it is scarcely necessary to make a detailed examination of the statements of Khire, Ramdayal Singh and Jagannath Singh. Khire is obviously under the thumb of the police, for he is related to Patwardhan police informer and is living in the same house as Patwardhan who was responsible for the apprehension and detention of Kale. Even if the evidence of these three witnesses, namely, Khire, Ramdayal Singh and Jagannath Singh were accepted at its face value, it would not in my opinion be sufficient to bring the guilt home to Dr. Parchure. The latter may have indulged in loose talk and may even have been gratified over the death of Mahatma Gandhi but that fact alone would not show that he had conspired to kill the Mahatma.

I am of the opinion that the confession was induced by improper means and is not admissible in evidence against Dr. Parchure. Even, if it were, I am of the opinion that it has not been corroborated in material particulars and ought not to be acted upon.

The statements of Kale and the other witnesses from Gwalior are perfectly valueless.

Towards the conclusion of his judgment, the learned Special Judge has made certain observations which appear to indicate that if the police had been more vigilant in the discharge of their duties, the tragedy which overtook Mahatma Gandhi on the 30th January may well have been averted. Mr. Daphtary contends that these observations are not warranted by the evidence on the record.

It is a fundamental legal principle that no one is to be condemned unless he has had an opportunity of being heard. Not a single question was put to any of the police officers with the object of ascertaining whether it was possible for them to save the life of Mahatma Gandhi and if so why the appropriate measures were not taken in this behalf. Had that question been pout and had an unsatisfactory answer been returned, the learned Special Judge would have been fully justified in making the observation that he made. That question was not put. The result therefore is that we are travelling in the realm of conjecture, because there is no proper evidence on the file on the basis of which it is possible to say with any degree of confidence whether the police were or were not negligent in the discharge of their duties.

Even on merits it seems to me that the remarks are not justified. It is common g4round that the very first occasion on which the authorities came to know about this particular conspiracy was at about 4 o'clock on the afternoon of the 20th January when Dr. Jain met Mr. Kher and Mr. Morarji Desai by appointment at the Civil Secretariat at Bombay. He told them that Madanlal who was responsible for the explosion of the 20th January was a refugee from the Punjab whom Dr. Jain had endeavoured to help; that before leaving for Delhi Madanlal had discussions with him; that Madanlal had told him that he (Madanlal) and his friends had decided to take the life of a great leader whose name he later stated to be Mahatma Gandhi; that dr. Jain had tried to dissuade Madanlal from his wild talk and wild plan; that Madanlal had introduced to Dr. Jain a person by the name of Karkare with whom Madanlal was working in Ahmednagar and who was on friendly terms with him; that Madanlal had spoken about his exploits at Ahmednagar; that Madanlal had told him that Karkare had taken Madanlal to Savarkar; that Savarkar had a long talk with him for about two hours and that Savarkar had praised him for what he had done, had patted him on his back and had asked him to carry on; that Madanlal had said that there was a dump of arms, ammunition and explosives at Ahmednagar and that Madanlal and his companions were to proceed to Delhi to carry out the objects of the conspiracy. Mr. Desai asked Dr. Jain as to why he did not tell him all about it immediately after he had come to know of it. Jain replied that refugees were in the habit of talking wildly and he believed that he had dissuaded Madanlal from doing what he had intended to do.

On receipt of this information Mr. Desai acted with commendable promptitude. He sent immediately for Mr. Nagarvala, Officer-in-Charge of the Intelligence Branch. Mr. Nagarvala was unable to come at once as he was busy at the time, and Mr. Desai accordingly asked him to see Mr. Desai at the Railway Station as he was leaving Bombay for Ahmedabad the same night. Mr. Nagarvala came to the Railway Station at about 8.15 p.m. and Mr. Desai told him that Dr. Jain had said and asked him (1) to take action in the matter. He asked Mr. Nagarvala (2) to arrest Karkare, (3) to keep a close watch on Savarkar's house and his movements and (4) to find out the names of the persons who were I involved in the plot. Mr. Desai reached Ahmedabad on the morning of the 22nd January and repeated to Sardar Vallabhbhai Patel the story that had been narrated to him by Dr. Jain.

Mr. Nagarvala complied with the instructions without loss of time. He organised an unobtrusive watch over the house of Savarkar from 5.30 p.m. that evening. He made arrangements for locating and arresting of Karkare. He made enquiries from the Ahmednagar police with the object of ascertaining whether Karkare whose detention had been ordered under the Public Security Measures Act 10 or 15 days before had been arrested. He contacted various informants of his to locate and apprehend Karkare and his associates. He also issued similar instructions to the various officials under him as he was giving top most priority to this particular enquiry.

In the meantime enquiries were being made from Madanlal by the Police at Delhi. He was interrogated by the Police immediately after his arrest on the 20th, but the enquiries do not appear to have revealed any useful information except in regard to Karkare. On being questioned under Section 342 of the Code of Criminal Procedure Madan Lal stated as follows:

> *"The police asked me names of the co-workers of Badge who were putting up in the Marina Hotel. I told them that I did not know their names. I told them that Badge had had told me that the co-workers were staying in a corner room on the first floor of the Marina Hotel."*

Birds have flown:

The police rushed to the Marina Hotel with the object of apprehending the conspirators. When they reached there they found that the **birds had flown.** Enquiries were made as to the persons who were occupying the corner room on the first floor but the only information that the management of the hotel could supply to the police was that two persons who had stayed under the names of M. Deshpande and S. Deshpande had settled their bills and had left the hotel immediately after the explosion in such haste they did not even care to take their clothes with them. The Police then visited the room in the Hindu Mahasabha Bhawan which was said to have been occupied by Badge, Shankar, Madanlal, and Gopal. This room was empty and the deserted for

Badge and Shankar had quitted the place almost immediately after the explosion. And what about Karkare and Gopal? Enquiry was made at the Sharif Hotel but no information could be obtained as to the whereabouts of Mr. B.M. Bias who had stayed there from the 17th to the 19th January and who had left the Hotel a day before the explosion. So far as can be judged even Madanlal did not know where his confederates had gone. Gopal was in Delhi but he too made himself scarce after the explosion. He did not dare go back to the Hindu Mahasabha Office where he was staying the previous night, for he did not know that Madanlal would not denounce him to the authorities. Both Karkare and Gopal are said to have spent the night of the 20th in the Frontier Hindu Hotel under the assumed names of G.M. Joshi and Rajagopalam. On the 21st January the position was that although the police were aware of the existence of a conspiracy to assassinate Mahatma Gandhi, the only conspirators who were known to them were Badge, Karkare, and Madanlal. A Deputy Superintendent and an Inspector of Police left Delhi **"by air"** and reached Bombay on the 22nd. They desired the arrest of Karkare and his conspirators in connection with the bomb explosion. They stayed in Bombay till the 23rd and after their departure Mr. Nagarvala continued the search for Karkare and his associates, if any. Karkare was not known to the Bombay City Police. On certain information received by him he issued instructions for the arrest of Badge on or about the 24th January, Mr. Rana, D.I.G., C.I.D. whose head quarters are in Poona came to Bombay on the 27th January and reported developments to him. On the same day Mr. Nagarvala had a telephonic conversation with the Director of Intelligence Bureau, Delhi to whom also the developments had been reported. Unfortunately Badge could not be traced till the 31st a day after the tragedy had been enacted at Birla House. The fatal shots were not fired either by Badge or by Karkare or by Madanlal and even if they had been arrested immediately after the explosion the tragedy could not be averted. The

evidence on record does not show that the names of the other conspirators were known. If their names were not known the police could not very well put them under arrest.

The movements of Karkare, Badge, and Shankar during the crucial period commencing with the 20th and ending with the 30th January are not known. Karkare is said to have gone to the Frontier Hindu hotel on the 20th January, to have spent the night of the 20th January in the hotel and to have left that hotel on the 21st. He was seen at the house of Mr. G.M. Joshi at Thana on the 25th and at the Railway Station at Delhi on the 29th. He was not known to the Bombay Police. He did not visit his regular haunts or if he did, his haunts were not known to the Bombay Police. Badge and Shankar could certainly have been arrested if they had gone back to Poona for they were well known the police. Orders for the arrest of Badge were issued on or about the 24th and Mr. Rana came to see Mr. Nagarvala at Bombay on the 27th in connection with the arrest. It is impossible to believe that if he had been anywhere near his house he would not have been arrested. He was arrested on the 31st when he was returning from a certain temple where he was presumably concealing himself. Shankar was arrested near Bhuleshwar on the 67th February. He too was arrested at a place where he was not expected to be.

The only person who could have been arrested if the police wanted to arrest him was Gopal younger brother of Nathuram. This prisoner was at the Frontier Hindu Hotel on the 20th January, in the Elphinstone Annexe Hotel for a short time on or about the 24th and in Thana on the 25th January. Neither the Elphinstone Hotel Bombay nor the house of Mr. G.M. Joshi at Thana are places which he was known to visit but in any case the police could not know that he was concerned in the crime. On the following day, i.e., on the 26th January he went and rejoined his appointment. He could obviously have been arrested on that day if the police had been aware that he was a member of this conspiracy but the police were not aware of this fact and he continued to be at large for a few days more. As soon as it was known that Mahatma Gandhi was the victim of a murderous assault furious mobs attacked the houses of persons who were said to be concerned in the crime. The house of Mr. Savarkar was attacked and was strewn with broken glasses and other missiles. The life of Gopal who was known to be a brother of the assassin was in imminent danger and police protection had to be given to prevent him from being lynched. He was rushed off to his native village where prejudice against him was probably not as strong as in the neighbourhood of Poona. He was arrested near Uksan on the 5th February, his name having probably been supplied by Badge who was arrested on the 31st January or by Madanlal who was brought from Delhi to Bombay on or about the 4th February.

Movements of Nathuram and Apte from 20th January till arrest:

And what about the movements of Nathuram and Apte? Nathuram and Apte left Delhi for Kanpur by train on the night of the 20th and stayed in a Retiring Room at the Railway Station at Kanpur on the 21st. they did not supply their names to the Booking Clerk. They left Kanpur on the 22nd and reached Bombay on the 23rd. They went to the Arya Pathik Ashram at about 9 p.m. and Apte asked for a room with two beds in the name of D. Narayan. No room with two beds was available but they were allotted two beds in a room containing eight beds. They left their luggage in that room and returned to the Ashram at 1 o'clock in the night. The accommodation provided for them was not suitable and Nathuram and Apte shifted to the Elphinstone Annexe Hotel on the 24th. They left Delhi by air under the assumed names of **D. Narayanrao** and **N. Vinayakrao.** They left Delhi the same afternoon, reached Gwalior at night, spent the 28th January in Gwalior and returned to Delhi on the morning of the 29th. Nathuram and Apte stayed in a Retiring Room of the Railway Station at Delhi

on the 29th and for a part of the 30th which had been booked by Nathuram in the name of **N. Vinayakrao.** On the 30th January, Nathuram went to the prayer meeting armed with a pistol and fired at Mahatma Gandhi. It was impossible for any police officer, however capable and efficient he might have been, to have prevented Nathuram from committing the crime on which he had set his heart. He was going about from place to place under assumed names, not staying in any one place for more than a day or two and it was impossible for any police officer top catch hold of him particularly if he was not known or suspected to be a co-conspirator. Apte was going about the Nathuram all the time. He too travelled about under assumed names. Even if the police were aware on the night of the 20th that Nathuram and Apte were concerned in the conspiracy it is extremely doubtful if they could have stopped them from achieving their end.

Third Class Tickets Passengers:

The police did all that was reasonably possible to do. Immediately after the explosion the police appear to have sent a number of persons to various railway stations in order to prevent the suspects from escaping by train. Badge states that as soon as the *Tonga* carrying him and his servant Shankar reached the Railway Station New Delhi and as soon as he had purchased **'2 Third Class Tickets'** from Delhi to Poona he found a great commotion on the platform. The police were moving about. Sensing danger to himself he came out of the platform, got into a *Tonga* and set off for the railway station at Delhi.[50]He slipped through their fingers[51] because the police do not appear to have known till that hour that he was concerned in the crime. Nor did they

---

[50] Old Delhi Railway Station and New Delhi Railway Station are there. Badge first attempted to escape by a train from New Delhi Railway Station; then changed his mind and moved by a train starting from Old Delhi Railway Station. Eds.

[51] Slip through fingers: An idiom that means "If you allow an opportunity or a person to slip through your fingers, you lose it or fail to catch him through not taking care or making an effort"

know an anything about Nathuram or Apte. If the statement of Madanlal is correct that he did not know the names of the conspirators and did not supply them to the police, it is idle to contend that the police could have prevented the tragedy notwithstanding the reticence of Madanlal. Nathuram had made up his mind and was prepared to risk his life in order to take that of Mahatma Gandhi. He took the risk of entering the premises of the Birla House armed with a pistol and he actually fired the fatal shots when he was surrounded by a large multitude of people. He did not care to run away. He had come to the Birla House with a particular object and he was determined to achieve it. He was prepared to take all risks and to abide by the inevitable consequences. Was it possible for the police to stop a person whom they did not know, or a person who was going about from place to place under false names or a person who was determined to commit this particular crime regardless of consequences to himself? The police were aware that something was afoot, but they did not know when or where or by whom the blow was to be struck. They were groping in the dark and could not find their way. We know what has happened and may be able to say that his precious life could be saved this way or that way, but **it is always easy to be wise after the event.**

The evidence on record satisfies me:

(a) that no opportunity was afforded to the police to explain the circumstances which prevented them from apprehending Nathuram before the 30th January and thereby saving the life of Mahatma Gandhi;

(b) that Madanlal failed to supply the names of the conspirators to the police;

(c) that even if those names were supplied, it was extremely difficult, if not impossible, for the police to arrest Nathuram who was going about from place to place under assumed names and who was determined to assassinate Mahatma Gandhi even at the risk of losing his own life.

Acquittal of Dr. Parchure:

"For these reasons, I am of the opinion that the prosecution have failed to bring the charges home to Dr. Parchure beyond reasonable doubt, I would accept the 'appeal' preferred by him, set aside the order of the learned Special Judge and direct that he be set at liberty."

Acquittal of Shankar Kistaya:

"The case against Shankar is also open to doubt and suspicion and I am clearly of the opinion that he was not a member of the conspiracy which was formed to take the life of Mahatma Gandhi. In addition to his conviction upon a conspiracy to murder, he was convicted for a contravention of the provisions of the Indian Arms Act and the Indian Explosives Act. His employer Badge was dealing extensively in arms and explosives and it is probable that this prisoner has committed offences in connection with the two said Acts. Unfortunately for the ends of justice no independent evidence has been produced in confirmation of the testimony of Badge that Shankar was in fact guilty of the said offences. I am accordingly of the opinion that although there is a very strong suspicion that he has offended against the provision of the appropriate enactments, no action can be taken against him. I would accordingly accept the appeal preferred by Shankar and acquit him of all the charges of which he has been convicted."

Nathuram and Apte: Death Sentence confirmed:

"The case against the remaining prisoners admit of no doubt whatever. Nathuram and Apte were so highly dissatisfied with the policy which was being pursued by Mahatma Gandhi that they started a newspaper for counter acting the said policy. They staged peaceful demonstrations with the object of dissuading Mahatma Gandhi from pursuing

**a course of action which according to them was suicidal to the interest of this country. When they found that neither written nor verbal protests could influence Mahatma Gandhi to alter his lie long policy they decided to remove this 'Apostle of Non-Violence" by violent methods. The murder was premeditated, cold-blooded and cruel and the only punishment that can be awarded to these two prisoners for the commission of so heinous a crime is that of death."**

Karkare and Madanlal and Crown's Power of Clemency:

*"**Karkare** and Madanlal have also been found guilty under Section 120-B/302 of the Indian Penal Code and of certain other sections of certain other provisions of law and have been sentenced to transportation for life. Karkare was imbued with the same ideas as Nathuram and Apte but the interest evinced by him in connection with this conspiracy was considerably less than that of his more experienced and more determined associates. They found a useful tool in the person of Madanlal and gave him an important part in the incident which was to take place at the Birla House on the 20th January. He lighted a gun-cotton-slab with the object of creating an explosion and if the other conspirators had played the parts assigned to them Mahatma Gandhi's life would have been terminated on the 20th January. He has taken an active though a secondary part in carrying out the nefarious designs of Nathuram, Apte, and Karkare but the fact that he actually set light to the gun-cotton-slab shows that the enormity of the crime committed by him is no less than that of the crime committed by Karkare. He is a misguided young man of about 20 years of age but he appears to have little or no regard for the sanctity of human life, and I can see no reason for commending his case to the Crown for the exercise of the Power of Clemency."*

Gopal Godse and Crown's Power of Clemency:

*"**I** must confess, however, that the case of Gopal has caused me a certain amount of anxiety. He is a young man of about 27 years of age. He was occupying a humble but respectable position in a Government factory and could have had no political views of his own. He probably entertained a warm regard for his brother Nathuram and his brother's friend Apte and I am inclined to think that he joined the conspiracy under the combined and powerful influence of these two men. The feelings of brotherly love and affection must have been supplemented by feelings of gratitude when Nathuram assigned his Insurance Policy in a sum of Rs. 3,000/- to his (Gopal's) wife. Gopal took little or no interest in procuring arms for the conspirators or in assisting them either on the 20th or 30th January. A raw and inexperienced youth as he is, he appears to have fallen prey to the natural temptation of supporting his brother without realising the full implications of the position taken up by him. It is true that he reached Delhi with a revolver which did not function properly and that he attended ht conference at the Marina Hotel at which a hand-grenade was given to him but he did not take either the revolver or the grenade with him to the scene of the outrage. He gave his revolver to Shankar and he left the grenade in the office of the Hindu Mahasabha. The facts and circumstances of the case make it quite clear that he did not enter into the conspiracy with zest or enthusiasm. He went to the Birla House but he appears to have been somewhat of a dazed spectator who had gone there because he considered it his duty to stand by his brother. He did not play any part at the Birla House. I am strongly of the opinion that the Power of Clemency which vests in the Crown should be exercised in his favour."*

21/06/1949	Sd/- A.N. BANDARI, Judge

Chapter 2

Mr. Justice Achhuru Ram

Judgment of

ACHHURU RAM, Judge

CHAPTER 2

Judgment of ACHHURU RAM J

These appeals have arisen out of the order of Mr. Atma Charan, I.C.S., Judge of the Special Court constituted under the provision of the Bombay Public Security Measures Act, 1947, as extended to the Provinces of Delhi.

Nathuram V Godse, Narayan D. Apte, Vishnu R. Karkare, Madanlal Pahwa, Shankar Kistayya, Gopal V Godse, and Dattaraya S Parchure appellants along with Mr. Vinayak D. Savarkar were tried by the learned Special Judge under Section 120-B of the Indian Pena Code read with Section 302 of the said code for having, between the 1st December 1947 and 30th January 1948, at Poona, Bombay, Delhi and other places agreed and conspired among and between themselves and Digambar R. Badge, who had been tendered a pardon, Gangadhar S. Dandwate, Gangadhar Jadhav and Suryadeo Sharma, who along with others not known were absconding, to commit the murder of Mahatma Gandhi, such murder having in fact been committed at Delhi on 30th January 1948. All the accused except Mr. Savarkar were found guilty of the charge, it being held that the conspiracy with which the accused had been charged had definitely been in existence from the first week of January 1948. Madanlal Pahwa and Shankar Kistayya were on conviction under this charge sentenced to Transportation for Life. No sentence was, however, passed in respect of this conviction on any of the other accused who were found guilty.

All the accused except Mr. Savarkar and Dattatraya S. Parchure were also tried:

(A)	(1)	**Under** Section 19-D of the Indian Arms Act for having in pursuance of the said conspiracy to murder Mahatma Gandhi transported without a licence to Delhi two revolvers with cartridges in contravention of the provisions of the Indian Arms Act.
	(2)	**Under** Section 19-D of the Indian Arms Act read with Section 119 and 114 of the Indian Penal Code for having in pursuance of the conspiracy abetted each other in the commission of the said offence;
(B)	(1)	**Under** Section 19-F of the Indian Arms Act for having two revolvers without a licence in their possession and under their control at Delhi in contravention of the provisions of Sections 14 and 15 of the said Act.
	(2)	**Under** Section 19-F of the Indian Arms Act read with Section 114 of the Indian Penal Code for having abetted each other in the commission of the above offence.
None of these charges was, however, found to be proved and all the accused were acquitted of them.		

All the accused excepting Mr. Savarkar and Dattatraya S. Parchure were also tried:		
(A)	(1)	**Under** Section 4-B of the Explosive Substances Act for having in pursuance of the conspiracy in their possession and under their control explosive substances, namely, two gun cotton slabs and five hand-grenades with detonators and wicks with intent to endanger life by means thereof or to enable any other person to endanger life by means thereof;
	(2)	**Under** Section 4B of the said Act read with Section 6 thereof for having, in pursuance of the conspiracy, abetted the commission of the above offence.
(B)	(1)	**Under** Section 5 of the Explosive Substance Act for having, in pursuance of the conspiracy, in their possession and under their control, the above mentioned explosive substances under such circumstances to give rise to a reasonable suspicion that they did not have them in their possession or under their control for a lawful purpose.
	(2)	**Under** Section 5 of the Act read with Section 6 for having in pursuance of the conspiracy abetted the commission of the above offence.

Nathuram V. Godse, Narayan D. Apte, Vishnu R. Karkare, Madanlal Pahwa, Shankar Kistayya, and Gopal V. Godse accused were convicted under Section 4-B read with Section 6 of the Explosive Substances Act and also under Section 5 of the said Act or Section 5 read with Section 6 thereof. Each one of them was sentenced to undergo rigorous imprisonment for three years in respect of the first and rigorous imprisonment for five years in respect of the second offence.

Madanlal Pahwa was tried under Section 3 of the Explosive Substances Act for having in pursuance of the conspiracy maliciously and unlawfully caused a gun-cotton-slab to explode which explosion was of a nature likely to endanger life and to cause serious injury to property.

Nathuram V. Godse, Narayan D. Apte, Vishnu R. Karkare, Shankar Kistayya, and Gopal V. Godse were tried under Section 3 of the aforesaid Act read with Section 5 of the same for the abetment of the above offence. All of them were found guilty of the offence with which they were charged. Madanlal Pahwa was sentenced to rigorous imprisonment for ten years. All the others were sentenced to rigorous imprisonment for seven years each.

All the accused whose names are mentioned in reference to the first charge except Dr. Parchure were tried under Section 302 read with Section 115 of the Indian Penal Code for having in pursuance of the conspiracy abetted each other to commit the murder of Mahatma Gandhi which offence was committed in consequence of the abetment. All of them except Mr. Savarkar were found guilty. Madanlal Pahwa and Shankar Kistayya were sentenced to undergo rigorous imprisonment for seven years each under this charge. No sentence was, however, passed on any of the other accused.

Nathuram V. Godse and Narayan D Apte were tried under Section 19-C of the Indian Arms Act for having, in pursuance of the conspiracy, between the 28th and 30th January 1948 brought without licence from Gwalior to Delhi automatic pistol No.606824 with cartridges in contravention of the provisions of Section 6 of the said Act. Both the above named accused and Dattatraya S. Parchure were also tried under Section 19(c) read with Section 114 for having abetted the above offence. Both Godse and Apte were convicted under Section 19(c) of the Indian Arms Act or in the alternative under Section 19(c) of the said Act read with Section 114 of the Indian Penal Code, Dattatraya S. Parchure being acquitted.

Gopal V. Godse was tried under Sec.19(f) of the Indian Arms Act for having in pursuance of the conspiracy at Delhi in his possession and under his control automatic pistol No.606824 with cartridges in contravention of Sections 14 and 15 of the Indian Arms Act. Narayan D. Apte and Vishnu R. Karkare were tried under Sec.19(f) of the Indian Arms Act read with Section 114 of the Indian Penal Code for having abetted the above offence. Nathuram V. Godse was convicted under Sec.19(f) of the Indian Arms Act and Narayan D. Apte and Vishnu R. Karkare were convicted under Section 19(f) of the Indian Arms Act read with Section 114 of the Indian Penal Code.

Nathuram V Godse was tried under Sec.302 of the Indian Penal Code for having, in pursuance of the conspiracy, on 30th January, 1948 committed the murder by intentionally and knowingly causing the death of Mahatma Gandhi. Narayan D. Apte and Vishnu R. Karkare were tried under Section 302 read with Section 114 of the Indian Penal Code for having abetted the commission of the above offence by Nathuram V. Godse which offence was committed in their presence. All the other accused mentioned above were tried under Section 302 read with Section 109 of the Indian Penal Code for having abetted the commission of the offence of murder, the murder having been committed in consequence of the abetment. Nathuram V. Godse was convicted under Section 302 of the Indian Penal Code and sentenced to death. Dattatraya S. Parchure, Narayan D Apte, Vishnu R. Karkare and Gopal V Godse were convicted under Section 302 read with Section 109 of the Indian Penal Code. Narayan D Apte was sentenced to death while Dattatraya S. Parchure, Vishnu R. Karkare and Gopal V Godse were sentenced to Transportation for Life. The other accused were acquitted of the offence under Section 302 read with Section 109 of the Indian Penal Code.

Feeling aggrieved from the judgment of the learned Special Judge, the seven above named convicts have filed seven separate appeals in this Court. Of the appellants, Nathuram V Godse has not challenged his conviction under Section 302 of the Indian Penal Code for the offence of the murder of Mahatma Gandhi on the 30th January 1948 nor has he appealed from the sentence of death passed on him in respect of that offence. He has confined his appeal and also his arguments at the Bar, he personally argued his appeal, I must say, with conspicuous ability evidencing a mastery of facts which would have done credit to any counsel only to the other charges which have been found proved against him. The appeals of the other appellants of course attack their conviction for all the offences of which they have been found guilty and the arguments addressed to us by their learned counsel naturally cover the entire field. The judgment shall dispose of all these appeals.

It may be noted that although in case of Nathuram V Godse and Narayan D Apte the sentences passed on them under Section 302 and Section 302 read with Section 109 of the Indian Penal Code respectively were those of death, the learned Special Judge did not, as he would have to do in any case tried by him the exercise of his ordinary powers as a Sessions Judge under the Code of Criminal Procedure, submit the record to this Court under Section 374 of the Code for confirmation of the aforesaid sentences. He was of the view, and I think rightly, that according to the provisions of the Bombay Public Security Measures Act as extended to Delhi under which the case had been tried a sentence of death passed by him was not subject to confirmation by this Court and that consequently the application of Section 374 of the Code was not attracted. Section 13(3) of the Act clearly provides that the provisions of the Code relating to Sessions Trials are to apply to the proceedings of a Special Judge appointed under the Act, subject, of course, to the provisions of the first two sub-sections, only in so far as they are not inconsistent with Sections

19 to 20 of the Act. Section 16 of the Act reads as follows:

> "A Special Judge may pass any sentence authorised by law."

A Comparison of the language of this Section with that of Section 31 of the Code should leave no doubt in one's mind as to the correctness of the interpretation placed thereon by the learned Special Judge. Section 31 of the Code runs as follows:

High Court may pass any sentence authorised by law;

A Sessions Judge may pass any sentence authorised by law but any sentence of death passed by any such Judge shall be subject to confirmation by the High Court."

It will be observed that the language of Section 16 of the Act is precisely the same as that of the first sub-section of Section 31 of the Code which defines the powers of High Court in the matter of passing a sentence. It follows, therefore, that the powers of a Special Judge appointed under the Act are, in the matter of sentence, the same as, and co-extensive with, those possessed by High Court under the Code.

Before proceeding to deal with the facts involved in the present appeals and the questions that arise for decision therein, it may be well narrate succinctly some facts relating to the lives of the appellants and their relations inter se because those facts are calculated, in my opinion, to conduce to a better understanding and a clearer appreciation of the events with which we have to deal. These facts have been taken from the Written Statements filed by the several appellants at the trial or from the Statements made by them in Court in answer to questions put to them by the learned Special Judge. In the circumstances so far as the appellants are concerned their accuracy may be deemed to be beyond question.

Nathuram V Godse is aged about 37. He is the eldest son of his parents and has three other brothers. Although he did not succeed in passing the Matriculation Examination he is quite widely read. In arguing his appeal in this Court he displayed a very fair knowledge of the English language and a remarkable capacity for clear thinking. For quite a considerable time he has been a very staunch advocate of ideology and the programme of the Hindu Sanghatanist movement (i.e. movement for the consolidation and the organisation of the Hindus). For some years he worked in the R.S.S. However he later dissociated himself from this organisation and, joining the Hindu Mahasabha, to use his own words, "volunteered himself to fight as a soldier under its pan Hindu flat."

Narayan D Apte is aged 34. He is a graduate in science and also in the art of teaching. He worked as a teacher in the American High School, Ahmadnagar, for about seven years. He joined the Hindu Mahasabha in 1939 and came in contact with Nathuram V Godse in 1941. In course of time they became very close and intimate friends. During the last War he got a Commission in the I.A.F. which he, however, resigned after a year. He also worked as an Assistant Technical Recruiting Officer for some time.

In 1944 Nathuram V Godse and Narayan D Apte started a daily Marhati paper named 'Agrani' with the object of, to use Apte's own language, "propagating the ideology of the Hindu Mahasabha and the Hindu Sanghatanist movement, opposing the pro-Muslim or Muslim appeasing policy of the Congress." This paper was later renamed as "Hindurashtra".The editorial charge of these two papers was throughout with Nathuram V Godse, while Narayan D Apte looked after its management. To place the paper on a sounder footing the two friends floated a Limited Company called the Hindu Rashtra Parkashan Limited to take charge thereof, they both being the managing directors of the Company.

Shahid Saheb:

Nathuram V Godse, in describing the reactions of himself and his friends to the atrocities committed on the Hindus in various parts of the country by Muslim, instigated by the Muslim League propagandists and encouraged by the British Officers, and the supposed attitude of the Congress and Mahatma Gandhi towards some of the alleged perpetrators of these atrocities and the Muslim community generally, has stated as follows in Para 35 of his Written Statement:

> *"In 1946 or thereabout the Muslim atrocities perpetrated on the Hindus under the Government patronage of Suhrawardy in Noakhali, made our blood boil. our shame and indignation knew no bounds, when we saw that Gandhi Ji had come forward to shield that very Suhrawardy and began to style him as 'Shahid Saheb', a 'Martyr Soul' even in his prayer meetings. not only that but after coming to Delhi, Gandhiji began to hold his prayer meetings in a Hindu temple in Bhangi Colony[52] and persisted in reading passages from Quoranas a part of the prayer in that Hindu temple in spite of the protest of the Hindu worshippers there."*

So bitter indeed were the feelings of Nathuram V Godse, Narayan D Apte, their friends against Mahatma Gandhi and the Congress that they did not even hesitate to raise a banner of revolt against older leaders of the Hindu Mahasabha itself when they counselled co-operation with the Congress Government. The activities of Gandhi in the matter of the restoration of communal cordiality in different parts of India had always been so utterly distasteful to them that even in 1944 and 1946 Apte, evidently with the approval of his friend, had staged demonstrations at the prayer meetings in Panchgani

and at Delhi respectively. That the demonstration hold at the Delhi Prayer Meeting in 1946 was in any case not a wholly peaceful demonstration is abundantly clear from the following significant statement contained in Para 36 of Nathuram V Godse's Written Statement:

> *"Mr. Apte with a large section of the refugees took out a procession in Delhi condemning Gandhiji and his Shahid Suhrawardy and rushed into his prayer meeting in the Bhangi Colony"*

The tragic happenings in the West Punjab appear further to having intensified the feelings of bitterness entertained by Nathuram V Godse and Narayan D Apte against Mahatma Gandhiji whom they considered to be responsible for what in their view was the weak kneed policy of the Congress and the Congress Government in dealing with the Muslims generally and the Muslim League particularly. They had also not taken kindly to the strong action taken by the Congress Government at the centre and in the provinces to protect the lives and the properties of the members of the minority community and against hostile attacks by the disorderly elements amongst the Hindus. Nathuram V Godse has given expression to his sense of exasperation in the following words in para 40 of his written statement:

> *"The Congress Government began to persecute, prosecute, and shoot the Hindus themselves who dared to resist the Muslim forces in Bihar, Calcutta, Punjab and other places."*

Vishnu R. Karkare is aged about 38 and is a kind of hotelier at Ahmadnagar where he has been residing for quite a number of years. During the general elections held in 1937 he took part in the election campaign carried on by the Hindu Mahasabha on behalf of the candidates who contested the elections on Hindu Mahasabha ticket. In 1938, he became an active member of the Hindu Mahasabha

---

[52] Scavengers' Colony

and in course of time was elected Secretary of the district Sabha. In 1942 he was returned to the Local Municipality on Mahasabha ticket. Quite naturally he came in contact with Narayan D Apte while the latter was employed in Ahmadnagar and it is an admitted fact that Apte helped him in securing election to the Municipal Committee. In 1946 he went to Noakhali with a Volunteer Corps to render assistance to the victims of the Muslim mob fury in that part of the country. He also took keen and active interest in making provision for refugees from the West Punjab. He made himself a person *nongrata*[53] with local Muslims who made several complaints against him to the Provincial authorities which resulted in the police keeping him, his family and his concerns under surveillance and the search of his house and later on, on an order for his detention under the Provincial Security Act, though he was able successfully to evade the execution of that order.

Madanlal Pahwa is a young lad of 20. He hails from some village in Pakpattan Teshil in the District of Montgomery. He passed his Matriculation Examination in 1945 and soon thereafter got employment as a wireless telegraphist in the navy. He was released from service in 1947 and since then had been residing in his village till he was evacuated therefrom with a refugee caravan. He was an eye witness to the atrocities committed by the Muslims in the West Punjab on the Hindu population there and his own family appears to have suffered a lot in consequence of these atrocities. As a refugee he reached Bombay in the last of September 1947 and was lodged at the Chembur refugee camp.[54] In his search for employment, he came in contract with one Mr. Gupta who introduced him to Dr. Jagdish Chandra Jain, a Professor in the local College. Dr. Jain began to take keen interest in him. For some time Madanlal sold Dr. Jain's books on commission basis. At sometime in November 1947, he went to

Ahmadnagar where he came in close contact with Vishnu R. Karkare an soon became the special object of the latter's bounty. Karkare helped him to do some business in cocoanuts and regarded him as his protégé.

Gopal V Godse aged 27 is the third brother of Nathuram V Godse who has been in Government service for the past seven years and was for some time on active service overseas during the last World War. At the time of his arrest he was employed as a temporary civilian Assistant Store Keeper in the Motor Transport Spares Sub-Depot at Kirkee which is at a distance of about six miles from Poona. It however appears from his address noted in his service book that he resides in Poona his address as noted there being, "282 Sukharwar Peth, Viyam Mandal, Poona, No.2 (vide Statement of Leslie Vernon Perceival Pounde P.W.75[55]). He denies having ever been associated with any of the activities of his elder brother, political or otherwise, and except in reference to the present case / there is no evidence or indication on the record to the contrary.

Shankar Kistayya aged about 20 is the private servant of Digambar R. Badge approver and had been in his service for some time. He used to prepare handless for daggers manufactured by Badge, to carry arms and ammunitions to Badge's customers and to do odd jobs.

Dattatraya S. Parchure is a medical practitioner in Gwalior where his father held a very high post in the Education Department and was otherwise held in high esteem. He and his brothers reside with their families in the same house. His brothers are in State service. He was the President of the Gwalior Hindu Sabha at the time of his arrest. Some years ago he organised a volunteer corps known as Hindu Rashtra Sena with which he was very intimately connected upto the time of his arrest. In connection with their

---

[53] non-grata: unwelcome
[54] Chembur is an upmarket large suburb in Central Mumbai, India.

[55] Leslie V Pounde P.W.75 was staff, M.T.T. Sub-Depot,Kirkee,Pune during the times of Gopal V Godse's employment there.

activities in the cause of the Hindu Mahasabha, Nathuram V Godse and Narayan D Apte came in contact with Dattatraya S. Parchure and were known to each other fairly well. It is, however, suggested that for some time the relations between Dr. Parchure and Nathuram V Godse had been strained because of the later not having accepted the former's proposal for the merger of the Hindu Rashtra Sena with Hindu Rashtra Dal organised by himself, Apte and others.

Digambar R. Badge approver hails from a village of the name of Chalisgaon but had been settled in Poona since 1937 where he seems to have gone in search of employment. He says that by offering Satyagrah at the house of one Mr. Atre, the leader of the Congress party in the local municipal board, he was able to secure a post carrying Rs. 18/- or Rs. 20/- per month. On being discharged from Municipal service he was employed by one Mr. G.V. Ketkar for collecting funds for the Hindu Anath Ashram and Hindu Sangthan Nidhi. In the end of 1946 or early in 1947 he became a member of the Hindu Rashtra Dal of Narayan D Apte and Nathuram V Godse. In 1942 with a capital of Rs. 75/- or Rs. 100/- raised by the sale of some household goods, he started a shop for the sale of arms and weapons under the name of Shastra Bhandar. Initially he dealt only in arms and weapons to which the provisions of the Indian Arms Act did not apply and which could be possessed by anyone without licence. In course of time, however he began an illicit traffic in firearms and explosives which he managed to obtain by surreptitious and clandestine methods from the Government Arsenal at Kirkee or otherwise. With the growth of Razakar[56] menace

in Hyderabad State the demand for such articles seems to have increased and Badge began to do quite a prosperous business. These articles were purchased through Badge by a number of persons, some of them connected with the State Congress, for being supplied to Hindus living on the border for use in case of any onslaught by the Razakars. Apte also purchased some stuff from Badge for this purpose. Badge seems otherwise also to have received some encouragement from Apte and Nathuram V Godse in his enterprise. He has stated that they used to give him monetary help now and then that their monetary help generally consisted in taking him in their car, introducing him to moneyed persons requiring arms and ammunitions and helping him in realizing the price thereof from them. Sometimes they also used to pay him in cash sums of money ranging between Rs. 5/- and Rs. 100/-.

Two of Badge's other customers figure very conspicuously in-the-present case, namely, Goswami Shree Krishna Jiwan Jee Maharaj, P.W.69 and his younger brother Goswami Dixitji Maharaj P.W.77. In the proceedings of this case as also in the judgment under appeal the former has been referred to as Dada Maharaj, his younger brother addressing him by that name. Dada Maharaj and Dixitji Maharaj are the direct descendants of Shree Ballabh Acharya the founder of one of the Vaishnava sects. Dada Maharaj is the head of that sect and as such has a very large following The property owned by the family fetches an income of over two lacs every year and both the brothers have also considerable income from their personal offerings. Dada Maharaj says that he is a member of the Congress since 1942. He has however quite unreservedly stated that he stoutly opposed, and

---

[56] Kasim Razvi (190-1970) was a politician in the Pincely State of Hyderabad. He was the founder of the Razakar militia in the Hyderabad State. Razakars operated Concentrated Camps and used 'rape' as weapon of war. The Razakar forces violated Geneva Conventions of War by participating in numerous massacres of civilians. The Dakra massacre was an instance of one such massacre where 646 Bengali Hindus were killed. Razakars were composed of mostly pro-Pakistani Bengalis and Biharis from Bangladesh (formerly East Pakistan). They were approximately 50,000. After the Indian Military Intervention in Hyderabad initiated by Sardar Vallabhbhai Patel, in an operation known as **Operation Polo** or the **Police Action** in September 1948, Hyderabad was integrated into India. Subsequently, the Razakars were disbanded, and their leader, Qasim Razvi, was arrested and and later imprisoned.

shall always remain opposed to, what he considers to be its appeasement policy towards Pakistan. He also admits having delivered the inaugural address at the All India Hindu Convention held at Delhi on or about the 9th August 1947 which was presided by Mr. Savarkar and at which he gave expression to his opposition to what he conceive d to be the policy of Nehru Government. According to Dada Maharaj he felt attracted to Apte by the knowledge that he shared his own ideology in relation to Pakistan and made his acquaintance when he stopped for the night at Poona on his way to Pandharpur. He further says that on his way back from Pandharpur he again met Apte because while at Pandharpur Karkare had taken a message to him from Apte that the latter wanted to see him. At the interview some plan with regard to Pakistan and some Pakistan leaders is said to have been discussed. On one or two occasions Nathuram V Godse is also said to have visited Dada Maharaj at Bombay in the company of Apte sometime after Diwali 1947. He, at the request of Apte, presided over some function connected with the Hindu Rashtraya Parkashan, (Dada Maharaj says that it was the opening ceremony, but Nathuram V Godse in course of his address pointed out that it was an annual function), which was also addressed by Nathuram V Godse. At sometime during this period Apte is said to have handed over either personally or through Karkare two pistols to Dada Maharaj with a request for the same being exchanged for two revolvers. Dada Maharaj says that he was unable to comply with Apte's request and returned one pistol to hi. He was however unable to return the other pistol because the same had been passed on to Hyderabad State Congress people by his brother, Dixitji Maharaj to whom he had given both the pistols for being exchanged for revolvers. Badge was introduced to Dada Maharaj by Dixitji Maharaj with whom, as will presently appear he had fairly extensive dealings. On the occasion of his visit to Poona to preside over the function connected with Hindu Rashtrya Parkashan, Dada Maharaj met Badge who was specially called for the purpose and discussed with him the question of the supply of some arms and explosives for certain purposes.

Dixitji Maharaj also professes to be a Congressite with socialist leanings. He seems to share the views of his elder brother on the question of Hindu solidarity and the need of the Hindus adopting a stiff and uncompromising attitude towards the Muslims. During the communal riots which took place in Bombay before the partition, he supplied daggers and other arms to the Hindus for what he describes as defensive use against attacks by the members of the opposite community. It was in connection with the purchase of these arms that he came to know Badge from whom he says he started purchasing them in December 1946. After the stoppage of communal disturbances in Bombay, and when arms were no longer required for local use, he continued to purchase arms from Badge for being supplied to the Hindus residing on the border of Hyderabad States and the State Congress which had undertaken the task of arming the Hindu subjects of the State in order to enable them to combat the great Razakar menace. Dixitji Maharaj became acquainted with Apte in August 1947 when he was introduced to him by his elder brother. He however did not know either Nathuram V Godse or Vishnu R. Karkare before the material events are said to have taken place. Madanlal Pahwa he had met once in October 1947 when he had come to his house for sale of Dr. Jain's books when Dixitji Maharaj purchased books worth Rs. 5/-.

Baba Sahib Paranjpe, Raghunath Keshav Khadilkar and Parvin Chandra Sethia were some of the other persons to whom Badge is said to have been supplying arms and ammunition for use in Hyderabad. They were presumably workers of the State Congress. Dixitji Maharaj has stated that on some occasions Badge used to deposit with him stuff for being delivered to Parvin Chandra Sethia.

Gandhiji's 'Ramdhun':

Mahatma Gandhi was staying at Birla House at Delhi in January 1948. He held his daily evening prayers in the open space lying behind the servants' quarters. Birla House has its front gate on the Albuquerque Road. As one enters this gate from the said road, one has the main building consisting of offices and living rooms on his right. The road by which one enters the front gate goes on to the lawn, the tank, the garages and other appurtenant buildings. There is also a gate on the back side presumably for use by servants, etc., because the servants' quarters open towards that gate. On the back of the servants' quarters there is a verandah and a slightly raised platform. Mahatma Gandhi's prayer meetings used to be held on this platform. Mahatma Ji himself used to sit on a *takht* in the verandah just at the back of the servants quarters. As stated by Chhotu Ram P.W. 16, an employee at the Birla House, and one of the inmates of those quarters, the prayer meetings in those days used to begin at 5 p.m. and to finish at 5.30 p.m. According to the said witness the recitation of the Quaran and the Gita and the singing of Mahatma Ji's favourite song named as 'Ramdhun' used to take about 20 to 25 minutes where after followed Mahatma Ji's daily discourse.[57]

Nathuram V Gods has annexed to his Written Statement a copy of the statement made by India's Deputy Prime Minister the Hon'ble Sardar Vallabh Bhai Patel at a Press Conference held at Delhi on 12th January 1948 wherein he had taken up a very stern attitude on the question of payment of cash balance (55 Crores) to Pakistan and had indicated that under the terms of the agreement arrived at between the two Dominions Pakistan could not demand the payment of these balances unless all outstanding questions between the said Dominions including the question of Kashmir had been settled. It is significant that the same night the All India Radio announced Mahatma Gandhi's decision to undertake "a fast unto death" with the object of restoring amicable relations between the two major communities in Delhi and of creating conditions under the Muslims could go back and live in their houses in Delhi and have a free use of their religious places. According to Nathuram V Godse this decision of Mahatma Ji was the direct outcome of the Hon'ble the Deputy Prime Minister's statement of the same day and was intended to coerce the India Government into reversing its decision in the matter of cash balances. That the decision of Mahatma Ji to go on fast not wholly unconnected with the announcement made by the Hon'ble the Deputy Prime Minister on the question of the cash balances may reasonably be inferred from the language of the communiqué issued on the 15th January 1948 by the Government of India announcing their decision to pay forthwith to Pakistan the said cash balances, a copy of which communiqué has also been annexed by Nathuram V Godse to his Written Statement. Sometime after this fast was broken on certain …… assurances[58] being given by some leading Hindus present in Delhi. It is in evidence that after breaking the fast Mahatma Ji held his first prayer meeting on the 20th January 1948.

It is not disputed that on 20th January 1948 while the prayer meeting was being held inside the Birla House at the place indicated above, Madanlal Pahwa placed a gun-cotton-slab near the back gate and ignited the same so as to cause an explosion. it is also not disputed that on Madanlal being arrested on the spot a hand-grenade quite ready for use was recovered from the inside pocket of the coat he was then wearing, although the defence does not admit that Ex.P.15 was that coat. It is further not disputed that Apte, badge and Shankar were present at the Prayer meeting at the time of the explosion.

---

[57] **"Raghupati Raghava Raja Ram"** also called "Ram Dhun" is a bhajan ie devotional song widely popularised by Mahatma Gandhi and set to tune by the Hindustani musician Pandit Vishnu Digambar Paluskar.

[58] One word is undecipherable in the text. Eds.

Karkare according to the defence arrived at the Birla House in a *tonga* a little after the explosion. Of course Apte and Karkare do not admit that they had any connection with or previous knowledge of Madanlal's act and give their explanations for having gone to Birla House which will be noticed at a later stage. Nathuram V Godse has admitted his presence in Delhi on the day but has denied his presence at the Birla House at the material time he has indeed "categorically denied his having visited Birla House at any time during his sojourn of four days at Delhi, namely between 17th and 20th January 1948. It is, however, an admitted fact that on 30th January 1948, Nathuram V Godse did fire shots at Mahatma Gandhi while he was on his way to the dais for the prayer meeting with his pistol Ex.P.39 which results in almost instantaneous death of Mahatma Ji. The assailant of Mahatma Ji made no attempt to escape and was arrested on the spot. He received some injury on the head as a result of an assault by someone from amongst the audience who found himself unable to control his anger at what he had witnessed.

As a result of investigations which naturally were prolonged and covered a wide range the investigating authority reached the conclusion that the acts done by Madanlal Pahwa and Nathuram V Godse on the 20th and 30th January respectively were not their isolated and individual acts but that they had been done in pursuance of a conspiracy entered into by6 the persons sent up for trial, the absconders, and may be some others whose identity it has not been possible to discover, for murdering Mahatma Gandhi. After the arrest of Nathuram V Godse, Badge was arrested in Poona on 31st January 1948. Gopal V Godse was arrested on 5th February 1948 while on his way to village Uksan. Where he has his ancestral home and where presumably his parents reside. From the evidence of Mr. Leslie Vernon Perceival Pounde, P.W.75, who is an assistant Security Officer in the Sub-Depot, in which Gopal V Godse was, employed at the time of his arrest it appears that the latter rejoined duty after the expiry of his leave on 26th January 1948. He attended office upto 30th January 1948. The office happened to be closed on 31st January and 1st February. When he attended office on 2nd February he had to be given some police protection for his safety presumably due to the hostility of the office staff by reason of his connection with the assassin of Mahatma Gandhi. He remained on leave on the 3rd February. He attended office on 4th February and it again became necessary to give him police protection. He had eventually to be given leave from the office as a safety measure in order to enable him to go to his village for the period of the popular excitement and it was when he had almost reached the village that he was arrested.

Shankar Kistayya was arrested at Bhuleshwar near the residence of Dixitji Maharaj and Dadaji Maharaj on the 6th February. Apte and Karkare were arrested in Pyrkes Apollo Hotel at Bombay on the 14th February.

Dattatraya S. Parchure was apprehended by the Gwalior Police early in the morning on the 3rd February under the Maintenance of Public Order Ordinance of the Gwalior State and detained in the Fort under Military Custody to avoid, it is suggested, demonstration. He was shown as 'under arrest' in connection with Mahatma Gandhi Murder Case from the morning of the 17th February 1948. Searches were made for Gangadhar S. Dandwate, Gangadhar Jadhav and Suryadeo Sharma the alleged absconders but without any effect.

The seven appellants and Mr. Savarkar were eventually sent up for trial for the offences mentioned in an earlier part of this judgment after obtaining the sanction of the District Magistrate under Section 29 of the Indian Arms Act in connection with the offences under the said Act and after obtaining the sanction of the Central Government under Section 7 of the Explosive Substances Act in respect of the offences under that Act as well as under section 188 of the Code of Criminal Procedure for trial of Dattatraya S. Parchure in respect of the offence committed by him in Gwalior State.

According to the prosecution case as put before the learned Special Judge all the accused except Parchure, who was stated to have joined the conspiracy on 27th January 1948 at Gwalior, entered into a conspiracy to murder Mahatma Gandhi at sometime in December 1947. In furtherance of the object of this conspiracy Badge the approver and his servant Shankar were made to carry to Bombay in the evening of the 14th January 1948 two gun-cotton-slabs and five hand-grenades which were, during the night between the 14th and 15th January 1948, kept with a servant of Dixitji Maharaj at the latter's residence. Apte and Nathuram V Godse had also arrived at Bombay the same evening and had accompanied Badge when he had gone to Dixitji Maharaj's house with the stuff. Vishnu R. Karkare and Madanlal Pahwa had arrived in Bombay earlier and were putting up in Hindu Mahasabha Bhawan where Badge and Shankar also stayed for the night. On the 15th, Apte, Karkare, Nathuram V Godse, Badge, and Madanlal Pahwa went to the house of Dixitji Maharaj, took the stuff from there and made over the same to Karkare and Madanlal who were to leave for Delhi the same day. The stuff is said to have been tied up in the bedding and to have been carried to Delhi. Badge and Nathuram V Godse returned to Poona, the former because he wanted to make some arrangement about his household affairs before proceeding on such a risky venture and the latter because he wanted to fetch his brother Gopal V Godse who had promised also to provide a revolver. It was agreed that they would meet at Bombay on the morning of the 17th January. During the sojourn of a day at Poona Badge handed over, with certain instructions as to its disposal, to one Amdar Kharat whatever was left with him of arms, explosives, and cognate stuff which he had secured and was keeping clandestinely and in contravention of the law of the land and also succeeded in exchanging a pistol given to him by Nathuram V

Godse for a revolver which sometime before he had sold to a customer of his known as Sharma. Badge and Shankar, who is also said to have accompanied the former to Poona, left Poona by a late night train, and reached Bombay early on the morning of the 17th. At Bombay they along with Apte and Nathuram V Godse visited several places and several men inter alia with the object of collecting some money for expenses which they might be required to incur for the fulfilment of their scheme. Nathuram V Godse and Apte left for Delhi by plane the same afternoon. They arrived at Delhi late in the evening and put up at the Marina Hotel. Madanlal Pahwa and Karkare had arrived at Delhi the same day at about 12.00 p.m. and having failed to get accommodation at the Mahasabha Bhawan were staying at the Sharif Hotel. Badge and Shankar had been asked to leave for Delhi by the night train on the 17th. They however actually left on the 18th and arrived at Delhi late in the evening on the 19th. They put up at the Hindu Mahasabha Bhawan. Gopal V Godse who had taken casual leave for one week with effect from the 17th January had also in the meanwhile arrived Delhi. Karkare and Madanlal had also left the Sharif Hotel that evening. Badge, Shankar, Gopal, and Madanlal stayed at the Mahasabha Bhawan for the night. The suggestion about Karkare appears to have been that he spent the night at the Marina Hotel in the room occupied by Nathuram V Godse and Apte. All the conspirators except Nathuram V Godse, who was somewhat indisposed, met at the Mahasabha Bhawan next morning. Apte took Badge and Shankar with himself in a taxi to the Birla House and made a survey of the prayer ground on the back of the servants' quarters. After they had returned to the Mahasabha Bhawan, the two revolvers, one brought by Badge and the other by Gopal, were tried out in the jungle behind the Mahasabha Bhawan and were found to be quite unserviceable. At attempt was made by Gopal Godse to repair his revolver. Thereafter all of them met in the Marina Hotel in the room occupied by Nathuram V Godse and Apte where behind closed doors the gun-cotton-slabs and the hand-grenades were put in order for immediate use and the plan for the evening was finalised. It was agreed that after the prayer had started Madanlal should explode one gun-cotton-slab near the back gate of Birla House so as to create a commotion and attract the attention of the people assembled at the prayer and taking advantage of the panic thus caused Badge and Shankar should fire at Mahatma Gandhi with the two revolvers and should also throw a hand-grenade each on him. Badge was to fire the revolver and throw his hand-grenade from the trellis work of the window of the room in the servants' quarters immediately behind where Mahatmaji used to sit at the time of the prayer. He was to enter the room posing as a photographer with the object of taking a photo of the prayer meeting. Gopal, Madanlal, and Karkare were to throw the remaining hand-grenades on Mahatma Ji at the same time. They were to get mixed up with the audience and to act at the crucial time. Apte and Nathuram were to give signals to the other actors of the drama at the right moment. In pursuance of this plan one gun-cotton-slab, and one hand-grenade were given to Madanlal, one hand-grenade and one revolver to Badge, one hand-grenade and one revolver to Shankar and one hand-grenade each to Gopal and Karkare. Madanlal and Karkare were the first to leave the Marina Hotel for the Birla House. The others except Nathuram V Godse left a little later in a taxi. Nathuram V Godse followed them sometime afterwards. It is not known what means of conveyance he used but it was suggested that he arrived not long after the taxi of Apte and others had parked near the back gate and its occupants had alighted. On its way to Birla House the taxi had been stopped for a short while near the Mahasabha Bhawan and Gopal had left the bag which was supposed to contain the spare gun-cotton-slab and some other spare materials in the cupboard. On getting the Birla House, Badge felt disinclined to do the job assigned to him in the manner originally planned because he felt that he might get entrapped into the room from the trellis work whereof he was to have fired the revolver and to have thrown the hand-grenade. He suggested to his comrades that he would much rather fire the revolver and throw the hand-grenade on Mahatma Ji from the front. After some hesitation his comrades fell in line with his views. Madanlal did carry out the part assigned to him by igniting the gun-cotton-slab near the back gate. However the others did not carry out their respective parts and Nathuram V Godse, Apte, and Gopal left immediately in the taxi. Madanlal was of course arrested on the spot. Karkare, Badge, and Shankar managed to get away. Apte and Nathuram V Godse left the same night for Kanpur. Badge and Shankar left for Poona; Gopal and Karkare, it was suggested, spent the night at the Frontier Hotel and left next morning. Apte and Godse arrived in Bombay on the 23rd and spent the night at Arya Pathik Ashram. On 24th Nathuram V Godse was able to get accommodation for the two of them at the Elphinstone Annexe Hotel. Apte spent the night at the Ashram with a lady friend of his and shifted to Elphinstone Annexe Hotel only next morning. On the 25th of January they met Karkare and Gopal at the house of G.M. Joshi at Thana at about … m. Gopal left for Kirkee the same night. Apte and Nathuram V Godse flow to Delhi on the 27th. While at Bombay they had made an unsuccessful attempt to get a pistol from Dadaji Maharaj and Dixitji Maharaj. From Delhi, they proceeded to Gwalior the same day arriving at Gwalior at about 10.30 pm. They stayed for the night and for the next day with Dr. Parchure at his house. They disclosed their plan to him with his co-operation and that of Dandwate and others whom they met at his place were able to get from one Mr. Goel the pistol Ex.P.39. They left Gwalior by a night train arriving at Delhi the next day. At Delhi they were joined by Karkare and the three spent the night in a retiring room at the Railway Station. Next evening Nathuram V Godse shot Mahatma Ji with the pistol Ex.P.39 which had been brought from Gwalior at the time and in the manner already indicated.

On behalf of the defence, it was not denied that Madanlal and Karkare had left Bombay by a night train for Delhi on the 15th January and had arrived at Delhi on the 17th at about 12.30 p.m. and had put up at Sharif Hotel. It was also not denied that they had left the hotel on the 19th. It was, however, denied that they stayed at the Mahasabha Bhawan for the night of the 19th. The allegation was that Madanlal had to come to Delhi in connection with arrangements for his marriage, that on hearing of Mahatma Gandhi's fast which he believed was intended to coerce India Government into paying to Pakistan the sum of 55 crores and into evacuating West Punjab Hindus from Muslim houses occupied by them, he had also planned to lead during his stay at Delhi a deputation of refugees to Mahatma Ji to place their grievances before him and that on his request Karkare agreed to accompany him to help him in both the matters. The allegation further was that after leaving Sharif Hotel, the two of them had stayed at the house of a relation of Madanlal. Apte and Nathuram V Godse admitted being at Bombay on the 14th and 15th January 1948 and having flown to Delhi on the 17th. They also admitted having met Shankar and Badge at Bombay on the aforesaid date and having gone with them in a taxi to certain places and having collected a sum of Rs. 1,100/- from two persons. Their allegation was that they had decided to stage peaceful but otherwise a powerful demonstration at Mahatma Gandhi's prayer meeting in order to lodge a vigorous protest against his pro-Pakistan and pro-Muslim activities, that Badge and Shankar had offered to accompany them and to help them in organising the proposed demonstration and that the offer had been accepted by them. It was also admitted that Apte and Nathuram V Godse on their arrival at Delhi on the 17th January 1948 stayed at the Marina Hotel. It was, however, stoutly denied that while staying there they had any talk with Madanlal and Karkare. The alleged visit of the aforesaid persons and Badge, Gopal and Shankar to the Marina Hotel on the 20th and the alleged conference behind closed doors in the room occupied by Apte and Nathuram V Godse were emphatically denied although Badge's having visited Apte and Nathuram V Godse in their room in the morning was admitted, it being suggested that he had come to ascertain what the prospects of the arrangements for the proposed demonstration were. It is admitted that Apte did go to the prayer meeting in the evening on the 20th, but it is explained that he went there for seeing if there was any prospect of holding a demonstration and came away on finding it impossible to hold any demonstration on that day on account of the failure of the microphone. It is alleged that Apte came to know about the explosion after his return from Birla House from Badge who told him about the arrest of Madanlal and also about his having sold some explosive stuff to the refugees including Madanlal. According to Madanlal he had met Badge at about noon in one of the barracks made for refugees when he had shown him a trunk loaded with firearms and explosives out of which he had given him one gun-cotton-slab and one hand-grenade by way of sample for canvassing the refugees to purchase the stuff and that he had ignited the gun-cotton-slab at a safe place after taking precautions that the explosion thereof should not harm anyone with the object of courting arrest in order to be able to bring grievances of refugees to the notice of Mahatma Gandhi. Nathuram V Godse is alleged not to have come out of the room in the Marina Hotel due to severe headache. Karkare admits having gone to the Birla House. He says that he arrived there at 5.30 p.m. after the explosion inasmuch as the driver of the *tonga* hired by him had in the first instance taken him by mistake to the Birla Mandir.

Nathuram Godse and Apte admit having entrained for Kanpur on the night of the 20th, having arrived at Kanpur on the 21st, and having stayed in the retiring room there till 11.20 a.m. on the 22nd when they left for Bombay. They also admit their presence in Bombay from 23rd to 27th January although they do not admit their alleged visit to G.M. Joshi's house at Thana on the 25th. They admit having flown to Delhi on the 27th January and to have left for Gwalior after their arrival at Delhi. They, however, say that they travelled by the Amritsar-Bombay Express which arrived at Gwalior at 5.30 a.m. on the 28th January. They admit having met Dr. Parchure but deny having stayed at his house. They say that they had gone to him to get some volunteers of his Hindu Rashtraya Sena for staging a demonstration at Delhi, that they reached his house at xx.00 a.m. when he was ready to go to his dispensary, that he asked them to see him in the afternoon and when they met him in the afternoon, he declined to lend them any volunteers for the purpose indicated above. It is denied that they got any pistol from Jagdish Prasad Goyel at Gwalior. It is alleged that Godse and Apte parted company at Gwalior. Godse entrained for Delhi where he reached about mid-day on the 29th and Apte proceeded to Bombay. It is denied that either Apte or Karkare were at Delhi on the 29th or 30th January. It is alleged that Godse alone stayed in the retiring room at the Delhi Railway Station. It is further alleged that it was after his arrival at Delhi that Godse decided to put an end to Mahatma Gandhi's life and that he did so with the pistol Ex.P.39 which he got from some refugee at Delhi. Karkare says that he proceeded direct to the Railway Station from Birla House on the 20th in the same *tonga* which he had come there and took the earliest train for ....ra from where he proceeded to Bombay at which place he stayed thereafter till his arrest on the 14th February. He further says that throughout the fourth week of January he was staying at the Chembur Refugee Camp.

Gopal Godse has of course totally denied having ever visited Delhi in the month of January 1948.

None of the accused produced any evidence to substantiate any of their allegations although Apte and Karkare did rely on some documents recovered from their respective persons at the time of their arrest in support of their pleas that they

were not and could not have been in Delhi on the 30th January.

The learned Special Judge has generally believed the prosecution evidence and has accepted the prosecution version except in so far as their allegations as to Savarkar being a party to the conspiracy and as to Gopal, Karkare and Badge having imported one revolver each into ... are concerned.

The first question that arises from decision in the present appeals is whether there was any conspiracy for .... murder of Mahatma Gandhi and Nathuram V Godse appellant committed the murder on the 30th January in pursuance of their conspiracy. In case this question is answered in the affirmative, the next question for determination will be .... of the appellants, if any, besides Nathuram V Godse himself was or were parties to the conspiracy. On the ......ngs of the learned Special Judge with reference to Madanlal and Shankar Kistayya and on certain..ents addressed to us by Nathuram V Godse in reference ... the case of Gopal Godse, although Gopal Godse's counsel [59] did not choose to stress the point, a question also arises if any of the appellants disassociated himself from the conspiracy before the accomplishment of its object and if so, what is the legal effect of such disassociation.

Before I proceed to examine the evidence led by the prosecution to substantiate their allegations as to the Mahatmaji having been murdered in pursuance of a conspiracy to murder him to which all the appellant and some others were parties, I propose to dispose of some legal points stressed by Mr. Bannerji, who argued the appeals of Apte and Madanlal Pahwa and by Mr. Inamdar Counsel for Gopal Godse and Dr. Parchure.

---

[59] Left margin portion of the Typed Page No.229 of the True Copy of the Judgment is in decipherable. Hence dotted words are left to the understanding of the readers. Eds.

The first contention of Mr. Bannerji was that where the offence to commit which a conspiracy is alleged to have been entered into is itself said to have been committed - i.e., where the object of the alleged conspiracy is itself said to have been actually achieved – before the trial starts, the offence of conspiracy must be deemed to have merged in the substantive offence which the alleged conspirators had agreed to commit and which has in fact been committed and that in such a case the accused can be tried on the substantive offence and not for the offence of conspiracy. He urged that Mahatma Gandhi having in the present case been actually murdered the accused could be charged and tried either under Sec.302, Indian Penal Code, for the offence of murder or under Sec.109 read with Sec.302 for abetment of murder but could not legally be charged under Section 120-B. After giving my careful thought to the argument addressed by the learned counsel in support of this contention, I find myself wholly unable to accept it.

The offence of "Criminal Conspiracy" has been defined in Sec.120-A of the Indian penal Code which reads as follows:

"**When** two or more persons agree to do, or cause to be done:-

an illegal act, or

an act which is not illegal by illegal means, such an agreement as designated a criminal conspiracy;

Provided that no agreement except an agreement to commit an offence shall amount to a criminal conspiracy unless some act besides the agreement is done by one or more parties to such agreement in pursuance thereof.

Explanation: It is immaterial whether the illegal act is the ultimate object of such agreement, or is merely incidental to that object".

The punishment for the offence is provided in Section 120-B which runs as follows:

1) "**Whoever** is a party to a criminal conspiracy to commit an offence punishable with death, transportation or rigorous imprisonment for a term of two years or upwards, shall, where no express provision is made in this Code for the punishment for such a conspiracy, punished in the same manner as if he had abetted such offence.

2) **Whoever** is a party to a criminal conspiracy other than a criminal conspiracy to commit an offence punishable as aforesaid shall be punished with imprisonment of either description for a term not exceeding six months, or with fine or with both."

These two sections were introduced into the Code by the Criminal Law Amendment Act of 1913 (Government of India Act No.8 of 1913). Under the law as it existed before the coming into force of the Amending Act of 1913, the subject of conspiracy was dealt with directly only by two sections of the Penal Code, namely, by Section 107, Secondly, and by Section 121-A. Section 107 defined "abetment" and by the clause Secondly as occurring in that section abetment was made to include the engaging with one or more person or persons in any conspiracy for the doing of a thing, if an act or illegal omission did take place in pursuance of that conspiracy and in order to the doing of that thing. Under Section 121-A of course it was an offence to conspire to commit any of the offences made punishable by Section 121, or to deprive the King of the sovereignty of British India or any part thereof, or to conspire to overawe, by means of criminal force or the show of such force, the Government of India or any Local Government. Thus except in cases falling within the purview of Section 121-A, according to the law of this country, a mere agreement to commit an offence, of however serious a nature, was not indictable unless some act or illegal omission took place in pursuance of the agreement and in order to the carrying out of such agreement. The law was, however, different and far more stringent *in* England. In the Queen v Aspinall *(1876, 2 Q.B.D.48) in describing the essentials of the offence of criminal conspiracy, Broot J.A. observed as follows at Page 58 of the report:*

> **"Now,** first, the crime of conspiracy is completely committed, if it is committed at all, the moment two or more have agreed that they will do, at once or at some future time, certain things. It is not necessary in order to complete the offence that any one thing should be done beyond the agreement. The conspirators may repent or stop or any have no opportunity, or may be prevented, or may fail. Nevertheless, the crime is complete; it was completed when the agreed."

In the Mughal Steamship Company Limited v McGregor Gow and Company and Others (57 Law Journal Q.B.544) Lord Coleridge said at Page 549:

> **"It** cannot be, nor indeed was it, denied that in order to found this section there must be an element of unlawfulness in the combination on which it is founded ******* But whereas in an indictment it suffices if the combination exists and is unlawful, because it is the combination itself which is mischievous and which gives the public an interest to interfere but indictment, nothing need be actually done in furtherance of it. In the Bridgewater Case (unreported) referred to at the Bar, and in which I was Counsel nothing was done in fact; yet a gentleman was convicted because he had entered into an unlawful combination, from which, almost on the spot, he withdrew, and withdrew altogether. No one was harmed but the public offence was complete. This is in accordance with the express words of Justice Bayley at Page 76 in **the King v Berenger**(3 M & S 67)."

Similar observations were to be found in the judgment of the House of Lords in ***Quinn v Lethem (1901A.C. 495).***

The object of the amendment of 1913 was to bring the Indian Law in line with the English Law in so far as conspiracies to commit offences were concerned. In case of a conspiracy other than a conspiracy to commit an offence, Section 120-A still requires some overt act to be done in pursuance of the agreement before the parties entering into the agreement can be held chargeable for the offence of criminal conspiracy. However, in cases where the agreement is to do or cause to be done, an act which is itself an offence, no overt act done by the parties to the agreement in pursuance of such agreement is required to be proved, and the crime of criminal conspiracy is complete as soon as the agreement has been formed. As observed by Sir Ashutosh Mukerjee in his judgment in ***Pulin Behary Das v Emperor (16 I.C.257)*** at Page 312, although conspiracy is usually actually bound up with the overt acts because in many cases it is only by means of the overt act that the existence of a conspiracy can be made out. Yet the criminality of the conspiracy is independent of the criminality of the overt acts.

The offence of criminal conspiracy which must be deemed to be complete the moment a number of persons agree amongst themselves to commit some offence cannot be wiped out when such offence has been committed in pursuance of the conspiracy. It may be that where the commission of the offence itself can be brought home to the conspirators and they are convicted of and sentenced for such offence, a separate conviction and sentence for the offence of conspiracy may become redundant and unnecessary. The punishment prescribed by Section 120-B for being a party to the criminal conspiracy to commit an offence punishable with death, transportation or rigorous imprisonment for a term, of two years or upwards being the same as for abetment of the offence, if, in a case where some persons are being tried on a charge of having conspired to commit such an offence, as well as on a charge of having either actually committed the offence, or of having abetted the same, the offence begin committed in consequence of such abetment, on the facts proved at the trial, the Court is able to convict such persons or any of them on the second charge, it is obvious that a separate conviction or sentence on the charge of conspiracy will be wholly unnecessary. it may, however, well be that on the facts proved that Court is unable to find the accused guilty of anything more than a mere concert to commit the offence. It may be of the opinion that the accused are not proved to have committed the actual offence, or even to have done any overt act in furtherance of such concert and for the carrying out of the common object. It may hold that although it was the accused who initially planned the offence, before they could do anything in furtherance of the plan, somebody else, of his own and without any reference to them, took the initiative and committed the offence. It is obvious that in such a case they cannot be convicted either of the offence itself or of its abetment as defined in Section 107 Secondly. The only offence of which they can be convicted is the one made punishable by Section 120-B. In the circumstances, I do not see how it can possible be said that trial on the charge of a conspiracy to commit an offence is not legally permissible when the prosecution also alleges that the offence itself has in the meanwhile been committed in pursuance of the conspiracy. The two offences are quite distinct offences and there is nothing illegal in the accused being charged with both. However, the Court will exercise a wise discretion in refraining from convicting the accused on the charge of conspiracy in case they are found guilty of the offence itself and in any case will refrain from passing a separate sentence for conspiracy.

The English law and practice on the subject is thus summed up at Page 73 Harrison's Law of Conspiracy:-

"If a conspiracy to commit a crime is actually carried out, the conspiracy is not merged in the crime and it is technically possible for the accused to be indicated twice, once for the conspiracy and once for the crime (As explained by Lord Campbell in O'Connell v Reg (1844, 11, C.L. and F. 155), but this is discouraged by the Judges as being unfair the accused (see R v. Boulton, 1871, 12 Cox 87."

There is no reason to suppose that the law or practice in this country is, or should be, different.

Mr. Bannerji drew our attention to certain decisions, and, while conceding that none of them went to the extent of laying down the extreme proposition contended for by him, urged that the general effect of those decisions was to render trial and conviction under Section 120-B for the offence of entering into a criminal conspiracy to commit an offence illegal where the accused are also charged with having committed the substantive offence or with having abetted the commission of such offence within the meaning of Section 107, Indian Penal Code. After a careful consideration of those decisions, I am of the opinion that they really do not go further than lay down that a separate conviction or sentence under Section120-B is unnecessary where the accused have been convicted either of the substantive offence which they are found to have conspired to commit or of having abetted the commission of such offence.

In **_Punjab Singh v King Emperor_ (I.L.R.15 Lah.84)** referred to by Mr. Bannerji a separate conviction under Section 120-B, where the accused had also been convicted of the offence to commit which they were found to have conspired, was upheld but it was held that a separate sentence in respect of that conviction was not necessary.

In **_Harsha Nath Chatterjee v Emperor_ (I.L.R. 42 Cal.1153),** the other case referred to by him,

Mr. Bannerji relied on some dicta of Beachcroft J. to be found at Page 1168 of the report. The accused had in that case been charged with having entered into a conspiracy to manufacture arms, an offence punishable with imprisonment. It was pointed out that, in such a case, if the offence of manufacturing arms was not committed in pursuance of the conspiracy the maximum punishment awardable under Section 116 would be imprisonment for one-fourth of the longest term provided for the offence, while in case of the offence being committed in pursuance of the conspiracy, the conspirators could under Section 109 be sentenced to the same term of imprisonment which was provided for the offence. Referring to the latter contingency Beachcroft J. observed:-

"**Perhaps** strictly speaking in such a case there should not be a conviction for conspiracy but for the abetment of the offence, for conspiracy followed by an act done to carry out the purpose of the conspiracy amounts to abetment."

In Jogeshwar Singh v King Emperor (I.L.E.15 Patna 26) the third case referred to by Mr. Bannerji, the accused had been committed by the Committing Magistrate to take their trial before the Court of Session for the offences of forgery and perjury and for having abetted the said offences. On the case coming up before him for Trial, the Sessions Judge framed an additional charge under Section 120-B against the accused for having entered into a conspiracy to commit the offence of forgery and perjury. He convicted them not only on the charge of conspiracy but also on the charges of having committed the offences of perjury and forgery. On appeal the High Court set aside the conviction under Section 120-B. In dealing with the subject Rowland J. observed:-

"**Whereas** Section 120-B provides an extended definition of criminal conspiracy covering acts which do not amount to abetment by conspiracy within the meaning of Section 107, and Section 120-B provides a punishment for criminal conspiracy where no express provision is made in the Code for the punishment of such a conspiracy, therefore where a criminal conspiracy amounts to an abetment under Section 107, it is unnecessary to invoke the provisions of Section 120-A and 120-B because the Code has made specific provision for the punishment of such a conspiracy.******** The appellants having been convicted on the substantive charges framed were not liable to be convicted also of conspiracy"

It is true that the Bench was also of the view that the Sessions Judge ought not to have framed the additional charge and ought to have proceeded with the trial on the charges framed by the Committing Magistrate. I take this only to mean that in view of the circumstances disclosed on the record of the Committing Magistrate the framing of the additional charge was unnecessary. I do not think that the Hon'ble Judges did, or meant to, lie down that the framing of the additional charge was illegal or otherwise open to any legal objection.

A.I.R. 1936 Rangoon 358 which was next relied on by Mr. Bannerji appears to me to be wholly irrelevant because all that was held there was that no one can be tried for abetment of the offence of conspiracy inasmuch as conspiracy is not an act committed which can be abetted.

In A.I.R. 1938 Mad. 130, the last case referred to by Mr. Bannerji, six persons were committed to take their trial before a Court of Session. Out of them four were committed on a charge under Section 386, Indian Penal Code (Committing of extortion by putting any person in fear of death or of grievous hurt to that person or to any other), and all six on a charge under Section 120-B for having entered into a conspiracy to commit the offence under Section 386. According to Section 196(a) (2), Criminal Procedure Code, no Court can take cognizance of the offence of criminal conspiracy under Section 120-B of the Indian Penal Code in any case where the object of the conspiracy is to commit a non-cognizable offence, unless the Local

Government, or a Chief Presidency Magistrate, or District Magistrate empowered in this behalf by the Local Government, has, by order in writing, consented to the initiation of the proceedings. The offence under Section 386 is a non-cognizable offence and in the particular case no such consent to the initiation of the proceedings under Section 120-B had been obtained. By means of a petition for revision presented to the High Court, the accused moved for the order of commitment being quashed on the ground of want of such consent. The learned Single Judge who heard the petition for revision declined to quash the commitment order **inter alia** on the ground that Section 120-B had been wrongly applied to the case and that instead of being charged under that section, the accused should be charged under Section 386 read with Section 109.

As pointed out by Rowland J. in the Patna case just adverted to and as will otherwise appear on a comparison of the language of Section 120-B with that of the clause **Secondly** in Section 107, the offence of criminal conspiracy becomes the offence of abetment by conspiracy as soon as any act or illegal omission has taken place in pursuance of the conspiracy and in order to the carrying out of the object thereof. Inasmuch as direct proof can scarcely, if over, be afforded of a conspiracy, and, as pointed out by Earle J. in the celebrated case of **Rex v Duffield** (1851, 5 Cox C.C. 404 at Page 434), "it does not happen once in a thousand times that anybody comes before the jury to say:- "I was present at the time when the parties did conspire together when they agreed to carry out their unlawful purpose", Very generally it is by means of the overt acts done by the conspirators or some of them that the existence of conspiracy can be made out. It is for this reason that it has been said by some Judges that conspiracy is usually actually bound up with the overt act done in pursuance thereof. In a very large majority of cases, therefore, where the accused are charged with having conspired together to commit an offence, the real offence with which they are to be tried will be found to be one of abetment by

conspiracy. Inasmuch as the latter offence may sometimes be more serious and punishable with severe punishment, but is nevertheless serious or punishable with less severe punishment, than the offence of conspiracy, pure and simple, and inasmuch as it will neither be fair nor just to punish a man twice for the same wrongful act or acts, it may sometimes be considered to be unnecessary or redundant to charge the accused under Section 120-B for having conspired to commit an offence where they can properly be charged with having abetted the commission of the offence. Sometimes, it may indeed become necessary to refrain from framing a charge under Section 120-B in order to avoid an awkward situation as was the case in A.I.R. 1938 Mad. 138 It cannot, however, be said as a matter of law that the offence of conspiracy to commit an offence which consists in the mere agreement to commit the offence is abrogated or wiped out when either some act or illegal omission has taken place in pursuance of the agreement so as to bring the case within the purview of clause **Secondly** of Section 107,or the offence itself has been actually committed. The offence of conspiracy still remains as an independent offence and the accused may quite properly be charged with and tried for it even though they are at the same time charged with and tried for the actual commission of the offence which they are alleged to have conspired to commit, or the abetment of such offence. I am accordingly unable to hold, as contended by Mr. Bannerji, that the learned Special Judge acted illegally in charging and trying the appellants under Section 120-B for having conspired together to commit the murder of Mahatma Gandhi because they had also been charged under a separate count for having abetted such murder.

Mr. Bannerji next attacked the legality of the trial on the ground of the misjoinder of charges and the accused persons. He conceded that if the appellants were lawfully charged with and tried for the offence under Section 120-B, no objection could legally be taken to the trial on the ground of misjoinder. In view of my decision that the indictment of the appellants for the offence of conspiracy under Section 120-B was not illegal or improper, the question of misjoinder does not therefore arise. Even, however, if it could be held that they were improperly charged under Section 120-B, I would have no hesitation at all in repelling the objection to the validity of the trial on the ground of misjoinder. As pointed out in section 239(d) Criminal Procedure Code, persons accused of different offences committed in the course of the same transaction may be charged and tried for all those offences. It has been repeatedly held that the word "transaction" as used in Clause (d) of Section 239 of the Code is not to be interpreted in any artificial or technical sense, and that, in each case, the Court has to decide with reference to the facts of the particular case whether the offences complained of were committed in the course of the same transaction, continuity of action or purpose being the main test to be applied. In I.L.R. 1944 Bom. 728 it was held that ordinarily a series of acts may be said to be so connected together as to form the same transaction when they are so related to one another in point of purpose, or cause and effect, or as principal and subsidiary acts, as to constitute one continuous action. In the present case all the acts which formed the subject matter of accusation were alleged, and have even been found, to have been done for one purpose and for one object, viz., the murder of Mahatma Gandhi. In the circumstances, there can be no reasonable doubt as to all the offences with which the accused were charged having been committed in the course of the same transaction. In this connection, it may be interesting to note that, according to the construction consistently placed by all the High Courts on the language of Clause (d) of Section 239 of the Criminal Procedure Code, which construction received imprimatur[60] of their Lordships of the Privy Council quite recently in the

case of Babu Lal Choukhani (I.L.R. 1938 (2) Calcutta 295 P.C.), it is the accusation as laid, and not the final decision of the Court, which should determine the applicability or otherwise of the Clause. In the case which went to the Privy Council the accused had been charged with, and tried for, conspiracy to commit criminal offences and also some substantive offences said to have been committed in pursuance of the conspiracy. The High Court found the charge of conspiracy having fallen through, the different offence which the different accused were found guilty of, could not be said to have been committed in the course of the same transaction, and that their joint trial for their separate individual acts was, accordingly, illegal. Their Lordships repelled this contention and held that the question of the validity or otherwise of the trial had to be decided with reference to the accusation and not with reference to the actual findings.

It was next contended by Mr. Bannerji that the procedure adopted by the learned Special Judge in the trial of the case was not proper and according to law, that the case should have been tried in accordance with the manner provided by the Code for the trial of warrant cases, and that the learned Judge acted illegally in framing charges against the accused without recording any evidence and merely on the basis of the charge sheet supplied by the police. These contentions of the learned counsel are also without any force.

In an earlier portion of this judgment, I have had occasion to refer to the third sub-section of Section 13 of the Bombay Public Safety Measures Act as extended to the Province of Delhi. According to that sub-section, subject to certain modifications, the provisions contained in the Code for the trial of Sessions cases are to apply to the proceedings of the Special Judge whose Court is to be deemed to be a Court of Sessions for the purposes of those provisions. One of the modifications of the provisions governing Sessions Trials as enacted in the aforesaid Act is that a Special Judge may take

---

[60] Imprimatur means authoritative approval. In earlier days it was an official licence issued by the Roman Catholic Church to print an ecclesiastical or religious book.

cognizance of offences without the accused being committed to his Court for trial. The procedure laid down in Chapter XXI of the Code for the trial of Warrant Cases applies only to proceedings before a Magistrate. The procedure for trial of cases in a Court of Session is to be found in Chapter XXIII. Unlike Chapter XXI this Chapter does not require the Judge to hold any enquiry or record any evidence before framing a charge. On the other hand, as provided in Section 271, the trial in a Court of Session has to commence with the arraignment of the accused and the reading out of the charge to him. This was precisely the procedure followed in the present case and I fail to see how it can be said to be open to any legal objection.

Mr. Bannerji next objected to the form in which the charge of conspiracy had been framed by the learned Special Judge, on the ground that it did not allege or indicate what, if any, plan or design had been formed by the accused for the accomplishment of their object. This contention is equally without force. As I have pointed out above, the offence of criminal conspiracy consists merely in the agreement to commit any illegal act and is complete as soon as the agreement is reached. In order to justify conviction for the offence of criminal conspiracy it is not necessary for the prosecution to prove anything more than the agreement. If the agreement is proved the accused are liable to be punished even though they may not yet have formed or even considered any plan or design for the achievement of their common object. In the circumstances, an indictment for criminal conspiracy need not allege or indicate the plan or the design formed by the alleged conspirators for carrying out the object of the conspiracy nor need it even allege that any plan or design has been formed.

The question as to what an indictment for criminal conspiracy must allege or indicate was considered in the case *"the King v. Gill and Henry"* (20 R.R. 407). In that case the defendants were found guilty upon an indictment which charged that "they unlawfully did conspire and combine together, by diverse false pretences and subtle means and devices to obtain and acquire to themselves of and from P.D. and G.D. divers large sums of the money of the respective monies of the said P.D. and G.D." The validity of the indictment was impugned on the ground that the words used therein gave no information to the defendants of the specific charge against which they were to defend themselves and did not state the overt acts of the conspiracy. In repelling this contention Abbot C.J. observed: *"It is objected that the particular means and devices are not stated. It is, however, possible to conceive that persons might meet together, and might determine and resolve that they would b some trick and device cheat and defraud another, without having at that time fixed and settled what the particular means and devices should be. Such a meeting and resolution would nevertheless constitute an offence. If, therefore, a case may reasonably be suggested in which the matters here charged would, if there were nothing more, be an offence against the law, it is impossible, as it seems to me, to conclude that the law should require the particular means to be set forth. The offence of conspiracy may be complete, although the particular means are not settled and resolved on at the time of the conspiracy."*

Bayley J. who was the other member of the Bench in dealing with the same question observed as follows: "When parties have once agreed to cheat a particular person of his monies, although they may not have then fixed on any means for that purpose, the offence of conspiracy is complete. This case appears to me not distinguishable in principle from the **King v Eccles** which decided that the means need not be stated; and there **Buller J.** said, that the means were matter evidence to prove the charge and not the crime itself."

In this country the question was discussed at great length and with his characteristic lucidity and thoroughness by **Sir Asutosh Mookerjee** in his judgment in the case of *Amrits Lal Hazra and*

Others v Emperor (I.L.R. 42 Cal. 957) at Page 975 to 981 of the report. The accused had in that case been charged with having conspired to manufacture explosive substances. The legality of the charge was attacked at the hearing of the appeal on the ground that it did not specify the nature of the explosive substances which the accused had agreed to manufacture. The objection was overruled by the Bench and the charge as framed was held to be quite legal and proper. In dealing with this subject **Sir Asutosh Mookerjee** observes:- *"In the second place, it has been contended that the charge under Section 120-B, Indian Penal Code, is bad, because it does not specify the explosive substances, which it is alleged, the accused had conspired with one another and with other persons to make and keep. The substance of the argument is that to make and keep explosive substances generally is not an offence which, it is contended means according to Section 4, Clause (o) of the Criminal Procedure Code, 'any act or omission made punishable by any law for the time being in force,' and according to the second paragraph of Section 40, Indian Penal Code denotes, 'a thing punishable under that Code or under any special or local law,' as defined in Section 41 and 42. Reference has also been made to Section 10 of the Indian Evidence Act, where the expression is used, 'two or more persons have conspired together to commit an offence or an actionable wrong.' *******We are unable to accept as well-founded the contention of the accused that where the illegal act, charged under Section 120-B, is the unlawful and malicious possession of explosives substances, within the meaning of Section 4 of the Explosive Substances Act, 1908, it is essential to specify in the charge the explosive substances which the accused have conspired to have in their possessions or under their control. It is indisputable that a person may be guilty of criminal conspiracy, even though the illegal act which he has agreed to do or cause to be done has not been done. As was observed by **Cleasby B.** in *Reg. v. Hibbert*((1875) 13 Cox

82) conspiracy differs from other charges in this respect, that in other charges the intention to do a criminal act is not a crime of itself until something is done amounting to the doing of or attempting to do some act to carry out that intention; conspiracy, on the other hand, consists simply in the agreement or confederacy to do some act, no matter whether it is done or not. We very often get facts sufficient to establish the guilt of parties to a conspiracy other than acts which have been done in pursuance of it. **Baron Cleasby** then gives an example: *'there may be a conspiracy to set fire to London at different places at once, and that conspiracy may be fully proved, though no part of London has in fact been set on fire, inasmuch as the crime of conspiracy consists only in the agreement or confederacy to do an illegal act by legal means or a legal act by illegal means. ********** If the contention of the accused in the case before us were well-founded, there could be no prosecution for a conspiracy to commit murders or dacoities till a murder or dacoity had been actually committed in pursuance of the conspiracy, though it might be conclusively proved that the conspiracy had been formed, even before a single overt act was done. The gist of the offence is in the conspiracy or agreement, and if the offence goes no further, it may not be possible to say what murders or dacoities it is proposed to commit, or in a case such as that before us, what particular explosives the accused intend to obtain. **** The indictment in all cases of conspiracy must, in the first place we, charge the conspiracy, but that in stating the object of the conspiracy the same degree of certainty is not required as in an indictment for the offence conspired to be committed, *** We are clearly of opinion that the conspiracy charge is not open to objection on the ground that it does not specify the explosive substances for the preparation and possession whereof the alleged conspiracy was formed."*

In arriving at the above conclusion **Sir Asutosh Mookerjee** quite exhaustively considered and reviewed a number of English authorities relevant to the subject that had been cited at the Bar.

Lastly, Mr. Bannerji sought to place on Section 10 of the Indian Evidence Act a much narrower interpretation than its language warrants. The section runs as follows:- *"Where there is reasonable ground to believe that two or more persons have conspired together to commit an offence or an actionable wrong, anything said, done or written by any one of such persons in reference to their common intention, after the time when such intention was first entertained by any one of them is a relevant fact as against each of the persons believed to be so conspiring, as well for the purpose of proving the existence of the conspiracy as for the purpose of showing that any such person was a party to it."*

Under the English Law statements or acts made or done by one conspirator, in order to be admissible against the others, must have been made or done **in furtherance** of the common purpose and **in pursuance** of the conspiracy. However, as will appear from the wording of the section quoted above, this rule of the English Law has not been adhered to by the framers of the Indian Evidence Act. Mr. Bannerji had to admit that according to the plain language of the Section a statement or act made or done by one conspirator should be admissible in evidence against the others for the purpose of proving both the existence of the conspiracy and their participation therein, if it has been made or done in reference to their common intention, and it is not necessary that it should have been made or done in furtherance of such intention. He, however, contended that in *Mirza Akbar v King Emperor* (A.I.R. 1940 P.C.176) the Privy Council had held that the scope of Section 10 of the Indian Evidence Act is not wider than that of the relevant rule of the English Common Law. After a careful perusal of the Privy Council judgment, I am quite clearly of the opinion that it does not at all support the contention of the learned Counsel. The question that arose for decision in that case was whether a statement made

to a third person by an alleged conspirator about past acts aftcr the common intention had ceased to operate was admissible. This question was answered in the negative relying on the judgment of the House of Lords in **Queen v Blake** ((1844) 6 Q.B.126), their Lordships being of the opinion that in this respect the rule of Indian Law was not different from that of the English Common Law as laid down in the above decision. The judgment of the Privy Council is no authority at all for reading into the section a sense quite different from that clearly implicit in the words used. That in this respect the rule embodied in the Indian Act is much wider that the corresponding rule of English Law has been noticed and commented upon in quite a large number of reported cases to which it is hardly necessary to refer in view of the most unambiguous language used in the section.

Mr. Inamdar wanted us to hold the evidence of the approver to be legally inadmissible on the ground that the pardon tendered to him by the learned Special Judge was illegal and in excess of the powers conferred on him by the statute under which the Special Court had been established. The relevant provision of the statute is contained in sub-section 2(a) of Section 13 of the Bombay Public Safety Measures Act of 1947 as extended to the Province of Delhi which was introduced into the Act by Ordinance 14 of 1948 which was subsequently replaced by the Central Act 52 of 1948. The sub-section runs as follows: "A Special Judge trying an offence under this Act may, with a view to obtaining the evidence of any person, supposed to have been directly or indirectly concerned in, or privy to, the offence, tender a pardon to such person on condition of his making a full and true disclosure*****".

According to Mr. Inamdar's way of reading the above sub-section, a Special Judge could tender pardon only while trying an offence created by the Act itself. His contention was that the words "under the Act" had been used in the Sub-Section to qualify the immediately preceding word "offence" and not the word "trying" occurring earlier. I find myself unable to accept the contention and have little doubt that the words "under this Act" have been used in the Sub-section as qualifying the "trial" and not as qualifying the "offence". Then interpretation of the Sub-section suggested by Mr. Inamdar seems to be wholly inconsistent with the general tenor and the language of Section 13 which was obviously enacted to provide generally for the procedure to be followed by a Special Judge in the trial of all the offences or classes of offences which he may be required by the Provincial Government to try and it appears to be wholly unreasonable to assume that, while conferring on him all the powers exercised by a Sessions Judge, in the trial of Sessions cases, with certain additions, the Legislature intended to restrict his power to tender pardon only to the two petty offences created by Sections 7 and 9 of the Act.

Before proceeding to examine the evidence by which the prosecution have sought to establish the existence of the conspiracy and the participation of the appellants therein, I wish to make a few general observations as to the considerations by which, I think, we must be guided in our appraisal of the said evidence in the present case.

As I have had occasion to remark before, it is well settled that conspiracy can seldom, if ever, be proved by means of direct evidence, and has almost invariably to be inferred from circumstantial evidence consisting generally of evidence as to the conduct of the parties on certain occasions and in relation to certain matters. In **R. v. Parsons** ((1702) IWMBL 391) Lord Mansfield told the jury that there could be generally no occasion to prove the actual fact of conspiracy and that the same had to be collected from collateral circumstances. In **Parnoll's Case**((1881) 5 Cox C C 505) Fitzgerald J. observed: *"There is no such necessity that there should be express proof of conspiracy, such as providing that parties actually met and laid their heads together and then and there actually agreed to carry out a common purpose, nor is such proof usually examined. It may be that the alleged conspirators have never seen each other and have never corresponded; one may never have heard the name of the other, and yet by the law they may be parties to the same common criminal agreement."*

In the ***King v. Brisac*** and Scott (7 R.R. 551) the question which directly arose for decision was whether the offence of having conspired to cheat the Crown by fabricating false vouchers for which the Captain and purser of a man of War had been indicted could properly be tried within the body of any county in England or was triable only under the Admirality Commission. In considering the question it became necessary for the Bench to consider also the question as to how the offence of conspiracy could generally be established against a set of persons indicated for such offence. Dealing with that question Grose J. made the following observations: *"Conspiracy is a matter of inference, deduced from certain criminal acts of the parties accused, done in pursuance of an apparent criminal purpose in common between them."*

These observations were cited with approval by the House of Lords in their judgment in **Denis Dowling v. The Queen**((18688) L.R. 3 H.L. 306).

In Barindra Kumar Ghose and others v. Emperor (also known as the **Maniktolla Conspiracy Case**)[61] (37 Cal.478) Sir Lawrence Jenkins C.J., who wrote the main judgment of the Division Bench, held that in a trial for conspiracy the agreement to do the unlawful ct has generally

---

[61] The Maniktala Conscpiracy Case also known as the Alipore Bomb Case or the Muraripukur Conspiracy case. The Alipore Conspiracy Case held at the Alipore Sessions Court in Calcutta. The trial spanned from May 1908 to May 1909. The case dealt with the assassination attempt on Presidency Magistrate Douglas Kingsford in Muzaffarpur by Bengali nationalists Khudiram Bose and Prafulla Chaki in April 1908. Prafulla Chaki committed suicide and Khudiram Bose was arrested and sentenced to death when he was only 18 years old. The other people tried in the case were Aurobindo Ghosh, his brother Barin Ghosh, Satyendranath Bose, Kanailal Dutt, and more than thirty others.

to be inferred from circumstances raising a presumption of a common concerted plan to carry out the unlawful design. Similar observations are to be found in the judgment of the High Court of Lahore in the case of Punjab Singh v. The Crown (I.L.ER. 15 Lah.84) to which a reference has already been made and the judgment of the Nagpur High Court in *B.N. Mukerji and Ors. v. King Emperor* (47 Cr.L.J.69).

In all criminal trials where the guild of the accused is sought to be proved by means of circumstantial evidence, it becomes incumbent on the Court to scrutinise such evidence with the utmost care, always bearing in mind, the well settled rule that in cases dependent upon circumstantial evidence, the incriminating circumstances must, in order to justify the inference of guilt, be wholly incompatible with the innocence of the accused and incapable of explanation upon any reasonable hypothesis other than that of his guilt. As observed by a Bench of the Chief Court of the Punjab in *Gurudatt v. Emperor* (136 P.L.R. 1909) there must be a chain of evidence so far complete as not to leave reasonable ground for a conclusion therefrom consistent with the innocence of the accused. While this is true of all criminal trials, a Court has to be particularly careful in dealing with the offence of conspiracy in which evidence may be given of statements said to have been made, orally or in writing, and acts alleged to have been done, by any one or more of the alleged conspirators without the knowledge of the others at places for removed from where they have ever been and even at a time when, even according to the prosecution, they were not parties to the alleged conspiracy. In a case like this, there is always the danger of witnesses, even where they are honest and want to speak the truth, quite unconsciously and without meaning it, confusing what they actually saw or heard with inferences which they feel inclined to draw from what they did see or hear and even from what they have otherwise seen or heard. As pointed out by Sir Lawrence Jenkins C.J.

in his judgment in the Maniktolla Conspiracy Case referred to above at Page 508 of the report, in such cases conjecture or suspicion may easily take place of legal proof. The learned Chief Justice has, in his above judgment, made a very pointed reference to the following passage occurring in Baron Alderson's summing up to the jury in *Reg. v. Hedge* (1838, 2 dem 227): *"The mind is apt to take a pleasure in adopting circumstances to one another, and even in straining them a little, if need be, to force them to form parts of one connected whole; and the more ingenious the mind of the individual, the more ...... is it, considering such matters, to over reach and mislead itself, to supply some little link that is wanting, to .... for granted some fact consistent with its previous theories and necessary to render them complete."*

It is particularly necessary to keep constantly in mind the above warnings of Baron Alderson and Sir Lawrence Jenkins in weighing the evidence in the present case where the person to murder whom the accused are said to have conspired amongst themselves and with others, and who was in fact murdered, according to the prosecution, in pursuance of the alleged conspiracy, was one whom the overwhelming majority of his countrymen including, presumably most of the witnesses and those charged with the duty of investigating the case, regarded with feelings of the highest esteem and deepest affection and whose assassination by one from amongst themselves had filled them with shame and indignation.

The events which the prosecution has sought to prove in the present case and from which we are asked to draw the inference as to the existence of the conspiracy fall under three heads via:

Events which took place up to 20th January, 1948 when a gun-cotton-slab was admittedly exploded by Madanlal at the Birla House.

Events which took place after the above explosion upto 30th January, 1948 when

Mahatma Gandhi admittedly shot dead by Nathuram Godse with a pistol; and

Events which took place subsequent to the aforesaid act of Nathuram Godse, thee events being merely those …. evidence the subsequent conduct and movements of the various accused up to the times of their respective arrests.

The principal witness relating to the events falling under the fist head is Digambar R. Badge, the approver, P.W.57. A very large part of the arguments addressed to us by Nathuram Godse and the counsel appearing on behalf of the other appellants, quite naturally, was directed against his evidence. The learned Special Judge while dealing with his evidence has observed:

> **"The** examination and the cross-examination of the approver went on from 20/07/1948 till 30/07/1948. He was cross-examined for nearly seven days. There was thus an ample opportunity to observe his demeanour and the manner of his giving evidence. He gave his version of the facts in a direct and straightforward manner. He did not evade cross-examination or attempt to evade or fence with any question. It would not have been possible for anyone to have given evidence so unfalteringly stretching over such a long period and with such particularity in regard to the facts which had never taken place. It is difficult to conceive of anyone memorizing so long and so detailed a story if altogether without foundation."

It was pointed out by Nathuram Godse that Badge had given his evidence in Marahti which language, the learned Special Judge did not understand and that, therefore, the latter was not in a position to make any estimate of his demeanour while he was in the witness-box. I do not agree that merely because the learned Judge did not understand the language in which the witness gave his evidence

and had, therefore, to make use of the services of an interpreter as he was not also in a position to form an estimate as to his general demeanour while he was in the witness-box. It certainly did not require any knowledge of the language in which the evidence was given to be able to observe if the witness gave his answers to the questions put to him in cross-examination without any attempt at evasion or prevarication.

After a very careful perusal of the approver's evidence, the impression left on my mind is that generally he gave his evidence in a straightforward manner and without any attempt at prevarication and without betraying an anxiety to withhold facts. Questioned about his original financial position and antecedents he quite candidly admitted that, on coming to Poona, he had been able to secure a job carrying a salary of only Rs. 18/- or Rs. 20/- *per mensem* after resorting to satyagrahaat the residence of the Chairman of the Municipal Board. He also admitted that when he started the Shastra Bhandar in 1942 he had to dispose of his household goods in order to be able to raise a small capital of Rs. 75/- or Rs. 100/- for the purpose. He made no secret of his having exploited the communal troubles and the trouble in Hyderabad to enrich himself by means of illicit traffic in arms, ammunition and explosives. He unhesitatingly admitted facts which he need to have admitted and which might be made use of against the prosecution. For instance, he admitted that Godse was suffering from headache on the 20th January. He also admitted having been frequently visited, while he was in police custody, by his brother Narayan who is a police employee at Poona. In answer to questions put by the counsel for Karkare about the latter's activities in connection with refugee work he stated: ***"He is greatly interested in the Hindu refugee work. I know that he spends money over the Hindu refugee work. Nathuram V Godse and Apte had told me that he was giving free board and lodging to the Hindu refugees. Karkare had been introduced to me by Apte. It was at that time***

that he was going to Noakhali to do the Hindu refugee work."

I do not of course suggest that his testimony should be placed on any higher plane than that of an ordinary accomplice or that it is not necessary, in his case, to insist on all those safeguards which, according to every civilized system of jurisprudence, must be satisfied before conviction can be based on such testimony. All that I mean is that if such safeguards are satisfied there do not exist any *a priori* grounds for its wholesale rejection.

In support of the plea for the wholesale rejection of the approver's evidence, our attention was drawn to a number of events narrated by him and it was pointed out that there was no independent corroboration of his testimony as regards these events. It is, however, not necessary that every fact deposed to by an approver should be so corroborated. The law on the subject of accomplice evidence was re-examined and re-stated by the House of Lords in 1916 in Rex v. Baskerville ((1917) 86 L.J.R.28), a Bench of five Law Lords presided over by Viscount Reading, C.J., having been specially constituted for the purpose, in view of some conflicting decisions on the subject. The following passages appearing at Pages 33 and 34 of the report lay down what their Lordships considered to be the correct law applicable to the subject: "After examining the authorities to the present day we have come to the conclusion that the public opinion of the law upon this point is that stated in Reg. v. Stubb, (25 L.J.M.C.16) by Baron Parke, namely, that the evidence of an accomplice must be confirmed not only as to the circumstances of the crime, but also as to the identity of the prisoner. The learned Baron does not mean that there must be confirmation of all the circumstances; as we have already stated, that is unnecessary.

It is sufficient if there is confirmation as to a material circumstance of the crime and of the identity of the accused in relation to the crime Baron Parke gave this opinion as the result of 25 years' practice.

It was accepted by the other Judges, and has been much relied upon in later cases. ******** We hold that evidence in corroboration must be independent testimony which affects the accused by connecting or tending to connect him with the crime. In other words, it must be evidence which implicates him—that is which confirms in some material particular not only the evidence that the crime has been committed, but also that the prisoner committed it.   **.....test** applicable to determine the nature and extent of the corroboration is thus the same, whether the case falls within the rule of practice at common law or within that class of offences for which corroboration is required by status.[62] ******
The nature of the corroboration will necessarily vary according to the particular circumstances of the offence charged. It would be in a high degree dangerous to attempt to formulate the kind of evidence which would be regarded as corroboration except to say that corroborative evidence is evidence which shows or tends to show that the story of the accomplice that the accused committed the crime is true, not merely that the crime has been committed; but that it was committed by the accused.

The corroboration need not be direct evidence that the accused committed the crime: it is sufficient if it is morally circumstantial evidence of his connection with the crime. A good instance of this indirect evidence is to be found in *Reg v. Birkett* (8 Car and P.732).Were the law otherwise, many crimes which are usually committed between accomplices in secret, such as incest, offences with females, or the present case (sodomy), could never be brought to justice."

The Counsel for one of the appellants pleaded for the outright rejection of the approver's evidence in this case on the ground that most of the facts stated by him being true and he having only interposed, in a very clever and astute manner, an

---

[62] Continuity from the previous page (Page 260-261) seems affected. Readers are to verify from original source Mahatma Gandhi Murder papers available with the National Archives, New Delhi. Eds.

untruth here and an untruth there, with the object of presenting a wholly distorted picture to the Court, the ordinary rule relating to accomplice evidence, as laid down in the judgment noticed above, and now generally accepted as the Rule of Law by Courts in this country, should not be applied. The argument though ingenious is hardly sound Speaking generally where the major and the material facts deposed to by an approver are either admitted or otherwise proved to be true, their truth reflects also on the other facts disclosed by his evidence, and, in a very large majority of cases, is found to render their existence so highly probable that, to use the language employed by the Legislature in the interpretation clause in the Indian Evidence Act in defining the expression "proved", a prudent man aught, under the circumstances, to act on the supposition that they exist. As the discussion that is to follow will show, if the events narrated by the approver in the present case which have been corroborated by the other evidence are held to have actually taken place, the conclusion becomes inescapable that most, at least, of the other incidents related by him must also be true.

From what I have said above I should not be understood to lay down that independent corroboration of the material parts of the evidence of an accomplice imposes any obligation on the Court to accept the rest of his evidence or relieves it of the duty to scrutinise such evidence, nor is that, I imagine, the effect of the House of Lord's judgment quoted above or of the decisions of the Courts in this country in which the principles laid down in that judgment have been followed. The law, as I understand it, is that while the uncorroborated testimony of an accomplice can, in no circumstances, justify conviction and, has, therefore, unless it is corroborated in the manner and to the extent indicated by their Lordships, to be completely ignored, a Court may, on such corroboration, accept even the uncorroborated part of his testimony. This of course always presupposes

that the Court is satisfied that there is otherwise no ground for rejecting such testimony or any part thereof. If it finds that the whole or any part of such testimony is either inherently improbable or unnatural, or is inconsistent with other admitted or proved facts, there is nothing to prevent it from rejecting the same, and indeed it will be its duty to do so. I do not entirely ruled out the possibility of the evidence of an accomplice being manipulated[63] in such a manner that incontestable facts which are easily capable of being proved by means of other evidence are interspersed with untruth, but I also cannot rule out the possibility of the accused cleverly admitting just those out of the f…. deposed to by his accomplice of which independent corroboration is available. Such a subterfuge cannot, however, destroy the effect of the corroboration of the accomplice's evidence in the manner required, and no Court can reasonably be expected to entertain the plea that in such a case the accomplice's evidence should be eliminated from consideration because the facts regarding which it has been corroborated are only those which were otherwise admitted by the accused.

It was also contended that the evidence of the approver should be completely disregarded because his statement was recorded by the police at quite a late stage of the investigation and after recording the statements of almost all the witnesses who were produced to corroborate him, and because even in Court he was not examined till at a somewhat late stage of the trial when quite a number of the above witnesses had already given evidence. It was urged that his statement as recorded by the police was presumably cocked in the light of the other statements recorded earlier and made to fit in with them. It was further urged that at the time the witnesses whose evidence was subsequently relied on as corroborating the approver's testimony were

---

63 The underlined word is not conspicuously readable. Readers are to verify the same from the Mahatma Gandhi Murder Papers available with the National Archives, New Delhi. Eds.

examined the accused did not know at all what the latter was going to say, and could not, accordingly, cross-examine them on and in the light of the facts deposed to by him. It was pointed out that the least the Court should do, under the circumstances, is to disregard the evidence supposed to corroborate the approver and, in the result to reject the latter's testimony as uncorroborated. After giving due weight to all the arguments addressed to use in support of these contentions I feel no hesitation in holding that they are wholly devoid of force. Digambar R. Badge, the approver, was arrested at Poona on the 31st January, 1948. The evidence of Mr. Deulkar, Deputy Superintendent of Police, C.I.D. Poona, P.W.123 shows that on that day he was interrogated by the witness for about an hour although his statement was not regularly recorded. On the 2nd February Badge was ordered by Mr. Nagarvala, Deputy Commissioner of Police, P.W.133, who eventually came to hold the Principal Charge of the Investigation, to be brought to Bombay. In pursuance of these orders he was brought to Bombay while Mr. Deulkar flew to Delhi on 3rd February, presumably pursuant to some information received by him in the course of Badge's interrogation on the 31st January. On 4th February Madanlal was flown to Bombay by the Delhi Police. At Bombay, Badge and Madanlal were interrogated after having been confronted with each other. On 5th February Badge *was* taken by Mr. Nagarvala and Sub-Inspector Pradhan (P.W.130) to Poona. Presumably in consequence of some information furnished by him, the police looked for Gopal V Godse and Shankar Kistayya. Gopal was arrested the same day in the manner already indicated and Shankar on the day following. On the 8th February Badge with Shankar and Gopal was again taken to Bombay where some recoveries were made on that day and on the day following in pursuance of information supplied by him. On 9th February the statement of Dixitji Maharaj (P.W.77) was recorded by Sub-Inspector Pradhan at Bombay at his residence due to his indisposition,

also presumably on information supplied by Badge. On similar information Aitappa Krishna Kotian, taxi-driver, P.W.80, was also traced on the same day at Bombay. On 10th February Shankar was taken by Mr. Nagarvala in a plane to Delhi where, on the day following three hand-grenades and some other stuff were dug out by him from two places in the jungle behind the Hindu Mahasabha Bhawan which purported to have been interred by Shankar at those places under the orders of Badge on 20th January, 1948 after the explosion. After his return to Bombay Mr. Nagarvala recorded the statements of Hon'ble Mr. Morarji Desai, Home Minister, Bombay, and Professor J.C. Jain on the 13th and the 17th February respectively in respect of some *communication said to have been made to the latter by Madan Lal during his stay at Bombay before he left for Delhi on 15th January. On 21st and 22nd February he recorded the statement of Badge. I do not see any reason to suppose that there was any unreasonable delay in recording this statement. Much less is there any reason to assume that the statement was cooked on the basis of, and with reference to, any other statements recorded by the police in the meanwhile. On the other hand, these statements themselves appear to have been recorded on information received from Badge himself during the course of his interrogations. It has to be remembered that on 21st and 22nd February there was no indication that Badge would turn the King's evidence. In the circumstances, there could, at the time, be no motive for the police to cook his statement in the manner suggested with a view to call in service[64] the persons who had already been examined to supply the necessary information.*

It is true that Badge was not examined as a witness till after 56 other prosecution witnesses

---

[64] It appears that some one or two words available in the right margin side of the scanned copy of the typed copies of the judgment, are missing in this sentence. Readers to refer the original documents pertaining to Mahatma Gandhi Murder Papers available in the National Archives, New Delhi. Eds.

had given evidence. It was not suggested by any of the learned counsel for the appellants that this amounted to any illegality or irregularity affecting the validity of the trial. It was indeed conceded that it is ordinarily the right of the prosecution to produce their witnesses in any order they choose. The contention was that the accused had been very seriously prejudiced by reason of the witnesses whose evidence was subsequently sought to be made use of for corroborating Badge's testimony having been examined before Badge and their consequent inability to cross-examine them in the light of his deposition. A reference to the record shows that out of the 56 witnesses examined before Badge, the evidence only of Mehar Singh (P.W.9), Surjit Singh (P.W.14), Shrimati Sulochana Devi (P.W.15), Chhotu Ram (P.W.16) and Bhur Singh (P.W.17) is being used to corroborate his evidence with regard to two of the incidents that took place on the 20th January, 1948. The evidence in corroboration of his testimony regarding the incidents that took place before the 20th was produced after he had himself been examined. Of the five witnesses mentioned above we expressly indicated, while hearing the appellants' arguments, that, subject of course to what the learned counsel for the Crown might have to say on the subject, we did not feel inclined to attach any importance to the evidence of Mehar Singh (P.W.9) Mr. Daphtary having said not a word touching the evidence of this witness, and having made no reference at all to the incidents sought to be proved by means of his evidence, he may be left out altogether. That leaves only four witnesses regarding the incident of the 20th evening at the Birla House. I would not rule out altogether the possibility of the accused having been handicapped, to some extent in the cross-examination of these witnesses by reason of their not being in a position to anticipate Badge's evidence on the subject, and would certainly keep this fact in mind when I come to consider their evidence on its merits. I, however, cannot see my way to hold that the approver's evidence should, on that account, be regarded as uncorroborated even to the extent to which corroboration is sought for it from such evidence much less can I reject it in its entirety.

I propose to deal with the relevant events in their chronological order and to consider the evidence relating to each event separately.

I have said in an earlier part of this judgment that Badge had been previously supplying arms and ammunition to Apte. This fact was admitted by Apte in his statement before the learned Special Judge. Reference may in this connection be made to the following passage at Page 70 in the Second Volume of the paper-book: "I have been knowing Badge for about four years. He did supply me some arms and ammunition for the State Congress in connection with the affairs of the Hyderabad State."

According to the evidence of Badge, he met Apte at Yerandawane while he himself was on his way to Bhor State on a pilgrimage and was told by him that they wanted him to supply some arms and ammunition to them. Badge further says that he returned to Poona about eight or ten days after this and within a day or two of his arrival at Poona he was able to arrange to get the stuff required. Thereafter he went to the Hindu Rashtra Office and informed Apte who told him that the members of his party had gone out and would purchase the stuff after their return.

According to Badge's evidence Apte visited the Shastra Bhandar in the last week of December 1947 and told the witness that the stuff would be collected by Karkare in two or three days.

Badge goes on to say that Apte came to his place at about 6 or 6.30 p.m. on 9th January, 1948 and told him that Karkare and others would be seeing him in a short time and requested him to show the stuff to them. Sometime after Apte had left, Karkare accompanied by Pahwa, Om Parkash and Chopra came to the witness's place and after introducing his three companions to him asked him to show them the stuff. Thereon Badge asked Shankar, his servant, to bring the stuff which on being brought was found to consist of gun-cotton-slabs, hand-grenades, cartridges, pistols, and fuse wire. It was shown by Badge to Karkare and his companions who left after having looked thereat. The next day at about 10 a.m. Apte again came to Badge's place and took him to Hindu Rashtra Office where Nathuram V Godse was doing his work in a tent pitched in the compound which was presumably being used him as his office. Apte asked Badge to supply them with two gun-cotton-slabs, five hand-grenades and two revolvers. Badge expressed his inability to supply any revolvers. He, however, expressed his readiness to supply the rest of the material asked for. Apte asked for the gun-cotton-slab and hand-grenades being delivered at Bombay. Badge agreed but told Apte that he would be unable to do so immediately because he wanted to go to his village Chalisgaon to sell his house. Apte agreed and told Nathuram V. Godse who had in the meanwhile come out of the tent that Badge was willing to hand-over the stuff and that their one work was over. Both Apte and Nathuram Godse then told Badge that the stuff was to reach Hindu Mahasabha Office at Dadar by the evening of the 14th January. To this Badge agreed.

On the 12th January, 1948 Badge, according to his evidence, went to his village Chalisgaon and sold the house. He returned to Poona the following day i.e., the 13th January and on his arrival at that place told his servant Shankar in the evening that they had to reach Bombay with the stuff by the evening of the next following day. The stuff was accordingly put in a khaki cloth bag. The stuff put in the bag consisted of two gun-cotton slabs, five hand-grenades and fuss wire and detonators.

It may be observed that all the above mentioned incidents narrated by Badge wee denied by the accused and that excepting the evidence of Badge himself there is no independent evidence to prove them. To what extent his evidence about these incidents can be said to receive any support from the other circumstances will be seen later. Much capital

was made by Nathuram Godse and the counsel for the other appellants of the prosecution having failed to produce Om Parkash and Chopra who were said to have accompanied Karkare and Madanlal at the time they went to see the stuff at the place of Badge. The evidence led by the prosecution shows that every possible effort was made to trace the aforesaid persons but the prosecution found themselves unable to do so. I am in the circumstances satisfied that no inference adverse to the prosecution can possibly bed drawn from their omission to produce them.

In order to prove that Karkare was not a stranger to Badge and had actually had dealings with him in relation to arms and ammunition the prosecution produced and relied on P.90 consisting of eight pieces of a torn letter pasted on a piece of paper purporting to have been written by Karkare to Badge on 29th May 1947. The letter was in Marahti and translated in English reads as follows:

"To Badge,

The person who has come to you is a trustworthy gentleman. I could not come yesterday due to great difficulties. I am specially sending this man. You must have received Rs. 400/- sent by telegraphic money-order. The copies of the 'pusta' which you have brought may be sent with that person, who has been instructed in regard to the arrangements made for the payment. Every time ten 'vastu' are to be handed over, and for each 'vastu' Rs. 150/- should be charged. I will come on the 2nd and settle my account. Do not worry about moneys. The gentleman from Bombay must have arrived. Confusion arose because the wire from you was received one day late."

The eight pieces of the torn letter were recovered from the possession of Badge's wife on 23rd May, 1948 by Sub-Inspector Pradhan (P.W.130). The aforesaid witness has stated that he had been asked by Mr. Nagarvala to see that she did not carry any papers or articles with her when she went to have an interview with her husband that on finding her carrying these pieces he seized them and had a **panchnama** or recovery list prepared after sending for the **panches** or the witnesses to the recovery, P.229 being the recovery list. Badge in his evidence stated that the letter had been written by Karkare to him and that the words **"pustak'** and **"vastu"** i.e. books and articles as used therein connected in fact bombs. In explaining the circumstances under which his wife carried on her person the torn pieces of the letter when they were seized on 23rd May, 1948 Badge has stated that when his wife came to see him sometime in May 1948 he had asked her to go back to Poona and to bring the Promissory-Notes and the letters that she found to be important ones and that she had again come to see him 15 or 16 days later. He was unable to tell whether she had actually brought the pieces of the letter which now make up P.90 with her on this occasion and in pursuance of the said request for Promissory Notes and letters being brought. Badge's wife from whose person the said pieces of the letter are said to have been recovered has not been examined and there is no other evidence to explain the circumstances under which these pieces happened to come into her possession and were brought by her with herself when she went to see her husband. Excepting these pieces no other letter or *pro-note* is said to have been recovered from her on that occasion or on any other occasion. Although Badge has said that the letter was written by Karkare, he does not profess to be acquainted with this handwriting and does not even say that he identifies the writing as that of Karkare. A handwriting expert was examined before the learned Special Judge who after comparing P.90 with some specimen writings of Karkare obtained by the police from him while he was in custody deposed that the writing in P.90 was that of Karkare. The learned Special Judge, however, rejected this evidence and did not choose to place any reliance on P.90. The learned Advocate-General did not, in his address to us seek to place any reliance on the evidence of the handwriting expert. He, however,

drew our attention to the following passage in the statement of Badge made in answer to questions put to him in cross-examination by the counsel for Karkare: *"Exhibit P.90 is in eight pieces pasted on a piece of paper. The pieces have not been pasted on the paper under my instructions. It is not true that the price of Rs. 150/- per article as given in the letter refers to the price of steel waist-coats. Had it referred to steel waist-coats, then it would have been mentioned so in so many words with impunity. It is true that the T.M.O. for a sum of Rs. 400/- was not sent to me direct."*

It was suggested by the learned counsel that the statement was made in answer to questions containing a suggestion that the word **"vastu"** as used in P.90 connoted a steel waist-coat and also a suggestion that the telegraphic money-order of Rs. 400/- mentioned therein had not been sent to Badge direct but to someone else. It was urged that these suggestions must be taken as implied admissions of the letter being in the handwriting of Karkare. Our attention was also drawn to an application made by the Counsel for Karkare on 29th July, 1948 i.e. on the day following that on which Badge was cross-examined by him with reference to P.90, which is to be found printed at Page 59 in the 6th Volume of the paper-book. It was contended that in the second part of the application objection was taken to the **admissibility of P.90 on the ground that it was a torn document and as such a document which did not exist according to law and could not be considered as a valid and legal piece of evidence, but there was no denial of its being in the handwriting of Karkare.** It must confess that there is considerable force in these contentions of the learned Advocate-General. However after giving my very careful thought to the question I find myself unable to hold P.90 to have been proves satisfactorily to be in the hand of Karkare. The questions in cross-examination in answer to which the above quoted statement was made by Badge might have been intended to imply no more than this that the word **"vastu"** as used in the letter by whomsoever it was written need not necessarily have meant a bomb but could have been used in an altogether different sense and that no telegraphic money-order of Rs. 400/- was ever received by Badge from the writer of the letter whoever he was. Similarly it might be that at the time of making the application dated 29th July, 1948 the counsel wanted to give only the ground on which, he thought he could ask for the absolute exclusion of P.90 from the record. The question whether P.90 was in the handwriting of Karkare was a different question which had to be decided on a consideration of the relevant evidence. The counsel could evidently not ask for the total exclusion of P.90 from the record as being no evidence in the eyes of law on the ground of its not being in the hand of Karkare because that matter could not be decided except after a consideration of the evidence and therefore not before the conclusion of the trial. In these circumstances and in view of the circumstances under which P.90 purports to have been seized I could not treat it as any evidence of any previous dealings between Badge and Karkare in illicit arms.

On 13th January, 1948 Nathuram V. Godse assigned in favour of Mrs. Champutai Narayan Apte wife of Narayan D. Apte his life policy for Rs. 2,000/- which he held in the Oriental Government Security Life Assurance Company, Limited, by means of an endorsement which was attested by Apte himself, vide P.129. On the next following day i.e., on the 14th January, 1948 Nathuram assigned his other life policy for Rs. 3,000/- in the same Company in favour of Mrs. Sindhutai Gopal Godse, wife of Gopal Godse, by means of a similar endorsement which was also attested by Narayan D. Apte vide P.128.

On the same day Gopal V. Godse made an application for leave for seven days, from 15th January, 1948 to 21st January, 1948, it being stated in the application that the leave was needed for some immediate farm affairs at his village. P.132

is the original application. This application was forwarded by the applicant's immediate officer with a recommendation for its being granted. It, however, appears that when it came before the final sanctioning authority it was discovered that the applicant had to appear before some Board on the 16th January. The final order passed on the application accordingly was that the applicant could avail of the leave after the 17th January.

On the same day i.e., 14th January, 1948 Gopal V. Godse was admittedly paid a sum of Rs. 250/- by his brother Nathuram Godse. There is an entry to that effect in Nathuram's diary Exhibit P.218. In his statement in Court Nathuram has said that the aforesaid sum was paid by him to Gopal on that day when he came to have his lunch with him, it being a Maghar shakrant day, inasmuch as Gopal had asked for it. The significance of the entry in the diary lies in this that the sum of Rs. 250/- paid to Gopal seems to form a part of the fund of Rs. 2000/- which evidently was earmarked by Apte and Nathuram for some purpose, which after some disbursements on the 14th January 1948 was divided into two lots, and out of which admittedly the sum required for booking air accommodation for the two from Bombay to Delhi was spent. The precise implications of this will be considered later.

Nathuram Godse and Apte left Poona for Bombay by the Poona Express which started from Poona at 3.20 or 3.30 p.m. They travelled in a 2nd class compartment. This fact is proved by Miss Shantabai B. Modak, a film actress, P.W.60, who was their co-passenger in the same compartment and whose brother, who had come to receive her at Dadar Railway Station, gave them a lift in his jeep car upto Savarkar Sadan from the said Railway Station. These facts deposed to by Miss. Shantabai was admitted by both Nathuram and Apte. Miss Shantabai also gave evidence with regard to the conversation which the aforesaid Nathuram and Apte had with her brother in the car. According to her on her brother saying that he was thinking of disposing of the car they said that they might purchase it adding that for a few days they were not going to be at Bombay, Poona or roundabout and that they would see to the matter on return. She admitted that she had not stated this fact in her statement to the Magistrate recorded under Section 164, Criminal Procedure Code. She explained this omission by saying that she did not consider the matter to be of importance for the case. Nathuram and Apte on being questioned by the learned Special Judge admitted having travelled from Poona to Bombay by the train mentioned by Miss Modak and in the same compartment with her and also admitted having been given a lift by her brother form Dadar Railway Station to Savarkar Sadan. Neither of them was questioned about the conversation which according to Miss Modak they had with her brother *en route*. In their lengthy Written Statements they did not make any reference at all to their having travelled with Miss Modak or to their having been given a lift by her brother. However both of them stated that they had come to Bombay with the avowed object of proceeding to Delhi in order to stage a demonstration by way of protest against the fast undertaken by Mahatma Gandhi which they believed to be intended to coerce the Government of India into paying the sum of fifty-five crores of rupees to the Pakistan Government and may therefore, well have told Miss Modak's brother that they are not likely to be in Bombay or Poona or near about for the next few days. The incident is otherwise of little importance and it is scarcely necessary to lay any emphasis on it. It is, however, important, to note that according to Nathuram although he did agree to Apte's suggestion about staging a peaceful demonstration at Mahatmaji's prayer meeting he was all the while conscious that such demonstration was not likely to prove fruitful. Reference may in this connection be made to the following passage occurring at the end of para 16 of his Written Statement:

"Apte suggested the same old method to stage a strong but peaceful demonstration at the prayer meetings of Gandhiji. I consented to this half-heartedly, because I could easily see its futility. However I agreed to join him as no alternative plan was as yet fixed in my mind."

The implications of this part of Nathuram's statement will be considered later.

According to Badge's evidence he and Shankar also left Poona for Bombay by the evening train on the 14th taking with themselves the bag containing the stuff mentioned above which Badge had undertaken to deliver to Apte and Nathuram at Bombay the same evening.

Nathuram Godse stressed two points in connection with the alleged journey of Badge from Poona to Bombay. He urged in the first place that if he had undertaken the journey as stated by him in pursuance of an agreement between himself and Nathuram and Apte, he could not have started from Poona without contacting the aforesaid two persons after his return from Chalisgaon and reassuring himself that they would meet him as agreed at Bombay that evening. It was next urged by him that it was rather queer that although he and Shankar travelled by the same train by which he himself and Apte travelled, Badge did not care or choose to contact them at any place *en route*. I, however, can see no force in either of these contentions. In the absence of any communication from Apte or Nathuram which could be taken to modify the previous agreement and in the absence of any other indication that they had changed their minds there was no necessity for Badge to entertain any doubt about Nathuram and Apte being in Bombay at the proper time as already agreed or to seek further assurance that they were still ready and willing to perform their part of the agreement. The second contention presupposes that Badge and Shankar travelled by the same train by which Apte and Nathuram had travelled, namely, the Poona Express, although there is no evidence at all on the record to that effect. Badge undoubtedly says that he and Shankar left by an evening train but there may be other trains leaving Poona in the evening than the Poona Express. Be that as it may, even if they did travel by the same train, undoubtedly Badge and Shankar did not travel by the 2nd class. They would, therefore, be in different compartments separated from each other by some distance. In any case, Badge, who was carrying with himself very objectionable stuff, could not be expected to come out of his compartment at any Wayside Station[65] in order to try to make a wholly unnecessary contact with Nathuram and Apte, even assuming that he knew that they were also travelling by the same train and had not left earlier.

According to Badge, he and Shankar got down at Dadar Railway Station and immediately proceeded to the Hindu Mahasabha Office. On getting there they did not find Apte or Nathuram Godse there. Badge on making an enquiry was told that they would be arriving in a short time. He waited for them for about half an hour where after he and Shankar left the office to take some tea. While going out they met Apte who told Badge that arrangements had to be made for keeping the stuff and asked him to come with him. Badge, according to his evidence, took the bag from Shankar who was asked to stay at the office. After Badge and Apte had gone four or five paces they met Nathuram on the pavement. The three then proceeded to Savarkar Sadan. On getting there Nathuram and Apte went upstairs with the bag while Badge stayed downstairs. Apte and Nathuram came back after a few minutes. All three then returned to the Mahasabha Office and then left with Shankar in a car which had been brought by Apte. They drove to Dixitji Maharaj's house in Bhuleshwar and finding him asleep (it being already 10 or 10.30 p.m.) the bag was left with a servant. As stated by Badge, when they

reached Dixitji's house Shankar was asked to sit in the hall while the three of them went into the house. They asked the servant of Dixitji Maharaj to keep the bag in the house and told him that they would take the bag back next morning. Badge says that he had said to the servant that the bag would be taken back by himself, Apte, and Nathuram. The servant to whom the bag containing the stuff is said to have been made over had been, according to Dixitji Maharaj, in his service for about 12 or 13 months. Badge says that he knew that servant before and that the latter was fully aware of his dealings with Dixitji Maharaj. Badge further says that he used to deliver stuff to Parwin Chandar Sethia at Dixitji's place and had so delivered stuff worth thousands of rupees. This is also admitted by Dixitji Maharaj.

Badge has not given any indication as to the person or persons from whom he made enquiries about Nathuram and Apte after his arrival at the Mahasabha Office. As we proceed with the consideration of the rest of his evidence we will find further references to incidents which are said to have taken place at that place and when we come to his evidence about the events said to have taken place at Delhi we will come across a number of quite important incidents connected with the Delhi Hindu Mahasabha Bhawan. No evidence has been produced by the prosecution either from the Bombay Mahasabha Office or from the Delhi Mahasabha Bhawan to corroborate Badge's evidence about these incidents. On behalf of the appellants much capital has been made of this fact and it has been contended that the Court should draw therefrom an inference averse to the prosecution. It has been very strenuously urged that in any case the uncorroborated testimony of the approver regarding these incidents should be rejected because corroboration of the testimony was available and yet not availed of.

After giving to this argument all the weight which it deserves I have unhesitatingly reached the conclusion that in the circumstances of this case it will be wholly unjustifiable to draw any inference

---

[65] Wayside Station in Railway parlance means Wayside Railway Station *i.e.* a small Railway station where the traffic will be less. Eds.

adverse to the prosecution from their omission to produce any evidence either from the Mahasabha Office at Bombay or from the Mahasabha Bhawan in Delhi in corroboration of the approver's evidence as regards the incidents which, according to him, occurred at these two places. We have it in the statements of both Nathuram and Apte that whenever they happened to be at Bombay they invariably visited the Mahasabha Office at Dadar. Naturally their relations with the people running the office or otherwise connected therewith would be quite intimate. Both of them profess to have been, and presumably were, quite well known workers of the Hindu Mahasabha and claimed to have played a very important role during the deliberations of the meetings of the working committee of the All India Hindu Mahasabha and of the All India Hindu Convention, both of which were held at Delhi on 9th and 10th August, 1947, when, they say, they and their friends strove very hard to make the Mahasabha adopt a fighting resolution. In the circumstances, it would not be unreasonable to suppose that they had made contacts even in the Mahasabha Bhawan at Delhi. Indeed, while arguing his case, Nathuram himself referred to these contacts in trying to support the statement of Apte as to their having had a private car at their disposal during their sojourn there from 17th to 20th January. Besides, as appears from the statements of some of the police officers examined in this case, immediately after the assassination of Mahatma Gandhi quite a number of people connected with the Hindu Mahasabha at Delhi and other places were placed under arrest. Mr. Savarkar, the foremost leader of the Mahasabha in the country, and the idol of the Maharashtra Hindus, about whom even Badge has said in his evidence that he still regards him not merely as a great Hindu leader but as a devta (God), himself was arrested on 5th February, 1948. Although initially the order for his arrest purported to have been passed under the Bombay Public Security Measures Act, and he was shown as under arrest in connection with the Mahatma Gandhi murder case only from 11th March 1948 it was commonly believed that he had been arrested on account of his supposed complicity in the murder. In these circumstances it would be to put too much strain on human nature to expect any person connected with the Mahasabha to furnish any information to, or otherwise co-operate with, officers charged with the duty of investigating the case, and it is not at all surprising that they were not able to get any clue from the two Mahasabha Office with which we are concerned in the present case or to produce any evidence from there in respect of the relevant incidents.

The position is, however, quite different with regard to the other incident of the 14th night deposed to by Badge i.e., the incident about the bag containing the stuff having been handed over to Dixitji Maharaja's servant. Narayan Vithal Angre is said to be the name of this servant. His statement was recorded by Sub-Inspector Pradhan of the Bombay Police as early as the 16th February, 1948. He was cited as a witness for the prosecution and it is undeniable that he actually came down to Delhi to give evidence. He, however, was sent back without being examined. The explanation given by Mr. Nagarvala for having done so is that his evidence was superfluous, having regard to the evidence already on record of the case. I must confess that I am not in the least impressed by this explanation. The evidence of Dixitji Maharaj, to which a reference will presently be made, no doubt establish that a bag containing some stuff comprising gun-cotton-slabs and hand-grenades had been left with Angre at sometime in the night on the 14th January. There is however, no evidence, except that of Badge himself, that he was, at the time he left the bag with the aforesaid Angre, accompanied by Nathuram and Apte, or, for the matter of that, by anyone. It is true that the identification parade held on 2nd March, 1948 Angre was not able to identify either Apte or Nathuram and could identify only Badge. He could, however, certainly have given evidence as to whether Badge whom he admittedly knew before had come alone or was accompanied by any other person or persons when he handed over the bag to him. had he said that there were two other persons with him at the time, in view of the admitted presence of Nathuram and Apte in Bombay at the time, and in view of his master's evidence about their having come with Badge for the stuff next morning, his evidence would have furnished corroboration of no mean importance for the evidence of Badge regarding the particular incident. In the circumstances, the appellants can, in my judgment, quite legitimately claim that from the fact of the non-production of Angre an inference should at least be drawn that, had he been produced he would not have supported Badge's statement as to two other persons being with him when he came to Dixitji Maharaja's house on the night of the 14th and handed over the bag to him.

According to Badge's evidence, from Dixitji Maharaja's place, he, Shankar, Apte and Nathuram Godse went back in the taxi to the Hindu Mahasabha Office where he and Shankar were asked to get down and he was paid a sum of Rs. 50/- on account of his travelling expenses by Godse to whom the same had been handed over by Apte. In corroboration of his evidence regarding this last incident reliance was placed on Ex.P.323, an entry in Nathuram Godse's diary Ex.P.218, in which there is a note as regards the payment of a sum of Rs. 50/-to one Bandopant on 14th January, the suggestion being that Bandopant was a fictitious name for Badge. In the absence of any evidence to show that by the name Bandopant, Badge was intended to be referred to the learned Special Judge declined to accept this entry as a corroboration of Badge's evidence and I myself see no reason to take a different view.

Badge goes on to say that on entering the Mahasabha premises he was accosted by Madan Lal who enquired from him when he had arrived. According to Badge, he could not recognise Madanlal till the latter reminded him of their interview of the 9th January at Poona. Badge further says that on an enquiry by him as to where Karkare was, he was told by Madanlal that he was at Thana.

There is of course no independent corroboration of this part of Badge's testimony. Mr. Daphtary sought to find corroboration in the following sentence to be found in the statement of Badge made during the course of his cross-examination by Madanlal's counsel: "It is not a fact that Madanlal told me on 14th January 1948 that Om Parkash and Chopra were at Bombay and had come to do refugee work at Chembur."

From the above statement it can, of course, be inferred, and legitimately, that the cross-examining counsel was not denying that the witness and Madanlal had met each to her on the 14th January, I cannot, however, read into the question, in answer where to the above statement was presumably made, that they had met at the Mahasabha Office and at the time and in the manner deposed by Badge. Madanlal has in his statement admitted is presence in Bombay from 12th to 15th January, but has stated that he was, during the above period, staying not at the Mahasabha Office but at the Chembur Camp. It may well be that the question was put by the Counsel in order to elicit, if possible, from the witness an answer in support of this part of Madanlal's statement and to show that the latter and his companions had come to Bombay to do refugee work and not for any other purpose.

In narrating the events of the 15th January, Badge says that t about 8.30 a.m. Nathuram and Apte came to the Hindu Mahasabha Office. Both the wits and Shankar left with them, not yet being ready, not having dressed up, was left behind. The four met Karkare somewhere near the Agrani Printing Press. They all entered the press premises. Shankar was asked by Apte to sit down on the planks lying in front of the press. Apte, Godse, Karkare, and Badge met G.M. Joshi, the Proprietor of the Press. Badge was asked to wait outside the office while others went inside. They came out after about an hour.

Thereafter all of them excepting G.M. Joshi went back to the Mahasabha Office. On reaching there, Karkare asked Madanlal to take his bedding and go with them. In the meanwhile Apte brought a car. All of them excepting Shankar who was left behind got into the car. Madanlal took his bedding also with himself. They drove to the house of Dixitji Maharaj. Madanlal kept his bedding in the hall. All of them then went in further into the interior of the house where they found Dixitji Maharaj. Badge asked Dixitji Maharaj for the bag that he had left there the previous evening. After about an hour or so the bag was produced and was opened by badge who showed the contents to Apte. Thereafter the bag was closed and was handed over to Apte who in turn handed it over to Karkare and asked him to leave for Delhi that evening by the Frontier or the Punjab Mail along with Madanlal. Karkare then handed over the bag to Madanlal and asked him to tie it up in the bedding. Karkare and Madanlal then left the place and went away. After they had left Apte told Dixitji Maharaj that they were proceeding on some important work and asked him to give him a revolver or two. Dixitji Maharaj stated that he had no revolvers and that the pistol which he had he could not give. Apte then requested Dixitji Maharaj to do all that was possible to obtain a revolver for him. Dixitji Maharaj promised to do so. After this the three came out of the house of Dixitji Maharaj.

This part of Badge's evidence is very substantially corroborated by the testimony of Dixitji Maharaj who was examined as P.W 77. As has been pointed out in an earlier part of this judgment, indisputably Badge and Apte were quite well-known to Dixitji Maharaj from before. Madanlal was also known to him by face, although, as he says, he did not know his name till he read the same in the newspapers and learnt about it more definitely t the identification parade held on the 2nd March 1948 when he identified him as the Punjabi body who had visited him for the sale of some books and who was one of the five persons who

had come to his residence on the morning of the 15th January. The three others out of the five whom he identified at the said parade were Nathuram V Godse, Apte and Badge. In his evidence in Court he has stated that the name of the fifth visitor, whom, however, he was unable to identify at the said parade, had been given by Badge at the time of the visit as Karkare.

It may be note that according to the witness, Karkare and Nathuram Godse had come to his place for the first time on the 15 January. Of them, as will presently be seen, Nathuram Godse admittedly met him twice again on the 26th January, once in the morning and a second time in the afternoon at a meeting held at their place under the auspices of Dada Maharaj to consider the situation created by certain inroads committed by the Pakistani Forces into the territories of Jaisalmer State. Both Nathuram Godse and Apte admit having attended this meeting and also the presence of Dixitji Maharaj there. The witness says that when on hearing the name of Godse mentioned as the assassin of Mahatma of Gandhi, he had enquired from Dada Maharaj who Godse was he had been told that he was the same person who had, with Apte, attended the aforesaid meeting. Having met Nathuram Godse thrice, and having heard, within four days of the last interview, about his association with the great national tragedy that had been enacted at Delhi, he, quite naturally, was able to retain a vivid recollection of his features in his memory and identified him at the identification parade. Karkare met only once i.e. on the 15th January. Although Karkare has said to have been in his presence for about forty-five minutes it has to be remembered the Dixitji Maharaj was not too well on that day and was bed-ridden by reason of suffering from scabies. Therefore, he found himself unable to identify him.

The evidence of Dixitji Maharaj is to the effect that on the morning of the 15th January, five persons came to his room on the first floor of his house where he was lying bed-ridden as he was suffering from scabies. Badge asked the witness to produce the bag which he had left at the latter's place with his servant the night before. The witness asked him to give him the description of the particular servant because he himself did not know anything about the matter. While Badge was describing the servant to whom he said he had handed over the bag, the witness's servant named Narayan Vithal Angre, also called Narayan or Angre or Agre, happened to drop in whereon badge at once pointed him out as the servant concerned. The witness thereon asked Angre to bring the bag, if any, handed over to him by Badge. It took Agre about half, or three-quarters of, an hour to fetch the bag. During this interval, the witness asked Madanlal if he was the Punjabi boy who had been to him sometime before to sell some books and got a reply in the affirmative He also enquired from Bade as to who the fifth man with them was and was told that he was Karkareji. Thereafter the witness left and went to the bathroom, which was situate at a distance of about 30 feet from the door of his room, in order to have his bath. It took him about 25 or 30 minutes to walk to the bathroom, have his bath, and walk back. When he entered his room he saw Badge showing the contents of the bag to his four companions and found the five talking amongst themselves although he could not hear their talk. Amongst the articles that he saw were two hand-grenades and two white bricks. He then saw Badge trying to explain to his companions the method of using a hand-grenade. Discovering that Badge was not doing correctly, the witness himself explained to them the correct method, telling them that the spring was to be kept tightly held down and then the pin was to be pulled out the teeth. After this the contents which had been taken out of the bag were placed back into it. Thereafter Nathuram Godse, Karkare, and Madanlal left the room, Badge and Apte remaining behind. The witness asked Badge the object of their visit to his house that morning and of exhibiting those things in his room. The curiosity of the witness had been excited, and the question had been prompted, by the

fact that although his contact with them till then had been in regard to the affairs of the Hyderabad State, and he had at first thought that that visit also was in the same connection, none of them had at the time said anything about those affairs. Both of them told him that they were going on an important mission and asked for a revolver or a pistol. The witness enquired from them the nature of the important mission and told them that he would consider the question of handing over to them a revolver or a pistol on getting the information asked for. However, they both expressed their unwillingness to divulge the nature of their mission to the witness at that stage. As they started to leave the room, the witness asked Badge to stay on. Badge, however, did leave promising to come back later. He did come back after about 15 or 20 minutes and on the witness pressing him again for information about the nature of their mission, at first tried to put him off by telling him that Karkarji was from Ahmednagar and that the Punjabi boy who had come with him was a trustworthy person, and he eventually told him that he could not give him the information asked for. On the witness appealing to him in the name of their previous relations, however, he promised to come to his place the same evening and tell him the nature of the mission on which they were proceeding. According to the witness, Badge did come to his place in pursuance of this promise although he is not quite sure whether it was the same evening or one or two days thereafter. On the occasion of this second visit Badge is said to have asked the witness first to pay the money due to himself from Parvin Chandra Sethia and then to have shown him a revolver telling him that by reason of his not having given them a revolver on their asking for the same a day or two earlier they had to purchase that revolver for Rs. 325/- and that he ought at least to pay them the aforesaid sum. On the witness' replying that he would consider the matter only after he had been told the object for which the revolver was wanted by them, Badge told him that they had collected arms and ammunition worth about Rs. 30,000/- or

Rs. 40,000/- and were proceeding to Kashmir to use those things against the raiders and to do sabotage.

At this stage I propose to confine my attention only to that part of the evidence of Dixitji Maharaj which relates to the incident of the 15th January. I will deal with the rest of his evidence when I discuss the incidents of the 18th January because, according to Badge, his visit to Dixitji's place to which this evidence relates took place on the aforesaid date.

In explaining how he has been able to remember the precise date of Badge and his companions; visit to his place, the witness has stated that an astrologer had prophesied that he would meet with an accident on 17th January, that on the aforesaid date he had a fall as a result whereof he injured himself very badly and that he remembered that Badge and others had visited him two days before the incident. On being asked about the while bricks which he saw Badge showing to the others, the witness said that he did not know, and therefore could not tell, what they were used for.

The evidence of Dixitji Maharaj as regards the incidents of the 15th January was subjected to a very vigorous attack by Nathuram V Godse as well as by the counsel for the other appellants. It was pointed out that according to this witness Nathuram Godse had left with Madan Lal and Karkare and only Apte and Badge had been left in his room when the former requested him for a revolver, whereas according to Badge only Madan Lal and Karkare had left and besides himself and Apte, Nathuram Godse was also in the room when Apte made a request for the revolver. Stress was also laid on a further discrepancy between the statements of Badge and the witness as regards what happened after all had left the witness's room. According to the witness Badge alone came back to his room 15 or 20 minutes thereafter when there was some further conversation between the two, while Badge is quite definite that he did not go back at all to the witness's room after having left the same. Attention was also drawn to the facts that the witness did not depose to having seen more than two hand-grenades and that he did not support Badge's statement as to Apte having asked Karkare to leave with Madan Lal and as to the bag having been made over to Karkare. The witness when asked who had carried the bag from his room and answered that he did not remember. It was urged that in view of the witness's professed anxiety to know what the stuff contained in the bag was meant for, and also in view of his great interest in the Hyderabad movement, he could not have failed to take particular notice of the disposal of the bag. The alleged persistence of Apte and Badge in not disclosing to the witness the object for which they needed the revolver was described as unnatural and inconsistent with their previous relations with him and his brother and their knowledge about the extremely pro-Hindu Sympathies of the two brothers. Lastly, emphasis was laid on the witness's inability to identify Karkare and it was pointed out that no significance at all could be attached to his identification of Nathuram Godse whom he had certainly seen twice on the 26th January.

In attempting to explain the witness's motive for giving false evidence, it was suggested that by reason of his activities in the matter of collection and distribution of illicit arms and ammunition he was in the grip of the police and that it was quite likely that he had given evidence just to save his own skin.

I have given my most careful consideration to all these contentions. They have, however, wholly failed to impress me and I have not been able to discover any reasonable ground for rejecting the testimony of this witness as untrustworthy. Indeed, the more closely I have looked at, and scanned, his evidence, the more convinced have I felt of his being an honest and truthful witness. The evidence given by him appears to me very natural, and the considerations that have been urged in support of the plea for its rejection seem to me really to furnish very reliable indication of its general truth. Had he been giving evidence to order, as was suggested, there was nothing easier for him than to say that the two white bricks he saw Badge showing his companions were gun-cotton-slab, that there were altogether five hand-grenades in the bag, and that the bag was handed over, to his knowledge and in his presence, to Karkare. Like Badge, who had already given his evidence, he could have said that Madan Lal and Karkare left his room together, leaving the other three behind, and that those three also went away after the conversation about the revolver. He need not have stated that Badge came back alone, in pursuance of a request by himself, 15 or 20 minutes after having left with Apte. It is to be remembered that this statement was made by him in examination-in-chief and it is not that it was elicited in cross-examination. The witness could naturally not be interested in all the details of what passed between Badge and his companions while they were in his room, and therefore, remembers only the main incidents. On the bag being brought by Angre, it was quite natural for Badge to show its contents to the others. The witness, on his return from the bathroom saw him doing so. He appears to have noticed only two slabs and two hand-grenades. The remaining thee hand-grenades had either not been taken out of the bag or had been put back by the time the witness arrived. Badge was trying to explain to the others the method of using the hand-grenade and it would, accordingly, not be necessary to keep all the grenades out of the bag. The witness was very well acquainted with hand-grenades and even knew the method of using them and so, on finding Badge unable to do so properly, he himself proceeded to explain to the latter's companions the method of using them. He does not seem to have seen gun-cotton-slabs before and did not know their use and so described them just as white bricks. As soon as he saw the hand-grenades and noticed that those present were anxious to learn how to use them, he became curious to find out with what object the grenades had been brought and for what purpose

they were intended to be used, —— whether they were meant for the object nearest to his own heart, namely, the defence of Hyderabad Hindus against the Razakar menace or for some other purpose. Naturally therefore, the ascertainment of the purpose for which the grenades were meant became his obsession and he lost all interest in other details concerning them.

I have already dealt with the matter of the witness's failure to identify Karkare and his identification of Nathuram Godse. I want here only to refer to one other (o) in this connection which seems to me to furnish a very clear indication of the witness's general honesty in giving evidence. During his cross-examination his attention was drawn to his statement recorded by the Magistrate under section 164, Criminal Procedure Code. In that statement he had expressly said that he was not sure if he would be able to identify anyone except Apte, Badge and the Punjabi boy. At that time he was not even sure of his ability to identify Nathuram Godse, although he had seen him twice even after the 15th January and although at the parade he was actually able to identify him. As regards Karkare, though the witness could not identify him at the parade, he does appear not only to have mentioned his name but also to have given his description in his statement recorded by the police as early as the 9th February. In his cross-examination on behalf of Nathuram Godse and Karkare a distinct question seems to have been put to him on the subject in reply to which he stated: ***"It is a fact that I had given a description of Karkareji that I remembered at the time to the police."***

It is not denied that copies of the police statements of all the witnesses had been furnished to the defence. Accordingly it may be legitimately assumed that when the counsel asked the question to which he got the above reply, he must have had the copy of the witness's police statement in front of him. The fact that he did not pursue the matter any further is clearly indicative of the fact that the witness had given Karkare's description and that too a substantially correct description in his police statement. This I consider to be almost conclusive proof of the witness having actually seen Karkare at his place on the 15th.

As regards the persistent refusal of Badge and Apte to disclose the nature of their mission to the witness in spite of his pressing them to do so on that day and subsequently, I see nothing to be surprised at in this conduct of theirs, assuming that Badge himself was cognizant thereof at the time he and the others met the witness on the 15th because, according to Badge's evidence which will be referred to presently, it was after having come out of the witness's room that the object of the mission was disclosed to him by Nathuram Godse and Apte. Indeed, I would have been surprised if they had acted differently. Both the witness and his elder brother had been associated with the Congress. Although they, at the time, strongly different from it and Mahatma Gandhi's policy vis-à-vis the Muslims and Pakistan and were out to do their utmost to consolidate the Hindu community, they could not reasonably be expected to receive the news about any contemplated attempt on the life of Mahatmaji with anything except feelings of utmost horror. Dada Maharaj has expressly stated that the did not want anything untoward to happen within the Dominion of India and that all that they desired was to arm the Hindus for defensive purposes.

The so-called discrepancies between the statements of the witness and Badge as to whether it was only the latter and Apte or both of them and Nathuram Godse who were left in the former's room after Madanlal and Karkare had left and as to whether Badge alone returned to his room 15 or 20 minutes after having left the same with Apte appear to me to be of no moment at all. They seem to connote nothing more than a mere lapse of memory or some kind of confusion of thought on the part of the one party or the other. When I look at the statements of the two witnesses I feel more inclined to regard it as a case of lapse of memory on the part of Badge. In his obsession to find out the precise nature of the mission mentioned by Apte and considering it to be far easier to draw out Badge by reason of his previous relations and dealings with him, Dixitji Maharaj probably did ask the latter to see him alone, and it is quite obvious that Badge could not and would not turn down any such request proceeding from Dixitji Maharaj.

While on this subject I may note in passing that the existence of this so-called discrepancy is wholly inconsistent with another contention of the appellants, which I have already examined at some length, viz., the contention that the police statement of Badge was recorded later in order to be able to cook it up on the basis of and with reference to the statements of other witnesses whose evidence was eventually to be used as corroborative of the approver's testimony and who had been examined much earlier. Dixitji Maharaj's statement was recorded by the police eleven days before recording the statement of Badge and had the insinuation contained in the above contention any force there would be nothing easier than make Badge say precisely what Dixitji Maharaj had already stated on the subject. We have heard a lot at the Bar about Badge's wonderful capacity for memorising faked stories and coining apparently plausible statements, and I do not think he would have found any difficulty in making his statement to the police fit in with the statement already made by Dixitji Maharaj.

As regards the suggested motive of Dixitji Maharaj for giving false evidence, I consider it to be wholly fantastic. it is quite a notorious fact that collection and distribution of illicit arms and ammunition during the transitional period preceding and immediately following the partition of the country has, in view of the very special circumstances then existing, been generally condoned. The supply of arms and ammunition to the Hindus living on both sides of the border of Hyderabad State in order to arm them for purposes of defence against the daily increasing Razakar atrocities has also been considered in the same light. Quite naturally the authorities concerned did not, and could not be expected to overlook the stern realities of the situation and enforce the letter of the law against activities, though unlawful in a strictly legalistic and technical sense, indulged in with the sole object of suppressing lawlessness and restoring law and order in the real sense of the expression. I cannot believe, therefore, that Dixitji Maharaj in fact found himself in the grip of the police at any time and that a religious and spiritual leader of his position could stoop so low as to perjure himself in a case involving very serious consequences to a number of persons merely to shield himself from legal action for having done. What quite a large number of other highly placed persons had also done with perfect impunity.

For foregoing reasons I feel no hesitation in believing the evidence of Dixitji Maharaj in its entirety, with the result that I hold the following facts deposed to by Badge to have also been otherwise proved by means of independent evidence:

(1) **During** the night of 14th January, Badge handed over to Angre, a servant of Dixitji Maharaj, a bag containing some explosive material consisting of hand-grenades and gun-cotton-slabs;

(2) **In** the morning of the 15th January, Badge accompanied by Apte, Nathuram Godse, Madanlal and Karkare went to Dixitji Maharaj's place to fetch the bag;

(3) **On** being asked to do so, Dixitji Maharaj's servant produced the bag and handed it over to Badge who opened it and showed the contents to his companions. He also tried to explain to them the method of using the grenades. Dixitji Maharaj finding him incapable of doing so, himself explained the method;

(4) **The** bag containing the stuff was taken away by someone of these present; and

(5) **Karkare** and Madanlal at least left the place before Badge and Apte.

Before proceeding further it seems well to notice another point which was stressed by Nathuram Godse, viz., the extreme improbability of five persons having been driven in one taxi to Dixitji Maharaja's house which is situate in the heart of the town, the maximum number of passengers permitted in a taxi being four.

Excepting a statement made at the Bar by Nathuram Godse there is no evidence that no taxi plying for hire in Bombay can carry more than four passengers. Mr. Daphtary, Advocate-General, Bombay stated at the Bar that there were taxis plying the city of Bombay which could lawfully carry more than four passengers. Badge who deposed to five men having driven in the taxi was never questioned on the subject. I accordingly cannot attach any weight to this contention. Be that as it may, if Dixitji Maharaja's evidence as to five persons having arrived at his place on 15th January in the morning is believed, the question whether they went by taxi or otherwise loses all significance. Even if Badge is assumed to have lied in this matter, it is of little consequence. What is material is the presence of five persons at Dixitji Maharaja's house and not the means of conveyance used by them in getting there. On the first point we have got the sworn testimony of Dixitji Maharaj which I consider to be wholly unimpeachable and quite trustworthy. Dixitji Maharaja's

Some stress was also laid on the extremely mercenary character of Badge and it was argued that it was highly improbable that a man like him should undertake to travel as far as Bombay for the delivery of stuff which he himself priced at Rs. 1,150/- without not only satisfying himself that the price would be paid to him at Bombay but without even settling the price. It was, further, argued that it was still more improbable that he handed over the stuff to Apte at Dixitji Maharaj's place when the latter handed it over to Karkare without even asking for the price. In view of the previous dealings and relations between the parties, I can see no force in this argument. It is admitted that Badge had supplied arms to Apte before this and had been duly paid for them. Badge says with regard to the previous dealings that he used to be paid whatever he demanded. He was otherwise also beholden to Nathuram Godse and Apte for the monetary and other help he had been receiving from them. It would, in the circumstances, be unreasonable to expect him to be very rigid in this transaction and to ask for the payment or the settlement of the price before agreeing to leave or actually leaving for Bombay. From the evidence of Dixitji Maharaj It appears that Badge had been delivering the stuff on credit to others also e.g. Sethia and Dixitji Maharaj himself. It may be that in transactions like these delivery cannot always be made for cash and some mutual accommodation is inevitable. Till Apte got the stuff at Dixitji Maharaj's place and handed it over to Karkare there was indeed no occasion for Badge to expect or demand payment because till then the stuff was under his own control. He naturally could not expect to be paid in the presence of Dixitji Maharaj. On leaving his room, as will appear from Badge's evidence, presently to be adverted to, and assuming that evidence to be true, he himself agreed to become a party to the venture and thereafter the question of demanding payment could naturally not arise. The matter was put to Badge and he gave the same explanation.

Badge goes on to say that on coming out of the house of Dixitji Maharaj and while standing in the compound of the temple, Apte asked him if he was prepared to go to Delhi. On being asked the nature of the errand on which they were going to Delhi, Apte told the witness that Tatyarao Savarkar had decided that Nehru, Gandhiji, and Suhrawardy "should be finished" and had entrusted the work to them. Apte asked him to accompany them for the purpose and promised to meet his travelling expenses. He agreed but added that he could not go immediately and would have to go to Poona in order to make arrangements for some household affairs. On this Nathuram Godse said that he also wanted to go to Poona to fetch Gopal who had promised to secure revolvers. After this, the three came out of the temple and got into the taxi. Apte and Nathuram Godse stopped in the Cotton Exchange Building for about 15 to 20 minutes and then dropped Badge and Shankar at the Mahasabha Office. In the evening Madanlal met Badge in front of the Mahasabha Office and told the latter that they had missed the evening train, that Karkare was on the Railway Station with the bedding, that he himself had come on account of some work and that they could be leaving for Delhi by the night train. Badge himself left with Shankar for Poona the same night.

There is no independent corroboration of any of the incidents mentioned in the above paragraph and deposed to by Badge. Of the talk which is said to have taken place between the latter and the other two in the compound of the temple there could naturally be no corroboration because such delicate and confidential talk could not possibly take place within the hearing of any third party. The learned Special Judge has eliminated this incident altogether from consideration. My own view is that if eventually on a consideration of the evidence as a whole, it is found that Apte and Nathuram Godse, and may be any other person or persons had, before coming to Bombay agreed to murder Mahatma Gandhi, had decided to proceed to Delhi, and had ordered the stuff from Badge for the purpose, this part of the evidence of Badge will become so highly probable that it may quite reasonably be held to be true. If Badge's co-operation in the undertaking had to be enlisted, quite naturally, he would, at sometime, have to be told the object thereof, and to be taken into complete confidence. That could have been done either at Poona before leaving for

Bombay or at Bombay before leaving for Delhi. If it was done at all, I consider it far more probable that it was done at Bombay and just after taking over the stuff. The view I am inclined to take about the activities of Badge on the 16th January which will be considered later will appear very considerably to heighten such probability.

Nathuram Godse and Apte admit, in their Written Statements, having met Badge at the Hindu Mahasabha Bhawan at Bombay on the morning of the 15th January. They also admit that it was agreed between them and Badge that the latter would go to Delhi and join them there. They, however, add that he was to go to Delhi to join them in the proposed demonstration. They further say that it was Badge himself who, on being told by Apte the object of their visit to Bombay, had offered to come to Delhi and join them and that they had accepted the offer because they wanted men to back them and to shout slogans. These facts are also mentioned in the oral statement of Apte in Court.

It is not disputed that Nathuram Godse and Apte had, before meeting Badge on the 15th January, already booked their passage in the Air-India plane which was to leave for Delhi at 2 p.m. on the 17th January. It is also an admitted fact that they had booked their passage under false and assumed names, namely, under the names of Mr. D.N. Karmarkar and Mr. S. Marathe. Exs. P.262 and 261 are the passenger tickets purporting to have been issued in the above names on the 15th January 1948. Ex.P.262 is the Reservation Slip for two seats booked for the above-named two passengers, also issued on the same date. The residence of the passengers is given in the slip as "Room No.6 Sea Green Hotel". It is admitted that Nathuram Godse and Apte stayed at the aforesaid hotel during their sojourn at Bombay. Apte, in his oral statement, first tried to explain away the assumption of false names by saying that on going to the Air-India Office sometime on 14th January to reserve two seats for Delhi for 17th January he had met a person who had two tickets for

the aforesaid date which he wanted to get cancelled and that he had purchased from him the said two tickets which were in the name of D.N. Karmarkar and S. Marathe. He, however, appears to have at once realized the futility of this explanation in view of the date of issue as noted in the passenger tickets and the Reservation Slip. He, accordingly, admitted that even if he had purchased the tickets direct from the Booking Office he would have purchased them under assumed names, and offered the following explanation for this: *"The pitch of the editorials in the Agrani (Hindu Rashtra) had been rising higher and higher before 15th January 1948. The Government had held out a threat that if in future any articles in the paper tended to communal strifes or violence they would not rest content with demanding further security but would prosecute us. We have got a letter to the effect in writing with us. Nathuram Godse and I accordingly wanted to keep our identity concealed till we had staged the demonstration as we intended at Delhi."*

I find myself wholly unable to accept this explanation. The letter alleged to have been received from the Government containing a threat of Criminal prosecution has not been produced. The prosecution had called one Prabhakar Laxman Aphale, a Clerk in the District Magistrate's Office at Poona, whose duty it was to attend to press matters and declarations, to produce the records relating to the declarations filed from time to time by Nathuram Godse in respect of Shri Shivaji Printing Works and the "Daily Agrani" and to give evidence regarding orders demanding or forfeiting securities in respect of the said paper. He was examined as P.W.83. Not a single question was put to him about the warning alleged to have been given by the Government in respect of the editorials appearing in the Agrani. On the other hand, it appears from the evidence of this witness that the security deposits aggregating to Rs. 16,000/- that had been forfeited had been returned as a gesture of good-will after 15th August 1947. Assuming, however, that a warning of the kind alleged had actually been received by Nathuram Godse and Apte, or either of them, before 15th January, I would still have no hesitation in rejecting the explanation as wholly unsatisfactory and unconvincing. No proceedings had yet been started against them. The proposed demonstration could possibly not take more than a few days. There could be no reasonable danger of Nathuram Godse and Apte being followed to Delhi and arrested before they could give effect to their intention to stage a demonstration, even if a prosecution had been launched against them on or about the 15th January.

Both Nathuram Godse and Apte have stated that they told Badge, on his offering to go to Delhi and join them in their proposed peaceful demonstration, that they were to leave Bombay on the 17th January. According to the statement of Nathuram Godse, Badge told Apte that he had to give some stuff to Pravin Chandra Sethia and that he would do so in a day or two and see them on the 17th January 1948. Apte's own statement on the subject is more detailed. He says that when he and Nathuram Godse told Badge that they would leave for Delhi on or about the 17th January, the latter told them that he had come down to Bombay with some stuff for Pravin Chandra Sethia which he had kept at the place of Dixitji Maharaj; but that in view of his decision to go to Delhi he would prefer to take it there for sale to refugees or others inclined in that way and thus make much larger profits. Apte says that he told him in reply that they would not allow him to take any stuff with himself and that in case he intended to take any such stuff also with him they would rather not take him as a volunteer and Badge is said to have promised not to take any stuff to Delhi and to have requested Nathuram Godse and Apte to meet him at the Victoria Terminus Railway Station in the morning on the 17th January, the day on which the latter proposed to fly to Delhi.

Nathuram Godse and Apte of course deny having accompanied Badge to the house of Dixitji Maharaj either on the night of the 14th or at any time on the 15th January.

It is an admitted fact that Lal Pahwa and Karkare were at Bombay on the 14th and the 15th January and left for Delhi by the Peshawar Express at 9.30 p.m. on the 15th January. They, however, deny having met Badge, Nathuram Godse or Apte either on the 14th or on the 15th January, and to have accompanied them to the house of Dixitji Maharaj on the 15th. According to them Madan Lal Pahwa had to go to Delhi in connection with the arrangements for his marriage and also with the object of leading a deputation of the refugees to Mahatma Gandhi and place before him their grievances. Karkare is said to have agreed to accompany Madan Lal to help him in both the matters. According to Karkare's Written Statement he was staying at the Chembur Refugee Camp since the beginning of the second week of January and it was there that Madanlal had met him and had requested him to accompany him to Delhi. Madan Lal's statement is that he arrived at Bombay on the 12th January and stayed at the refugee camp till the 15th when he with Karkare left for Delhi.

I will presently show that Madan Lal and Karkare had been at Bombay since before the 12th January. Although excepting the evidence of Badge there is other independent evidence to prove that they stayed at Hindu Mahasabha Bhawan, the probabilities of the case do seem to point to that conclusion. We will presently see that an order for the arrest and detention of Karkare had been passed by the Home Government, Bombay, on or about the 9th January 1948. We will also presently see that after that Karkare had been doing everything possible to keep his identity concealed. In the circumstances it is highly improbable that he would stay at a more or less public lace like the refugee camp. It is true that by reason of his association with refugee work the atmosphere at the camp could not be assumed to be hostile to him. Still all kinds of people would be coming to the camp and it would be scarcely a place for a person hiding himself from the law to stay at. There would be more privacy in the Hindu Mahasabha Office and greater chances for the concealment of his identity by Karkare. Whenever, however, they came to Bombay, and wherever they had been staying, and whether or not Nathuram Godse and Apte met Badge on the night of the 14th and accompanied him in a taxi to Dixitji Maharaj's place for depositing the stuff there, as held by me above, Karkare and Madan Lal, as also Apte and Nathuram Godse did accompany Badge to the house of Dixitji Maharaj on the morning of the 15th when the bag containing gun-cotton-slabs and hand-grenades which Badge either alone or accompanied by Apte and Nathuram Godse had left with Dixitji Maharaj's servant the night before was taken back.

Professor J.C. Jain P.W.67 to whom reference has already been made in an earlier part of this judgment and Angad Singh P.W.72, a friend of the aforesaid Professor Jain, have given some evidence with regard to some of the activities of Madanlal during the period of his sojourn at Bombay. Professor Jain has also given evidence in respect of a visit paid to him by Karkare in the company of Madanlal. The Hon'ble Mr. Morarji Desai, Home Minister, Bombay Government P.W.78 has given evidence in respect of some information conveyed to him by Professor Jain on the 21st January regarding some communication made to him by Madanlal a few days earlier. I consider the present to be a proper stage for the consideration of the evidence of these three gentlemen.

Professor Jain is an M.A. of the Benaras University and Ph.D. of the Bombay University and, at the material time was a Professor of Hindi and Arghmagadhi in the Ram Narain Ruia College, at Bombay. The college is situate at Matunga quite close to Dadar. Angad Singh, as graduate and a textile broker seems to be a very intimate friend of Professor Jain. He lives at Lady Jamshed Ji Road, his house being only about two minutes walk from that of Professor Jain.

Angad Singh has been a congressman and according to him, he first came into contact with Professor Jain in connection with his electioneering campaign when he sought Election to the Provincial Congress Committee. Being a socialist, he left the Congress when his party decided to secede therefrom. Reference has already been made to the circumstances under which Madanlal came into contact with Professor Jain and also to the connections existing between the two. Angad Singh also met and came to know Madanlal at the house of Professor Jain who on one occasion had asked him to help the former in getting a job.

It seems that when Madanlal first left Bombay for Ahmednagar, he took with himself some books of Professor Jain. One Mr. Sood, also a refugee, was associated with Madanlal in the sale of these books. Some money, according Professor Jain Rs. 40/-, out of the sale proceeds of the books sold at Ahmednagar still remained with Madanlal and Sood and had not been paid to the Professor. On 9th December, 1947 Madanlal wrote to the Professor a post-card from Ahmednagar (Exhibit P.121) wherein he stated that his work was progressing well and enquired if Sood had paid him a sum of Rs. 30/-. He also wrote that he would himself pay the money in case Sood did not pay it and expressed great regret for its not having been paid till then. In this post-card Madanlal gave his address as care of Karkare Sahib, Deccan Guest House, Ahmednagar. On 21st December, 1947 Madanlal sent another post-card to Professor Jain, Exhibit P.122, in which after acknowledging the latter's reply to his first post-card, he expressed regard for Sood's having neither paid the money nor written to the Professor. He indicated that he was expecting a Money Order from his house. He wrote further that after doing an urgent piece of work, he would return to Bombay and asked the Professor not to worry. The address of Madanlal as given in this post-card was the same as given in the previous one.

According to the evidence given by Professor Jain (P.W.67), saw him at his house about the end of the first week of January, 1948 when he was accompanied also by another man whom he introduced to the witness as a Seth from Ahmednagar. Madanlal then went to tell the witness that he himself owned two fruit stalls at Ahmednagar and was otherwise doing very well. Madanlal then asked his companion whom he had described as Seth to arrange for the payment of the witness' money. Thereafter, the two left the witness' house. Madanlal, however, came back leaving his companion on the road and told the witness that the two fruit stalls mentioned by him earlier belonged to the Seth and not to himself and that he was only looking after then. He also told the witness that they had driven away all the Muslim stall-holders and held the sole monopoly of the business. After that Madanlal left promising to see the witness later. Two or three days thereafter, Madanlal met the witness near the Plaza Cinema which is very near his house and, saying that he had been to his house and wanted to have a talk with him, he walked with the witness to the latter's house. When they reached their destination, the witness asked Madanlal to come later as he felt tired at the time. Madanlal then turned up at 8 p.m. the same evening when Angad Singh also happened to be at the witness' place. Madanlal narrated his exploits in Ahmednagar in front of the two starting with an account of an assault which he claimed to have made, armed with a knife, on Rao Sahib Patwardhan at a meeting where he latter was preaching Hindu-Muslim unity, the police having not interfered with him at all by reason of their being Hindu-minded. He next said that he organised a volunteer corps for the benefit of the refugees and the Hindus and, producing a Marhatti newspaper, asked the witness to read the same and see how his work had been praised therein. According to the witness, Angad Singh left at that stage. After that Madanlal told the witness that the Seth who had accompanied him on the occasion of his previous visit was named Karkare

and was financing him. He went on to say that he had formed a party to Ahmednagar which was being financed by Karkare, and that the said party had been collecting arms and ammunition which had been dumped in a jungle. Next he told the witness that Vir Savarkar of the Hindu Mahasabha had, on hearing of his exploits at Ahmednagar, sent for him, had long talk with him lasting for two hours, and, patting him on the back had asked him to carry on. Then he told the witness that his party had plotted against the life of some leader. On the witness' asking him the name of that leader, Madanlal after considerable reluctance and after having at first professed ignorance of the name at last yielded to the witness' pressure and told him that it was Mahatma Gandhi. The witness asked Madanlal not to behave like a foolish child. Madanlal then said that he had been entrusted with the work of throwing a bomb at the prayer meeting of Mahatma Jee to create a confusion and that in the confusion so caused, the latter was to be overpowered by the members of his party. On hearing this, the witness had a long talk with Madanlal, trying to dissuade him from carrying out his design. Madanlal then left the witness' house promising to see him again and telling him that he with his associates was putting up at the Hindu Mahasabha Office at Dadar. He also told the witness that Karkare had an eye on him and would not allow him to move about alone. The witness has an impression that on this occasion Madanlal had paid him a sum of Rs. 15/- out of his dues.

Professor Jain says that he did not take the story as given by Madanlal very seriously because at the time the refugees of the locality used generally to abuse Mahatma Jee and the Congress. He met Angad Singh a day or two later and told him what he had heard from Madanlal. Angad Singh also advised the witness not to take the thing seriously. Madanlal again came to the witness after a couple of days and on the latter asking him if he had thought over his advice told him that he considered him like his father and that he knew that he would be doomed in case he did not listen to his advice.

A day or two later, Madanlal again saw the witness at about 8 p.m. and told him that he was proceeding to Delhi. On being asked the object of his going to Delhi he told the witness that he had some work there. He then left the witness' place promising to see him again on his return from Delhi.

The witness says that he was present at a meeting which was organised by the Poddar College which is managed by the same institution as his own College and was held in the Xavier's College Hall two or three days after Madanlal had left for Delhi and which was addressed by Shri Jai Prakash Narain leader of the Socialist Party. He intended to contact Shri Jai Prakash Narain and tell him what he had heard from Madanlal because he thought that the information might be of some use to the authorities at Delhi. By reason of his being surrounded by a large number of people, he was only able to tell Shri Jai Prakash Narain that there might be a big conspiracy at Delhi but was unable to convey to him any further details. He intended to contact Shri Jai Prakash Narain next day for the purpose but was unable to do so because of the illness of his child who had to be taken to a hospital. Thereafter he learnt that the gentleman had left for Delhi.

On the morning of the 21st January, on reading in the newspapers the news item about a bomb having been exploded at Mahatma Jee's prayer meeting the day before, and about Madanlal having been arrested in connection therewith, the witness, in consultation with Angad Singh who had come to his house that morning, decided to contact the Hon'ble Sardar Vallabh Bhai Patel and to tell him whatever he knew about the facts of the case. The witness attempted to ring up Sardar Jee at the house of his son but did not succeed. He then tried to contact Shree S.K. Patil, the President of the Bomaby Provincial Congress Committee on the phone but could not get him. He then rang up the Premier of Bombay, Shree B.G. Kher, and by appointment not him at his office at 4 p.m., the Home Minister Shree Morarji Desai also being present there. The witness told them all he knew about Madanlal.

On cross-examination by the counsel for Mr. Savarkar the witness stated inter alia that he had told the Premier and the Home Minister that he was prepared to assist them in unearthing the conspiracy and that he was told by the Home Minister that they would be making an investigation and would inform him in case his services were required in that connection. He also stated that he had told A.B. Yajnik of his college about the plot disclosed by Madanlal before the explosion at Delhi. (This A.B. Yajnik has not, however, been produced.)

On cross-examination by the counsel for Madanlal, the witness stated that he did enquire from the latter the names of his associates but that he did not give him those names. In one of the questions it appears to have been suggested to the witness that Madanlal had given the names of his associates who were staying at the Mahasabha Office as Jogendra Singh Chopra, Om Prakash and Ved Prakash. The witness, however, repudiated the suggestion. The other suggestions that seem to have been put to the witness by Madanlal's counsel were that Madanlal had introduced Karkare to him as a worker for the refugees at Ahmednagar and that Madanlal was going to Delhi to see his father in connection with his marriage. Both these suggestions were also repudiated by the witness. The witness further stated that he had been asked by the Home Minister why he had not reported the matter to the authorities concerned earlier and that he had replied that in view of the surrounding circumstances of the case he had not taken the matter seriously.

Angad Singh P.W.72's evidence is to the effect that he had gone to Doctor Jain's house at about 7 or 8 p.m. on 10th or 11th January, the day of the week being either Saturday or Sunday. Sometime after the arrival of the witness, Madanlal also turned up and began to talk to Doctor Jain of his exploits at Ahmednagar, the gist of the talk being that they had formed a part at Ahmednagar which was financed by Seth Karkare and which had been creating trouble for the Muslims with the object that no Muslims should be left in the town. Madanlal is said also to have told Doctor Jain that they had driven away all the Muslim fruit and vegetable stall-holders and that the stalls so vacated had been taken over by Seth Karkare and himself. Madanlal also said that on seeing Rao Sahib Patwardhan deliver a speech wherein he asked Hindus and Mohammedans to live like brothers, he rushed up to the speaker, whipped out his knife, caught hold of the speaker's collar, and asked him if he dared repeat those words and that the police had thereon intervened but had eventually allowed him to go. Madanlal had also produced a Marhatti newspaper and had asked Doctor Jain to read the same and see that it was full of praises for him. At this stage the witness left Doctor Jain's house.

According to the witness, he again met Doctor Jain a day or two later, very probably a day later, although he is not quite sure about it. On this occasion he had a long conversation with Doctor Jain who, during the course of the conversation, told him that according to Madanlal the party which he belonged had plotted to kill a leader, that leader being Mahatma Gandhi. Doctor Jain also told the witness that he had been informed by Madanlal that he members of the latter's party had been collecting arms and ammunition at Ahmednagar and that Barrister Savarkar was behind the party. This talk, according to what Doctor Jain told the witness, had taken place between himself and Madanlal the day before. Doctor Jain further told the witness that he had dissuaded Madanlal from engaging in such activities and also suggested that inasmuch as according to Madanlal, Savarkar was behind the plot and, therefore, there was the possibility of its coming out true, information regarding the same might be given to the authorities. The witness told Doctor Jain that it was a tall talk of a refugee, that

no importance should be attached to it inasmuch as the refugees in those days used generally to abuse Mahatma Gandhi and the others but that he agreed that the authorities should be informed about the talk. The witness, thereafter, saw Doctor Jain on the 21st January in the morning when the latter told him that what Madanlal had been talking about had proved to be partially rue and that the story about the plot against Mahatma Jee's life might also turn out to be true The two friends then decide to inform the Bombay authorities. The witness goes on to say that Doctor Jain, after unsuccessful attempts to contact Sardar Patel and Shree S.K. Patil on the phone at last succeeded in contacting Premier Kher and secured an appointment for 4 p.m. at the Secretariat. The witness could not accompany Doctor Jain on the occasion inasmuch as he had to appear in a personal case of his before a Magistrate that day and could not return from there in time.

In cross-examination the witness stated that he had not taken the facts about the plot as stated by Doctor Jain seriously and that during the time he himself was present at the house of Doctor Jain on the relevant date he had shown total lack of interest in the conversation because he thought that Madanlal was just bluffing.

The account given by the Hon'ble Shree Morarji Desai P.W.78 of the interview Doctor Jain had with him on the 21st January in the afternoon at the Secretariat may be summed up as follows. Doctor Jain told the witness that Madanlal who had been arrested in connection with the explosion at the Birla House was known to him. He explained to the witness the circumstances under which he had come in contact with Madanlal. He then told him that, before leaving for Delhi, Madanlal had discussions with him during the course whereof he disclosed that he and his friends had decided to take the life of a great leader, the name of the leader having been given, after very considerable pressure had been exercised by him, as Mahatma Gandhi. Doctor Jain also told the witness that he had tried to dissuade Madanlal. The latter was stated also to have introduced to Doctor Jain a friend of his, had taken him to Savarkar who had in turn, had a talk with him for about two hours, had praised him for what he had done, had patted him on the back and had asked him to carry on his work. Doctor Jain further told the witness that Madanlal had narrated to him his own exploits at Ahmednagar and recapitulated some of the details about such exploits as he had got them from the aforesaid Madanlal.The Doctor also informed the witness that he had been told by Madanlal that there was a dump of arms, ammunition, and explosives at Ahmednagar, and if the witness' recollection was correct some explosives were also said to have been stored at Poona. On being asked by the witness the reason for his not having conveyed the information to his earlier, the Doctor said that refugees were in the habit of talking wildly, that he believed that he had succeeded in dissuading Madanlal from doing what he had said he intended to do and that he came to realise his mistake only on reading about the explosion incident in the newspapers. The witness, after having heard all this, summoned the officer in charge of the Intelligence Branch, Mr. Nagarvala, who, however, was unable to come by reason of otherwise being extremely busy and who met him on the Railway station at 8 p.m. that night when the witness went there to catch a train for Ahmedabad. The witness narrated to Mr. Nagarvala what he had heard from Doctor Jain and asked him to take action in the matter, to arrest Karkare, to keep a close watch on Savarkar's house and movements and to find out who were the other persons involved in the plot. The witness, however, did not disclose to Mr. Nagarvala the name of his informant who had told him that, in view of the locality in which he lived and the persons involved, he would not like his name to be divulged for fear of danger to his own life, but had otherwise expressed his readiness to render, if required, all the help he was capable of in connection with the investigation. The witness had a second interview with Doctor Jain on the 24th

January and a third one on the 3rd February. At this last mentioned interview the Doctor told the witness that in view of the tragedy that had taken place, he would no more mind any personal danger and was quite willing to help the police openly. The witness thereon put him in touch with Mr. Nagarvala. The witness did not at any stage reduce to writing the information conveyed to him and did not direct Mr. Nagarvala to interrogate Mr. Savarkar and to find out from him if the story given by Professor Jain was true. The witness does not recollect Doctor Jain having made any reference to Angad Singh in the course of his talks with him. About the end of the first week of January, 1948 the witness learnt that one Karkare of Ahmednagar had been instigating the refugees to create trouble and passed an order for the arrest of the aforesaid Karkare about 10 or 12 days before 21st January. He admits that he issued no direct instructions to the Ahmednagar Police to make any investigations. He also admits that under his orders security had been demanded from the daily 'Agrani' and the 'Hindu Rashtra' of which he knew Nathuram Godse to be the Editor, and forfeited, although he could not tell how many times,on account of the Editor's preaching hatred against the Muslims and encouraging violence. He stated that so far, as he could recollect a position had been filed in the High Court against the order forfeiting the security but the same had been rejected. He added that all the securities forfeited had been returned on 15th August, 1947 as a gesture of good-will with an appeal for a better behaviour in the future. He admits that on the first occasion when security was demanded from the 'Agrani' by sheer oversight, the matter had not been referred to the Press Advisory Committee, that being the first or the second case of its kind under the present Government, but adds that on all subsequent occasions the matter had in the first instanced been referred to the said committee.

Mr. Nagarvala (P.W.133) has stated that after having seen Mr. Desai at the Railway Station on the 21ˢᵗ January, and in pursuance of instructions received from him, he organised an unobtrusive watch over the house of Mr. Savarkar and made arrangements for locating and arresting Karkare in which connection he made enquiries from the Ahmednagar Police as to whether Karkare whose detention had already been ordered had or had not been detained. On 24ᵗʰ January, he also issued orders for the arrest of Digambar R. Badge.

It is in evidence that Doctor Jain was first contacted by Mr. Nagarvala on 4ᵗʰ or 5ᵗʰ February, 1948. The statement of Doctor Jain was recorded by him on 17ᵗʰ February, that of Shree Morarji Desai having already been recorded four days earlier, i.e., on 13ᵗʰ February. Angad Singh's statement was recorded on 23red February. At the identification parade hold on 2ⁿᵈ March, 1948, Doctor Jain identified both Karkare and Madanlal.

Mr. Brown Chief Presidency Magistrate of Bombay recorded the statement of Doctor Jain under Section 164, Criminal Procedure Code, on 26ᵗʰ February. This statement was duly put to him and is duly exhibited as Exhibit D.11 Inasmuch as a good deal of argument has been based on the discrepancies alleged to exist between this statement and the evidence given by Doctor Jain in Court, I propose to reproduce here the said statement verbatim:

"I am a Professor Arahamagdi and Hindi, at the Ramnarain Ruia College, Matunga. In October, 1947 I met Madanlal. He was a refugee from the Punjab. He was introduced to me by Mr. Gupta of Amir Manzil Mahim. Madanlal was looking for a job and for a short time sold my books. He said he was going some fruit business with Ahmednagar. He told me that though the generosity of a Gujarati lady he also had an interest in doing cracker business. Madanlal introduced me to one Sood. Madanlal told me of a meeting which he attended at Ahmednagar and in which he opposed Rao Sahib Patwardhan who had spoken of Hindu and Muslims living peacefully together. Madanlal told me that the person who accompanied him was one Karkare, a big Seth of Ahmednagar. Madanlal said that a group had been formed at Ahmednagar and that Karkare, a big Seth of Ahmednagar. Madanlal said that a group had been formed at Ahmednagar and that Karkare was financing the Group. Madanlal stated that the party to which he belonged had plotted to do away with some great leader. Madanlal mentioned the name of Mahatma Gandhi. I was horrified at such a suggestion and tried to dissuade him. I tried to dissuade him for about 2 hours and said that he was making unnecessary troubles for himself and for others. I reminded him of all the repercussions and said that he was an intelligent young man and was merely being made a scapegoat by his party. Madanlal listened to me and thanked me for my advice, Madanlal met me on the following day. He said he was proceeding to Delhi and would return in a few days. I wanted to bring this to the notice of Jai Prakash Narain but merely told him that there would be a great conspiracy in Delhi but as he was in a great hurry to leave I could not tell him the details. On 21ˢᵗ January 1948 after reading the news of the explosion of a bomb at the prayer meeting of Gandhiji I tried to contact Vallabhbhai Patel. I failed to do so as he had already left for the Aerodrome on his way to Delhi. I also tried to contact Mr. S.K. Patel. He also had accompanied the Sardar. I rang up the Premier Mr. B.G. Kher. He gave me an appointment for 4 p.m. at the Secretariat. Mr. Morarji Desai, Home Minister was present. I gave the Prime Minister the whole statement as set out above. I also offered

my services to unearth this conspiracy. I requested them to take such action as they considered necessary. I will be able to identify Madanlal. I think I shall be able to identify Karkare also."

The evidence of Professor Jain, Angad Singh and Mr. Desai was subjected to very severe criticism by Nathuram and the Counsel for the other appellants particularly Mr. Bannerji, Counsel for Madanlal and Apte and Mr. Dange Counsel for Karkare. Nathuram described the entire evidence given by the three as pure fabrication. He urged that all three, of whom Professor Jain and Mr. Desai were admittedly staunch congressmen, and Angad Singh had been a very staunch congressman and had only recently seceded from the Congress along with his party because they felt that the Congress was not prepared to go far enough them in the execution of their socialistic programme, had combined together, out of political movies, in order to crush their political opponents particularly Mr. Savarkar, the leader of the Hindu Mahasabha. He drew our attention to what he described as the most hostile attitude of Mr. Desai towards his journals the 'Daily Agrani' and the 'Hindu Rashtra' as disclosed by the fact that theirs was almost the solitary case in which he had decided to take action under the Press Emergency Powers Act without reference to the Press Advisory Committee and the further fact that within a very short time the security deposits of the above-named journals aggregating to Rs. 16,000/- had been forfeited. He laid very great stress on the failure of Mr. Desai to take proper action on the alleged receipt of information by him from Professor Jain on the 21st January. He pointed out that even on his own showing Mr. Desai did nothing more than direct Mr. Nagarvala to arrest Karkare and keep a watch over Mr. Savarkar and does not even purport to have disclosed the name of his informant to him in order to enable him to contact the former although he himself has stated that Dr. Jain had expressed his readiness to give

every possible help in unearthing the conspiracy. As regards the statement of Mr. Desai that he had refrained from divulging the name of his informant to Mr. Nagarvala by reason of an express request to that effect having been made by the former, attention was drawn to the fact that Professor Jain himself had not said that he had made any such request to Mr. Desai, but that he had, on the other hand, deposed that he had expressed his readiness to give all possible assistance in unearthing the conspiracy. Attention was also drawn to the fact that beyond passing an order for the arrest of Karkare, an order for whose detention under the Provincial Security Act had already been passed as far back as about the 9th or 10th January, and placing an unobtrusive watch on the house of Mr. Savarkar, Mr. Nagarvala, admittedly, did absolutely nothing; did not take any steps to trace the alleged dump of arms, ammunitions, and explosives at Ahmednagar and Poona; did not direct that enquiries should be made at Ahmednagar as to the activities of Madanlal and his associates at the place; and did not even care to make any enquiries from the Hindu Mahasabha Office at Dadar as to who were the persons who had stayed there between the 11th and 15th January although, according to Professor Jain, Madanlal had distinctly told the later that his associates were staying at that place. It was urged that the conduct of Messrs. Desai and Nagarvala was hardly consistent with their being in possession of any information whatsoever as to Madanlal and his associates having a design on the life of Mahatma Gandhi and could not but lead to the conclusion that the whole story as to such information having been conveyed by Doctor Jain to Mr. Desai on the 21st January, and by the latter to Mr. Nagarvala the same evening, is faked, and that, not only Professor Jain, but also the two above-named officials, had lied.

Mr. Bannerji and the other counsel did not go to this extent and did not suggest that Mr. Desai had given false evidence. Their contention was that the conduct of Mr. Desai and Mr. Nagarvala showed that they had not taken the story told by Professor Jain to the former seriously at all and did not regard it as anything more than a yarn.

Nathuram also urged that even if there had been a conspiracy it was exceedingly improbable that Madanlal would divulge the same Professor Jain. He laid stress on the discrepancies between the evidence given by Professor Jain in the Court below and the statement made by him before the Chief Presidency Magistrate under Section 164, Criminal Procedure Code, much earlier, and also on the discrepancies between that evidence and the evidence of Angad Singh and Mr. Desai, and contended that Professor Jain appeared to be a wholly unscrupulous witness, who presumably in order to carry favour with the Congress Government, or, it may be to ward off a possible suspicions against himself by reason of his admitted association with Madanlal, had cooked up an entirely false story, and that Angad Singh had only come to his rescue as an obliging friend. The suggestion was that having heard from Madanlal that he and some of his friends had adopted a somewhat aggressive attitude towards the Muslims in Ahmednagar, and that they had formed a volunteer corps at that place for helping Hindu refugees which corps was being financed or otherwise encouraged by Karkare, Professor Jain had, on reading in the newspapers the account of the explosion caused by Madanlal and the suggestion that the said act of Madanlal had probably been done in pursuance of some conspiracy, quite unconsciously allowed his imagination to work, and had rushed to the Home Minister with the story that Madanlal had actually told him about such conspiracy being in existence, the object of contacting the Home Minister being to save himself from the possible consequences of his own connections with Madanlal.

The evidence of Angad Singh as to what he heard from his friend Professor Jain as to the talk the latter had with Madanlal after he had himself left his house, and the vi of Mr. Desai as to the communication alleged to have been made to him

by the Professor, have been admitted in evidence under Section 157 of Indian Evidence Act. While no objection was taken to the admissibility of Angad Singh's evidence under the aforesaid Section it was very strenuously contended by Mr. Bannerji that the section had no application the evidence of Mr. Desai and that the same ought, accordingly to be regarded as wholly inadmissible.

Before proceeding to examine the arguments regarding the merits of the evidence of the above-named three witnesses, of which I have attempted to give as complete a resume as possible, I should like to dispose of the objection as to the admissibility of the evidence of Mr. Desai. Section 157 under which that evidence has been admitted reads as follows:

> **"157.** In order to corroborate the testimony of a witness, any former statement made by such witness relating to the same fact at or about the time when the fact took place, or before any authority legally competent to investigate the fact, may be proved."

It is common ground that the alleged statement of Professor Jain to Mr. Desai, made admittedly more than a week after his alleged talk with Madanlal and the disclosures alleged to have been made to him by the latter, cannot be regarded as having been made at or about the time when the talk took place and the disclosures were made, and cannot, accordingly, be said to fall within the first part of the section quoted above. The learned Special Judge has, however, held that Mr. Desai being an authority legally competent to investigate the truth or untruth of the disclosures said to have been made by Madanlal to the Professor, the case did fall within the purview of the latter part of the section, and that, accordingly, the statement made by the Professor to him was legally admissible in evidence. After giving due consideration to the arguments of Mr. Bannerji, I have not been able to see any reason to differ from this view of the learned Special Judge. As very clearly stated by Mr. Desai, the police, crimes and the investigation of crimes fall within the portfolio of 'Home'. Accordingly, as a Home Minister of the Province, he was legally competent to investigate, i.e., to enquire into the truth or untruth of, the disclosures, if any, made by Madanlal to him. There can, in the circumstances, be no doubt at all that the statement paid to have been made to him the Professor about those disclosures has been rightly admitted in evidence.

I consider the contention as to the three witnesses having combined to give false evidence out of political motives to be wholly fantastic. There does not appear to be any truth at all in the suggestion that Nathuram or the papers edited by him were the special targets of the Home Minister's wrath. It is quite true that, as admitted by Mr. Desai, an order had been made demanding security under the Press Emergency Powers Act from the 'Agrani' without previous reference to the Press Advisory Committee, while in almost all other cases in which action was taken under the said Act, this was done after reference to the said committee. I, however, consider the explanation given by the witness for this to be quite satisfactory. As pointed out by him, this was the first or the second case of its kind since the assumption of office by the present Government and one can easily understand that the department followed, as a matter of routine, the procedure in vogue in the time of the old bureaucratic Government. The new administration could hardly have yet had time to formulate their policy on the subject in the light of their professedly democratic ideals. Mr. Desai has said that it was a case of sheer oversight. When a kind of general amnesty was granted by the Provincial Government to the press, and a decision was taken to refund all security deposits that had been forfeited, the Minister did not make any discrimination against the 'Agrani' and the 'Hindu Rashtra' and it is not denied that the latter were refunded a sum of Rs. 16,000/- which was the aggregate amount of their security deposits forfeited.

There is no reason at all to suppose that either Mr. Desai or the two other witnesses had any animus against any of the accused. None of the accused even suggested to have ever come in any kind of conflict with them and there does not seem to be anything common between Professor Jain and Angad Singh on the one side and Mr. Desai on the other. It seems to me to be a wholly ridiculous suggestion that the three had combined together to give false evidence against the accused simply on account of the difference in their political ideologies. I also cannot take seriously the suggestion that the combination was for the purpose of roping in Mr. Savarkar. The case against the latter failed for want of adequate evidence and not by reason of the evidence against him having been disbelieved by the Court. The only evidence against him was the statement of the approver that on 17th January when Apte and Nathuram went to have his darshan before leaving for Delhi, he came to the ground floor of his house to bid them good-bye and while doing so used words which meant "Be successful and Come Back".[66] The three witnesses we are dealing with at the present moment did not seek to prove anything against him except an alleged statement of Madanlal that he had expressed approval of the latter's activities at Ahmednagar in turning out the Muslim fruit and vegetable vendors and had encouraged him to continue such activities. Surely, if the three witnesses had combined together to commit perjury in order to implicate Mr. Savarkar, they could have made their evidence against him much more effective. They could at least have put into Madanlal's mouth some words showing that Mr. Savarkar had encouraged or blessed the plot against the life of Mahatma Gandhi. The combination of these three evidently intelligent and shrewd persons could not, if they had decided to stoop so low as not to mind perjuring themselves for the achievement of their object, have given

---

[66] On coming out Apte *told* Badge that *Savarkar* blessed them "*Yashasvi* houn ya"- "यशस्वीहोऊनया", - Be successful and return. Eds.

their evidence in such a lukewarm and half-hearted manner, if, as is suggested, they were laying for such high stakes as the removal of Mr. Savarkar from the political arena.

I do not regard the conduct of Mr. Desai or of Mr. Nagarvala as in any manner inconsistent with the former having received on 21st January from Professor Jain the information which he has deposed he did receive and which says he had communicated to Mr. Nagarvala with the necessary directions. The following extract from the statement of Mr. Desai which contains a full account, as given by him, of the conversation which took place between him and Professor Jain on the occasion fully bears this out:

"**Professor Jain** then spoke and told us his story. By the 'story' I mean his narrative. He told us that he had read about the explosion incident in the newspapers dated 21st January 1948 as also the name of the person who had been arrested and that he had personal knowledge of the various matters relating to that person which he wanted to narrate to us. He said that he knew that person Madanlal, who had come in contact with him as a refugee and whom he had helped monetarily. He also said that he had given him his books to sell so that he might earn some money and that he had been keeping in contact with him. He said that Madanlal had left Bombay for Delhi only about 3-4 days before the explosion incident. I am not sure about how many days Jain had mentioned. He said that before leaving for Delhi, Madanlal had told him that he (Madanlal) and his friends had decided to take the life of a great leader. He (Jain) then pressed him to give the name of that leader. Madanlal then gave the name of Mahatma Gandhi. Professor Jain then told us that he had tried to dissuade Madanlal from his wild talk and wild plan. He also told us that a friend of Madanlal with whom Madanlal was working at Ahmednagar had also been introduced by Madanlal to him "as Karkare. Professor Jain also told us that Madanlal had told him about his exploits at Ahmednagar, and gave us some details about them as narrated to him by Madanlal. He then told us that Madanlal had told him that Karkare had taken him (Madanlal) to Savarkar, that Savarkar had a talk with him for about two hours and that Savarkar had praised him for what he had done, had patted him on his back and had asked him carry on his work. Professor Jain had said that Madanlal had told him that there was a dump of arms, ammunition and explosives at Ahmednagar. If I remember right, Professor Jain had also said that Madanlal had told him that some explosives were stored also at Poona. Professor Jain had said that Madanlal had told him that he and his companions were to go to Delhi to achieve their object. I asked Jain as to why he did not tell me all about it immediately after he had come to know of it. He said that refugees were in the habit of talking wildly and that he believed he had dissuaded Madanlal from doing what he intended to do."

In the circumstances, I do not see how Mr. Desai as the Home Minister of a professedly democratic Government could have done anything more than what he actually did in this case. Madanlal was under arrest at Delhi and not available for interrogation at Bombay. Professor Jain did not furnish any clue about his associates or coadjutors except Karkare and for the latter's arrest directions were at once given by Mr. Desai to Mr. Nagarvala who also immediately set about locating him for the purpose of giving effect to those directions. We will presently see that Karkare was in the meanwhile, striving hard as possible to keep his identity concealed and it could not, therefore, be an easy task actually to locate him. It is true that Professor Jain has stated in his evidence that he had been told by Madanlal, at the time the latter disclosed to him the plot against the life of Mahatma Jee, that he with his associates was putting up in the Hindu Mahasabha Office at Dadar, but as the above extract from Mr. Desai's evidence would show he does not seem to have communicated this information the Home Minister. Even Angad Singh to whom Professor Jain is said to have narrated what he had been told by Madanlal within a day or two does not profess to have received any information from him on the subject. Whether this omission was accidental or deliberate, or whether it should, and if so, to what extent, affect the weight to be attached to the Professor's own evidence are questions which need not worry us at this stage and which will properly arise for consideration only at the time of the appraisal of the Professor's evidence. It is, however, quite clear that, on the information in his possession, Mr. Desai could not reasonably be expected to direct any enquiry from or at the Hindu Mahasabha Office nor could Mr. Nagarvala be expected to make such enquiry on his own. As regards Mr. Savarkar's connection with Madanlal the only information then in the possession of Mr. Desai was that when Karkare took Madanlal to his house he had a long talk with him, praised him for what he had done, patted him on his back and asked him to carry on. I do not think this information could reasonably be deemed to warrant any severer or more drastic action against Mr. Savarkar than that actually taken by Mr. Nagarvala, viz., an unobtrusive watch on his residence. Indeed, any severer action would have savoured of vindictiveness and might have been displayed as an attempt on the part of the Congress Government to stifle all political opposition. Much stress was laid by Nathuram on the inaction of Mr. Nagarvala in relation to the arms, ammunition and explosives which, according to Mr. Desai, Madanlal had told Professor Jain, had been dumped at Ahmednagar and the explosives which had been stored at Poona. At first sight, in the circumstances, the omission of the Home Minister or the police chief, to take immediate steps to trace and seize the dumps of arms, ammunition and explosives at Ahmednagar and the store of explosives at Poona does appear to be astounding, and to lay both open to a charge of gross, even criminal negligence. However, on a closer and more careful consideration of the situation, it seems to me that, in the absence of some clue as to where to look for the objectionable stuff, a precipitate action in this matter would have been imprudent and might have proved disastrous. Ahmednagar and Poona are not far removed from the Hyderabad border, and, on getting scent of a possible police raid, the parties concerned could easily have got rid of such stuff, if there was nay, across the border or otherwise placed it beyond the reach of the police.

For the foregoing reasons, I am unable to see my way to reject the testimony of Mr. Desai as untrustworthy on the round of his own conduct and that of Mr. Nagarvala, who was acting under his instructions, being incompatible with his being in possession of the information which he claims to have received from Professor Jain on the 21st January.

It was next urged by Nathuram that there were some obvious untruths in the evidence of Mr. Desai in view whereof he could not be regarded as generally a truthful witness. The only two such untruths of the witness to which our attention was drawn were:

1. **The** statement as to the appeal from the order passed under the press Emergency Powers Act for forfeiture of the security of the 'Hindu Rashtra' having been dismissed by the High Court and

2. **The** statement as to the witness having had no knowledge of the distribution of arms and ammunition by Dada Maharaj to the members of the Socialist Party till he read the account of the evidence given by the latter in the present case as reported in the press.

In so far as the first statement is concerned, it was admitted by Nathuram that there was no evidence on the record to justify the assertion as to its being untrue. It was, however, asserted by him that the appeal had in fact been admitted by the High Court. He challenged the learned Advocate General to deny the correctness of his assertion. Mr. Daphtary found himself unable to make any statement one way or the other. The correct position as I gather from certain remarks made by Nathuram in his final reply seems to be that although the appeal was admitted by the High Court in the first instance, it becomes infructuous when on 15th August, 1947 the amount of the forfeited security was refunded under Government orders, and was dismissed on that ground. In the circumstances, it cannot be said that Mr. Desai did not speak the truth when he made the impugned statement.

As regard the second statement, the contention of Nathuram was that it must be held to be false inasmuch as Dada Maharaj's evidence clearly showed that Mr. Desai was fully acquainted with his activities in the matter of collection and distribution of arms and ammunition long before the report of his evidence in the case appeared in the press.

The relevant portion of the evidence of Dada Maharaj P.W69 which was recorded on 10th August, 1948 reads as follows:

"It is true that I had gone to a high Government Officer and had told him that I would not help anyone whose intentions were to injure Muslims in the Dominion of India. That Government Officer was the Hon'ble Mr. Morarji Desai. I had heard that the Hon'ble Home Minister had some misunderstandings about my activities. I accordingly went and saw him to get those misunderstandings about me removed. It was on the Janamashtmi day in 1947. There was also a talk with the Hon'ble Home

Minister about my activities in regard to the collection of arms and ammunition."

The relevant portion of the evidence of Mr. Desai, which was recorded about a fortnight later on 24th August runs as follows:

"I know both Dada Maharaj and Dixit Maharaj. I had heard some rumours in 1947 that Dada Maharaj was concerned in the collection and smuggling of arms and ammunition. I did not know that Dada Maharaj was distributing arms and ammunition to the members of the Socialist Party. I came to know of it when I read the evidence of Dada Maharaj given in this Court in a newspaper."

Both the statements quoted above were made in answer to questions put in cross-examination by the counsel for Mr. Savarkar. I fail to see any discrepancy at all between the two statements, much less am I able to discover any indication of Mr. Desai not having stated the truth in making the above statement. According to Mr. Desai's statement, Dada Maharaj saw him once in 1947 when he heard rumours as to his being concerned in the collection and smuggling of arms. According to Dada Maharaj he heard about Janamashtmi of 1947 that the Home Minister had some misunderstandings about his activities, that he went to see him to remove those misunderstandings, and that on that occasion there was a talk about his activities in regard to the collection and distribution of arms and ammunition. I can see no material difference between the versions given by the two witnesses with regard to the circumstances under which they met and the subject discussed between them on the occasion. Dada Maharaj did not say that there was any talk at that time about is distributing arms and ammunition to the members of the Socialist Party. It cannot, therefore, be said that Mr. Desai lied when he said that before reading the press report of Dada Maharaj's evidence he did not know that the latter had been distributing arms and ammunition to the members of the Socialist Party. In fact, Dada Maharaj never said that he had distributed arms and ammunition to the members of the said party. It was his brother Dixit Maharaj who while giving evidence in this case made the following statement on 21ˢᵗ August, 1948:

> *"I had supplied revolvers, pistols, guns, carbines, rifles, hand-grenades, detonators, etc., to the Socialist Party."*

It seems that it was the report of Dixit Maharaj's evidence that Mr. Desai had read in the press but that he confused it with that of Dada Maharaj, or it may be, that the form in which the cross-examining counsel put the question misled him into the belief that it was Dada Maharaj who had stated in Court that he had been distributing arms and ammunition to the members of Socialist Party. Be that as it may, a comparison of the relevant portion of Dada Maharaj's evidence completely demolishes the entire fabric on which Nathuram based this part of his argument.

After giving my most careful thought to all that was urged at the Bar against the evidence of Mr. Desai, I can find no reason to hold that he was not a witness of truth.

I come now to the evidence of Professor Jain himself and that of his friend Angad Singh.

A lot of argument against the evidence of Professor Jain was based on the dates mentioned by him and an attempt was made to show that if the witness' evidence as regards the dates on which Madanlal met him is accepted, it will completely demolish the evidence of the approver as to his having gone to his place, along with Karkare, at some time in the night on the 9ᵗʰ January, in order to see the stuff which he had collected at Apte's request. There is undoubtedly some confusion in Professor Jain's evidence in the matter of dates. He originally said that Madanlal had seen him first in the end of the first week of January. Then he corrected himself by saying that Madanlal saw him about the end of the first week of January. On a question being put in cross-examination he said that he would consider the 6ᵗʰ or the 7ᵗʰ January as the end of the first week of the month. A closer examination of the evidence, however, would show that the confusion is more apparent than real and that there is in reality no conflict between the evidence of this witness and that of the approver. According to the witness, Madanlal saw him on four occasions, once when he came to him with Karkare, a second time when he told him about the plot against the life of Mahatma Gandhi, a third time when he assured him that he had accepted his advice, and a fourth time when he told him that he was leaving that night for Delhi. The fourth visit of Madanlal must, in the circumstances, have taken place, assuming of course that the witness is telling the truth, on 15ᵗʰ January. The witness puts the third visit as one or two days before the last visit. He puts the second visit two days, before the third and the first visit at two or three days before the second. Thus, according to him, the third visit of Madanlal was either on the 14ᵗʰ or 13ᵗʰ January, the second either on the 12ᵗʰ or 11ᵗʰ, and the first either on the 9ᵗʰ or 10ᵗʰ. In these circumstances, it cannot be said that the Professor's evidence is necessarily inconsistent with Madanlal and Karkare having visited Badge at his house at sometime on the 9ᵗʰ January. They could easily have reported what they had seen at Badge's house to Apte immediately and could have got some train for Bombay the same night or early next morning so as to be in Bombay on 10ᵗʰ January.

From the statement made by Madan Lal before the learned Special Judge, his Written Statement, the statements, written as well as oral, of his friend Karkare, and other material, to be found on the record, the impression left upon my mind about Madan Lal is that he is an impetuous, reckless and rash youth, impressionable in a very high degree, having a lot of bravado combined with a passion for notoriety, and one who would respond to the slightest favour shown to him with utmost gratitude. A helpless, homeless, refugee that he was, Professor Jain had received him kindly when he was introduced to him, had tried to get a job for him, and had otherwise evidence tried to get a job for him, and had otherwise evinced some interest in him, had given him his books for sale on commission basis without insisting on any kind of security for the payment of sale proceeds and had shown no impatience even when about Rs. 30/- or Rs. 40/- out of the sale proceeds of books at Ahmednagar had not been paid to him for a considerable time. In the circumstances, it was quite natural for a youth of the temperament and disposition of Madanlal to begin to regard him with feelings of uncommon affection and gratitude. How Madanlal did feel towards the Professor can be gathered from the language of his two post-cards which have been referred to above. In both of them he called the Professor's wife as his mother and his children as his brothers and sisters.

On going to Ahmednagar, Madanlal seems to have received particular kindness and consideration at the hands of Karkare and this fact, along with the solicitude shown by the latter generally for the refugees appears to have drawn him very close to Karkare can find no difficulty in believing that, while he was in Bombay with his Ahmednagar patron and benefactor, he, anxious as he was to remove from his benefactor's mind any unfavourable impression that might have been created by the withholding of sale proceeds of his books, went, on the day of his arrival at Bombay, with Karkare to Professor Jain's house, introduced the former to the latter as a big Seth and a great worker in the refugee cause, and told him that he would also pay the amount due to him from himself on account of the sale proceeds of the books. The Professor identified Karkare at the first identification parade held at Bombay as the person who had come to his house with Madanlal. This identification parade was held on 2nd March. Karkare was arrested as late as 14th February and was taken to Delhi on the 25th February. He was flown back to Bombay on the 1st March, i.e., just one day before the parade. In the circumstances, the genuineness of the identification cannot reasonably be doubted.

I see also no difficulty in believing that Madanlal saw Professor Jain again and narrated to him his exploits at Ahmednagar. He would be bursting with them and would avail himself of the earliest opportunity to communicate them to this benefactor, possibly with considerable exaggeration and I find nothing unnatural or improbable in his desire to impress Professor Jain with his own importance and that of his new associates, having blurted out that they had a design on the life of a leader, and, on being hard pressed by his benefactor to do so, having disclosed the name of that leader, even though he may subsequently have repented. From the evidence of Doctor Jain with regard to his third interview with Madanlal it appears that he did in fact repent and regret his impetuosity and tried to convince Professor Jain that the project previously disclosed to him had been abandoned.

Much stress was laid on the fact that Madanlal could not, assuming there was a conspiracy of the nature alleged, possibly have disclosed the fact to Professor Jain whom he must have known to be a congressman and who had gone to jail in 1942 in connection with the 'Quit India' movement launched by Mahatma Gandhi. This argument, however, ignore human nature and overlooks the fact that an impetuous and impulsive youth, in a moment of excitement and exultation, is generally apt to throw all prudence and foresight to the winds.

The only motive suggested for Professor Jain having concocted a false story was a desire for self-preservation. It was suggested that on reading, on the morning of the 21st January, in the newspapers the news item about the explosion at the Birla House the previous evening and the arrest of Madanlal in connection therewith, Professor Jain became nervous and, fearing that, by reason of his association and contacts with Madanlal, he might get into trouble and might be suspected of complicity in the crime, rushed to the Home and the Prime Ministers with a cock and bull story. The suggestion seems to be simply fantastic. With his antecedents, being a person who had actually served a long term of detention in connection with the 'Quit India' movement of Mahatma Gandhi, Professor Jain could not have the slightest apprehension of his being suspected of any complicity with Madanlal.

Lengthy arguments were addressed to us with reference to the conduct of Professor Jain after the alleged communication had been made to him by Madanlal. His inaction and his failure to give information to the authorities were described as wholly unnatural and it was contended that they were wholly irreconcilable with the Professor being in possession of such important information. I must say, however, that it is Professor Jain's evidence as to how he behaved after the communication of the news to him by Madanlal which has impressed me most. I consider it so natural, and it makes the rest of his evidence look so probable, that I cannot help being driven to the conclusion that the evidence given by the witness is at least substantially true. A young lad, in whom he had been taking some interest, who was the object of his sympathy and, may be also of his affection, who, though impetuous and rash, had some good attributes, had told him of a secret design formed by himself and his friends against the life of Mahatma Gandhi. As was natural, he tried his utmost to dissuade the boy from having anything to do with such design. After the boy had left, promising to see him again, his mind was literally torn up by conflicting feelings. He wished very much that there was no truth at all in what he had been told and that the boy had been merely bluffing. With his knowledge of the temperament of Madanlal, and with his knowledge of the bragging generally indulged in by the refugees, he felt very much inclined to believe that it was so. He could not, however, at the same time absolutely exclude

the possibility of there being some truth in what he had been told. He naturally felt chary of taking any immediate action for four of unnecessarily involving Madanlal in trouble in case in fact there was no truth in what the latter had told him. In the circumstances, he adopted the most natural course of confining the matter to, and seeking the advice of, an intimate friend like Angad Singh. The latter had agreed with him that what Madanlal had told him was no more than a tall talk of a refugee and should not be taken seriously at all. But, it was further agreed between the two friends that no risks should be taken and that the matter should be reported to the authorities. However, either the same or the following night, Madanlal again saw Professor Jain and assured him that he had accepted his advice. Otherwise being very strongly inclined to think that the story told him earlier about the plot against Mahatma Gandhi's life was no more than a bluff, and being anxious not to involve Madanlal in unnecessary trouble, Professor Jain naturally readily accepted this assurance as quite genuine and refrained from carrying out the decision taken by him conjointly with Angad Singh about informing the authorities. Element of doubt still, however, and quite naturally, lurked in his mind and he tried to satisfy his conscience by conveying some warning to the authorities in Delhi. With that end in view, he tried to contact Mr. Jai Prakash Narain but due to unavoidable causes did not succeed. All this is so natural, and its description as given by Professor Jain has such a ring of sincerity about it, that I feel no hesitation at all in accepting it.

Great stress was laid on the fact that while according to Professor Jain, Angad Singh had left his house after Madan Lal had recounted his own exploits t Ahmednagar and before he had said anything about the Seth who had accompanied him at the time of his previous visit and the party organised by himself and financed by the Seth, according to Angad Singh the talk about the Seth and his financing the party organised by Madan Lal had also taken place before he left. I do not consider that this discrepancy can be taken to thrown any doubt on the veracity of either of the two witnesses. It only shows that Professor Jain's recollection as to the precise moment at which Angad Singh left his house is not quite accurate. His impression seems to be that the latter left a minute or two – or say five minutes – earlier than he actually did. Of course Angad Singh is in a far better position than Professor Jain to say at what stage of the conversation between the latter and Madan Lal he did leave. Rather than case any doubt on the truthfulness of either of the two witnesses, this so-called discrepancy seems to me only to show that neither of them is a tutored witness and that, in spite of being so intimate with each other, they did not compare notes or discuss between themselves the evidence which each of them was going to give or had given. It is to be observed that this so-called discrepancy is to be found in the statements made by the witnesses in their examination-in-chief and there was an interval of four days between the dates on which they gave their evidence. Both are intelligent and educated men and if they had, during this interval, talked between themselves about the events regarding which one had already given, and the other was to give, evidence, this discrepancy could have been very easily avoided.

The other discrepancies pointed out between the evidence of Professor Jain and that of Angad Singh, and between the evidence of the former and of Mr. Desai, may be summed up as follows:

(1) **Professor Jain** did not say that Madan Lal had told him that Mr. Savarkar was behind his party while, according to Angad Singh, in narrating to the latter the account of what Madanlal had told him, Professor Jain did make a statement to that effect. Indeed, according to Angad Singh this was the reason why the Professor Jain felt worried and inclined to think that after all what Madan Lal had told him might not be pure bluff;

(2) **Professor Jain** had stated that Madan Lal had told him that he had been entrusted with the task of exploding a bomb at the prayer-meeting of Mahatma Gandhi when his companions would, in the commotion so caused, overpower the latter, and that he and his associates were putting up at the Hindu Mahasabha Office at Dadar. There is, however, no reference at all to any of these matters in the evidence of Angad Singh and Mr. Desai who do not appear to have been told by Professor Jain that any such statement had been made to him by Madan Lal;

(3) **Mr. Desai**has stated that he had been told by Professor Jain that according to that he had heard from Madan Lal the latter had been taken to Mr. Savarkar by Karkare, while in the evidence given by Professor Jain in Court as to what Madan Lal had stated to him there is not a word about his having been taken to Savarkar by Karkare, nor does Angad Singh say that this fact was mentioned by Professor Jain to him.

(4) **According** to Mr. Desai, Professor Jain told him that Madan Lal had informed him not only about arms, ammunition and explosives having been dumped by his party at Ahmednagar but also about explosives having been stored by them in Poona, while no such statement has been ascribed to Madan Lal in the evidence given by Professor Jain, nor does Angad Singh says that it was mentioned by the former while reporting to him the conversation which Madan Lal had with him.

To be continued in Volume-2

"THE HINDUSTAN TIMES"

New Delhi Edition, dated Staturday 31st January 1948

DIGAMBAR R BADGE'S SHASTRA BHANDAR, NARAYAN PETH, PUNE

Shastra Bhabndar of Digambar Ramchandra Badge
(Weapon Storehouse)
No.300 Narayan Peth, Poona Badge's residence cum
Weapons Storehouse
(Author: Smt. S. Padmavathi can be seen in this picture)

**Places of Bizarre Events
Mahatma Gandhi – Indira Gandhi – Rajiv Gandhi
Assassination**

**Place of Mahatma Gandhi Assassination, New Delhi.
30/01/1948 Friday Evening 5.17**

**Place of Indira Gandhi Assassination, New Delhi.
31/10/1984 Wednesday Morning 9.17**

Photo courtesy and credit: User:PlaneMad/email:arun.planemad@gmail.com

**Place of Rajiv Gandhi Assassination,
Sriperumpudur, Tamil Nadu. 21/05/1991 Tuesday
Night 10.21**

<table>
<tr><td colspan="3">High Court Judgment Repercussion on the Convicts/Appellants</td></tr>
<tr>
<td>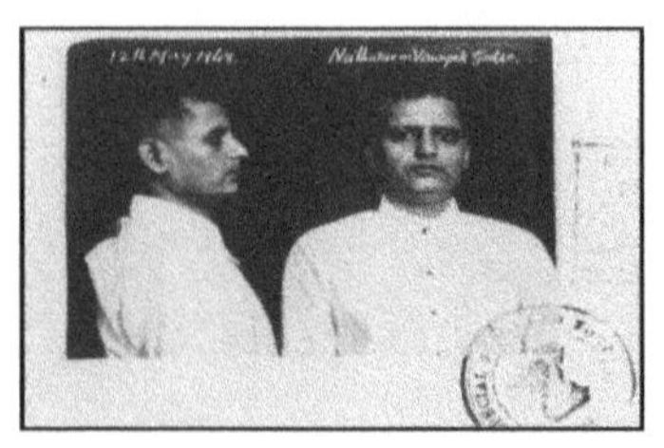</td>
<td></td>
<td></td>
</tr>
<tr>
<td>Nathuram V Godse</td>
<td>Narayan D. Apte</td>
<td>Vishnu R. Karkare</td>
</tr>
<tr>
<td>APPEAL DISMISSED:
Death Sentence
Confirmed</td>
<td>APPEAL DISMISSED:
Death Sentence
Confirmed</td>
<td>APPEAL DISMISSED:
Transportation for Life
Confirmed</td>
</tr>
<tr>
<td colspan="2" style="text-align:center"></td>
<td style="text-align:center">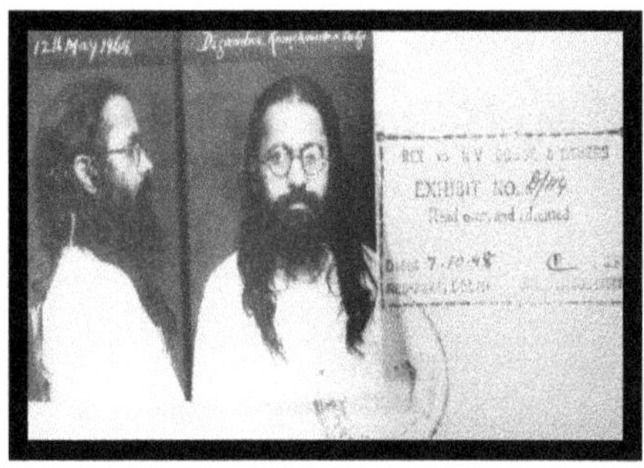</td>
</tr>
<tr>
<td colspan="2">HONOURABLE ACQUITTAL
at the Trial Court itself</td>
<td>GENERAL PARDON TENDERED
at the Trial Court itself</td>
</tr>
</table>

JUDGMENT OF

PUNJAB AND HARYANA HIGH COURT AT SIMLA

<table>
<tr>
<td>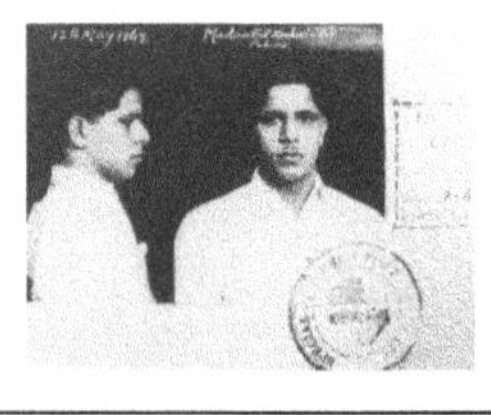</td>
<td></td>
<td></td>
<td></td>
</tr>
<tr>
<td>Madanlal K Pawa</td>
<td>Shankar Kistayya</td>
<td>Gopal V Godse</td>
<td>Dattarya S Parchure</td>
</tr>
<tr>
<td>APPEAL DISMISSED:
Transportation
for Life Confirmed</td>
<td>APPEAL ALLOWED:
ACQUITTED</td>
<td>APPEAL DISMISSED:
Transportation
for Life Confirmed</td>
<td>APPEAL ALLOWED:
ACQUITTED</td>
</tr>
</table>

(1869-1948)

"You can chain me,

You can torture me,

You can even destroy this body,

but you will never imprison my mind"

- **Mahatma Gandhi**

READERS' HAND NOTES